The American Political Economy

"There has long been a need for a readable introductory survey and synthesis of recent scholarship on the evolution of U.S. economic policy-making at the federal level over the last century or so. Dr. Eisner has now provided us with one that is both historically concrete and well aware of the most important methodological controversies in the literature."

Paul M. Johnson, Auburn University

"This timely book is a concise, clear, balanced, and thoughtful analysis of the nation's momentous economic problems and their origins. Eisner expertly synthesizes the intertwined growth of government and economic institutions over the past century, and shows that this history is indispensable for understanding today's American dilemmas of social welfare, globalization, the financial crisis, and the recession. *The American Political Economy* provides an essential foundation for coming to grips with contemporary American politics and policy."

David Robertson, University of Missouri

"Conventional approaches to the study of public policy tell us that there are states and there are markets and never the twain shall meet. Marc Allen Eisner persuasively demonstrates not only that they have met but that they are joined cheek to jowl."

Richard Bensel, Cornell University

Policy debates are often grounded within the conceptual confines of a state-market dichotomy, as though the two existed in complete isolation. In this innovative text, Marc Allen Eisner portrays the state and the market as inextricably linked, exploring the variety of institutions subsumed by the market and the role that the state plays in creating the institutional foundations of economic activity.

Through a historical approach, Eisner situates the study of American political economy within a larger evolutionary-institutional framework that integrates perspectives in American political development and economic sociology. This volume provides a rich understanding of the complexity of U.S. economic policy, explaining how public policies become embedded in bureaucracy and reinforced by organized beneficiaries and public expectations. This path-dependent layering process helps students better understand the underlying historical dynamics, which provide a clearer sense of the constraints faced by policymakers now and in the future. Thorough coverage of the entitlement crisis, globalization's impact on the U.S. political economy, and the recent financial crisis in the final chapters, demonstrates the importance of this historical institutionalist framework.

Marc Allen Eisner is Henry Merritt Writson Chair of Public Policy and professor of government at Wesleyan University. He is the author or co-author of several books on public policy and American political economy.

The American Political Economy

Institutional Evolution of Market and State

Marc Allen Eisner

 Routledge
Taylor & Francis Group

NEW YORK AND LONDON

First published 2011
by Routledge
270 Madison Avenue, New York, NY 10016

Simultaneously published in the UK
by Routledge
2 Park Square, Milton Park, Abingdon, Oxon OX14 4RN

*Routledge is an imprint of the Taylor & Francis Group,
an informa business*

Typeset in Galliard by
RefineCatch Limited, Bungay, Suffolk
Printed and bound in the United States of America on acid-free paper by
Edwards Brothers, Inc.

Library of Congress Cataloging-in-Publication Data
Eisner, Marc Allen.
    The American political economy: institutional evolution of market
    and state / Marc Allen Eisner.
       p. cm.
    1. United States–Economic policy.   2. United States–Economic
    conditions.   I. Title.
    HC103.E38 2010
    330.973—dc22   2010009839

ISBN 13: 978-0-415-99960-1 (hbk)
ISBN 13: 978-0-415-99962-5 (pbk)
ISBN 13: 978-0-203-88014-2 (ebk)

Contents

Figures

Acknowledgements

Scholarship is a rather solitary pursuit. Extended periods of time are invested in research in hopes of better understanding the wonderful complexity of the world. Then the real challenge begins: how does one best convey one's "discoveries" to those who have not had the opportunity, resources, or inclination to do their own research? For the past two decades, I have had the luxury of teaching political economy to students at Wesleyan University. Several iterations of the arguments in this book were "field tested" before a bright and, at times, combative set of students. Outside of the classroom, I have drawn on the insights of a number of colleagues, most notably, Gil Skillman, who has endured endless discussions of the day's discoveries, and Russell Murphy, whose mastery of US political history has been a rich resource since I arrived at Wesleyan. During the past two years, participation in the Tobin Project has expanded my thinking about political economy and public policy in ways that were, at times, unexpected. Michael Kerns, editor at Routledge, gave me the rare opportunity to develop this volume as I saw fit. Five anonymous reviewers for the press provided insightful comments and suggestions that helped me sharpen my arguments and avoid several errors (those that remain are mine alone). The greatest thanks are reserved, as always, for my wife Patricia. For three decades she has been my primary source of wise counsel and inspiration.

Abbreviations

AAA	Agricultural Adjustment Administration
AFDC	Aid for Families with Dependent Children
AFL	American Federation of Labor
AIG	American Insurance Group
BAC	Business Advisory Council
CBO	Congressional Budget Office
CEA	Council of Economic Advisers
CED	Committee for Economic Development
CIO	Congress of Industrial Organizations
COPE	Committee on Political Education (AFL-CIO)
CPI	Consumer Price Index
CRA	Community Reinvestment Act
CSE	Consolidated supervised entity
DIDMCA	The Depository Institutions Deregulation and Monetary Control Act
EPA	Environmental Protection Agency
ERTA	Economic Recovery Tax Act of 1981
FDIC	Federal Deposit Insurance Corporations
FERA	Federal Emergency Relief Administration
FSLIC	The Federal Savings and Loan Insurance Corporation
FTC	Federal Trade Commission
GAO	Government Accountability Office
GATT	General Agreement on Tariffs and Trade
GDP	Gross Domestic Product
GLBA	Gramm-Leach-Bliley Act
GM	General Motors
GNP	Gross National Product
GSE	Government sponsored enterprise
HHS	Department of Health and Human Services
HMO	Health Maintenance Organization
HUD	Department of Housing and Urban Development
ICC	Interstate Commerce Commission
IMF	International Monetary Fund

IRA	Individual Retirement Account
ISO	International Organization for Standardization
LDC	Less Developed Country
NAFTA	North American Free Trade Agreement
NASDQ	National Association of Securities Dealers Automated Quotations
NLRB	National Labor Relations Board
NOW	Negotiated Order of Withdrawal
NRA	National Recovery Administration
NWLB	National War Labor Board
OBRA	Omnibus Budget Reconciliation Act
OECD	Organization for Economic Cooperation and Development
OFHEO	The Office of Federal Housing Enterprise Oversight
OIRA	Office of Information and Regulatory Affairs
OMB	Office of Management and Budget
OPA	Office of Price Administration
OPEC	Organization of Petroleum Exporting Countries
OSHA	Occupational Safety and Health Administration
PAC	Political Action Committee
RFC	Reconstruction Finance Corporation
S&L	Savings and loan
SCHIP	State Children's Health Insurance Program
SEC	Securities and Exchange Commission
SSA	Social Security Administration
TANF	Temporary Assistance for Needy Families
TARP	Troubled Asset Relief Program
TNEC	Temporary National Economic Committee
TRA	Tax Reform Act of 1986
USDA	United States Department of Agriculture
WFC	War Finance Corporation
WIB	War Industries Board
WPA	Works Progress Administration
WMC	War Manpower Commission
WPB	War Production Board
WTO	World Trade Organization

Part I

Making Sense of the Political Economy

1 Beyond the Market-State Dichotomy

In 2007–8, a housing bubble collapsed bringing with it the largest investment banks on Wall Street, many of which were saved only through a massive infusion of government funds. The effects spread rapidly across the globe. Several nations, including the United States, fell into a deep and prolonged recession. General Motors, once the largest corporation in the country, entered bankruptcy (along with Chrysler). The resulting bailout left the US government holding a controlling share of stock in GM, a company that was once emblematic of American capitalism. The enormous injection of money into the economy, both to bail out failing corporations and stimulate demand, forced the largest issuance of debt since World War II. It also raised some profoundly important questions. First, how much debt could markets absorb? In the past several decades, the United States had undergone a remarkable transformation from the world's greatest creditor to the world's greatest debtor. A seemingly insatiable appetite for imports created persistent trade deficits and fueled the rise of China as a new economic powerhouse. As a result of this reversal of fortune, the capacity of the United States to raise funds would depend, in part, on China's willingness to continue to buy its debt.

Second, would the need to respond to the economic collapse divert attention from other long-term problems? For decades, analysts had issued dire projections about the future insolvency of Medicare and Social Security, the nation's largest policy commitments to the elderly. With a rapidly aging population, it was clear that the trust funds associated with these policies were going to be depleted when they were most needed unless policymakers introduced significant reforms. Year after year, the Government Accountability Office and the Congressional Budget Office issued warnings before Congress, only to be met with indifference. The political costs of reform were simply too great. Each year, the unavoidable day of reckoning came closer, and now, with a new set of pressing commitments there was almost no chance that elected officials would turn to entitlement reform.

Third, the collapse raised normative questions about the proper role of the state in the economy. Since the late 1970s, many analysts and elected officials had rejected the welfare-regulatory state that emerged over the course of the twentieth century. Markets, it was argued, were self-regulating and efficiency promoting. Policy interventions could undermine its beneficial effects. "Yes, a return to the market might create higher levels of inequality and, at times, instability," many reasoned, "but this was a small price to pay for higher rates of growth and innovation." But the magnitude of the economic collapse had a sobering effect on even the staunchest advocates of deregulation, welfare reform, and free and unfettered trade. Alan Greenspan, the former head of the Federal Reserve who had been one of the single greatest promoters of self-regulating markets, admitted that the collapse left him in a state of "shocked disbelief." The "whole intellectual edifice" had "collapsed."[1]

Indeed, a period that began with a seemingly unflappable faith in the marvels of the market ended with the passage of a large fiscal stimulus package and an earnest discussion of the merits of nationalization.

As this brief vignette suggests, these are exciting and uncertain times. How does one make sense of the problems, their sources, their interconnections, and the challenges they create for policymakers? To understand the financial crisis, for example, one needs to investigate the history of financial regulation and deregulation. One needs to consider the ways in which tax, regulatory, and monetary policy decisions created the real estate bubble, shaped corporate decisions about risk management, and magnified the impact once the bubble burst. To understand the challenges of funding the debt, one needs to consider the ways in which the post-war pursuit of international economic liberalization created the foundations for the emergence of new industrial powers willing to purchase US bonds, thereby facilitating an expansion of the national debt while placing new pressures on American policymakers. One must also understand the constraints facing policymakers. They work within a set of hard constraints imposed by the legal, budgetary and administrative resources at their disposal and established policy and political commitments. These constraints change overtime—to use an example from above, the potential impact of unfunded entitlement liabilities is far greater today, as the baby boom generation approaches retirement, than it was in 1960 when there were eight workers for each recipient of Social Security old age pensions.

The effort to make sense of the changes also demands that one explore changes in governing philosophies. As John Maynard Keynes once noted: "the ideas of economists and political philosophers, both when they are right and when they are wrong, are more powerful than is commonly understood. Indeed, the world is ruled by little else."[2] Governing philosophies and political-economic doctrines are powerful. They emphasize certain clusters of values over others. Policymakers and analysts draw on them to decipher a complex reality, to contemplate the trade-offs inherent in their decisions, to understand the ways in which public policies can be used to bring this reality into alignment with larger goals, and to justify their decisions to citizens. These doctrines often find an expression in public policies and institutions. But even after one set of ideas has been discredited and replaced by another, they can continue to exert an influence and give rise to contradictions and conflicts intrinsic to the state and core policies governing the economy. Indeed, many would suggest that the economic collapse was, in part, a product of a larger institutional incoherence that created perverse incentives for economic actors and limited the capacity of regulators to respond in a timely fashion.

The State and the Economy

Political economy is the study of the interactions between the state and the economy. There are myriad approaches to political economy and those who profess to work in the field often draw on far different analytical frameworks and assumptions that shape the focus of their analyses. As the above discussion suggests, the approach to political economy that will be adopted in this book will be concerned with the relationships between public and private institutions as they change in historical time. It will be particularly interested in those moments of crisis that have occurred periodically over the course of the past century because they both reveal the limitations of existing public policies, institutions, and political-economic doctrines and create an opportunity for significant change. We may be in the midst of such a crisis today. The looming entitlement crisis, the dislocations associated with globalization, and the recent collapse of the financial system all raise profound questions about the governing philosophy that has prevailed for the past several decades and the efficacy of the policy decisions it has shaped. These issues will occupy the final chapters of this book. It is a core assumption of this book that one cannot understand these problems without having a broader understanding of the historical record and the ways in which public and private institutions—and the relationships between them—have evolved. Before we can embark on this exploration, we need to address some preliminaries.

Political economy has a long and rich history that predates the contemporary fields of political science and economics. In 1848, John Stuart Mill provided a sense of the breadth of political economy, when he observed:

> Writers on Political Economy profess to teach, or to investigate, the nature of Wealth, and the laws of its production and distribution: including, directly or remotely, the operation of all the causes by which the condition of mankind, or of any society of human beings, in respect to this universal object of human desire, is made prosperous or the reverse.[3]

This broad vision disappeared with the professionalization of the social sciences in the late nineteenth and twentieth centuries. Political economy was fractured into separate disciplines, most importantly, economics and political science. Increasingly, economists focused on market behavior, a world of voluntary exchanges populated by rational utility maximizers and governed by the price mechanism. Most political scientists, in contrast, studied political power, coercion, conflict, and the rules and formal institutions that translate political demands into public policies. While this division of labor may have served some important disciplinary functions, it reinforced an illusion that there is a clear market-state dichotomy, a line of demarcation between two separate realms of human action governed by their own internal logics.[4]

Markets are remarkable institutions, to be certain. As Friedrich Hayek argued persuasively, the price mechanism communicates massive amounts of information that is dispersed among many actors. Changes in prices coordinate the production and consumption decisions of economic agents without their knowledge, thereby accomplishing feats that would be impossible for more centralized forms of control. As markets expand, they support a division of labor that results in higher levels of labor productivity and wealth generation, as Adam Smith illustrated with his classical example of the pin factory. Markets reward efficiency and innovation and there is little to suggest that the impressive record of growth of the past several centuries could have been realized absent market forces. There will be no effort at this point to argue against markets. Rather, the concern centers on the way in which markets have been understood relative to the state.[5]

The market-state dichotomy often carries with it a set of additional assumptions. If we assume that the market is an autonomous, self-constituting and self-regulating entity that functions according to its own intrinsic logic, and if we assume, furthermore, that the market has a privileged status, then there is an automatic bias against any policies that would constrain the behavior of economic actors. Charles E. Lindblom, for example, suggests that the market "seems to have imprisoned our thinking about politics and economics." Rather than seeing the market as a variable, analysts tend to "treat it as the fixed element around which policy must be fashioned."[6] Indeed, policy debates are often grounded, explicitly or implicitly, within the conceptual confines of the market-state dichotomy. They are replete with discussions of the limited conditions under which the state's *intervention* in the market can be justified. As David L. Weimar and Aidan R. Vining explain:

> When is it legitimate for government to intervene in private affairs? In the United States, the normative answer to this question has usually been based on the concept of *market failure*—a circumstance where the pursuit of private interest does not lead to an efficient use of society's resources or a fair distribution of society's goods.[7]

And yet, even market failure may not provide a sufficient justification for intervention. It may impose greater costs than market failure. The choice is often between imperfect alternatives, and thus analysts must compare the costs and benefits of each.[8]

The conceptual bifurcation intrinsic to the market-state dichotomy also carries significant analytical costs. If we equate the economy with the market, it becomes difficult to explore the variety of institutions subsumed by "the market." There is a rich literature in economic sociology, for example, that explores the various means by which economic organizations coordinate their behavior. They may employ a variety of governance mechanisms (e.g., trade associations, interlocking directorates, long-term contracting arrangements, collective bargaining) to manage uncertainty and increase stability. These arrangements have little in common with the anonymous, self-liquidating transactions that occur in classic markets. To the extent that they affect economic performance and the distribution of economic power, they are worthy of careful examination. Moreover, the bifurcation draws attention away from the role that the state plays in creating the institutional foundations of economic activity. Rather than constituting a natural outgrowth of the innate human "propensity to truck, barter, and exchange,"[9] the economy is, in a real sense, an expression—both intended and unintended—of public policies and institutions.

At first glance, this may seem counter-intuitive so let us explore the role of the state through the lens of property rights. Markets facilitate the exchange of property. Property rights are commonly understood as having three dimensions.[10] First, they must be *defined*. What kinds of things can be legitimately held and exchanged as property? Second, they must be *defensible*, that is, property holders must be able to defend their rights against the intrusion of others. Third, property rights must be *divestible*. Property holders must be able to exchange their property with others for markets to function. The state plays an indispensable role in each of these dimensions. Property is defined through legislation and court decisions; government institutions are central to the defense and exchange of property and the adjudication of contractual disputes. A failure of the state to establish a functional set of property rights can undermine economic growth. Without enforced property rights, individuals are subject to ongoing uncertainty over whether others will take their property through force rather than engaging in voluntary exchanges, and this undermines the incentives to invest and innovate. Indeed, the importance of property rights has become salient in recent years as analysts have sought to understand the factors that have impeded growth in some poorer nations.[11]

If property rights—as defined by the state—are fundamental to transactions even in classical markets, it is impossible to defend the notion that the market and state constitute separate realms of human action. The role of the state becomes even clearer when we consider the complex organizations that populate the economy. The most important actors in the economy—corporations, financial institutions and labor unions—are legally constituted entities. Incorporation is a legal act that conveys distinct benefits on a corporation while imposing conditions on organization and governance. Laws and regulations circumscribe the means corporations can adopt in seeking profit. Commercial banks must be chartered and, once again, abide by regulations regarding organization, governance, levels of capitalization, and the kinds of product they can offer. In the United States, the National Labor Relations Board must certify unions; its regulations delineate what can and cannot be addressed through industrial relations. Without exception, the economic organizations that constitute the economy are embedded in a dense network of public policies and institutions.

Some analysts have described property rights and public policies as a "membrane" connecting the state and economy.[12] The use of the term "membrane" is apt, given that the state and economy do not evolve in isolation. Rather, the two are best viewed as evolving together. New policies can dramatically alter the conditions under which economic production and investment occur, thereby shaping the trajectory of economic development. Corporations may alter their major capital investment or product and process design decisions in response to changes in regulations, and these decisions may have profound consequences for strategic and investment decisions. They may be forced to seek out new means of coordinating their behavior with other firms in response to changes in antitrust policy.

At the same time, as policymakers assume new responsibilities for responding to economic crises or regulating the negative externalities of industrial production, the state must develop new administrative capacities and policy instruments. New public policies often require bureaucratic expansion. Once they are in place, they are embedded in organizational routines and insulated by constituencies that seek to preserve or expand on existing commitments. This creates what is commonly referred to as a pattern of "path dependent development." That is, past decisions about policy and administration narrow the set of options open to future generations of policymakers. While change continues to occur, it occurs in an incremental pattern and reinforces past decisions. This pattern of development can engender serious problems. For example, as institutions evolve according to their own logic of path dependent development, they may not develop the capabilities they need to address new challenges or manage exogenous shocks. Although significant crises (e.g., the Great Depression, the stagflation of the 1970s) may lead to the introduction of policies and institutional changes that alter the trajectory of development, there is a major complication. New policies, more often than not, are layered on top of the old. The accretion of policies and bureaucracies—often grounded in very different theoretical and normative assumptions—creates problems of incoherence. Policies may work at cross-purposes and impose requirements on economic actors that are difficult to reconcile.

A Record of Growth and State Expansion

This book is an exploration of the American political economy as it has evolved since the early years of the twentieth century. Economically, the period has been one of impressive growth (see Figure 1.1). In 1929, the Gross Domestic Product (GDP) was $997 billion (all figures in this paragraph are in 2005 dollars to adjust for inflation). With a population of 121.9 million, the economy generated $8,016 per person. Four years later, when the economy was mired in the Great Depression, the GDP had fallen to $716.4 billion or $5,700 per person. While recovery from the depression was slow, beset by a host of policy miscues, at the height of World War II mobilization (1944), the economy produced an unprecedented $2.04 trillion, or $14,705 per capita. While the

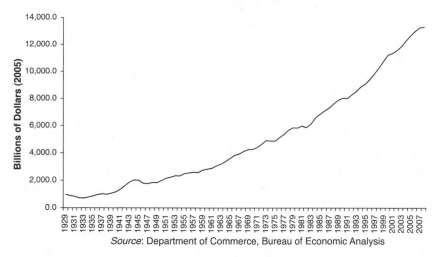

Source: Department of Commerce, Bureau of Economic Analysis

Figure 1.1 Real Gross Domestic Product, 1929–2008.

GDP fell with the cessation of war spending, the postwar economy was characterized by sustained growth. Between 1946 and 2008, the GDP increased from $1.79 trillion to $13.3 trillion, an increase of some 743 percent. Per capita GDP increased from $12,676 to $43,714 during this same period. To place things in the broader context, by 2008, the inflation adjusted GDP per capita was 545 percent greater than on the eve of the Great Depression.[13]

Advocates of *laissez-faire* economics commonly argue that the state should serve three essential functions: it should preserve stability in property rights, provide for domestic order, and protect the nation from foreign threats. To the extent that the state exceeds these bounds, it is argued, it may impose burdens that undermine the incentives to invest and produce. And yet, nations with growing capitalist economies vary dramatically with respect to the size of their states. As noted above, the nation realized sustained economic growth during the past century, resulting in dramatic increases in per capita income. During this same period, there was also a substantial growth in the size of the state. Although the government's claim on GDP has never approached the levels witnessed in northern Europe, it has nonetheless been significant.

At the beginning of the twentieth century, the American state was relatively small, with outlays of approximately 3 percent of GDP. Corporations and other economic organizations were largely unregulated and citizens, when faced with the vicissitudes of the business cycle and the life cycle, could harbor no expectation of federal assistance. The Constitution (most notably, the interstate commerce clause) and revenues (dependent on the tariff and land sale receipts) placed hard limits on the role of the state. And yet, over the course of the century, the state and the scope of public authority would expand dramatically. In 1929, on the eve of the Great Depression, federal government expenditures claimed 3.67 percent of GDP. The New Deal marked a clear sea change in government expenditures. By 1940, federal expenditures had reached 9.8 percent of GDP. But these levels of spending would pale relative to the peak years of World War II, when federal expenditures reached 43.6 percent of GDP. The levels of expenditures fell with the end of the war and depression, but they never returned to pre-war levels. As Figure 1.2 reveals, in the 1950s, government expenditures averaged 17.6 percent of GDP, increasing to an average of 18.7 percent GDP in the 1960s, and 20 percent of GDP in the 1970s. Even if Ronald Reagan won the presidency in 1980 on the claim that government was the problem, not the solution, during the decade of the 1980s, spending averaged 22.2 percent of GDP. President Clinton's second term of office brought a decline in the size of government to 18 percent of GDP by 2000, reflecting a number of factors including the end of Cold War levels of defense spending. But with the election of George W. Bush, the levels of spending increased once again such that by his second term in office, the federal claim on GDP once again exceeded 20 percent. As a share of GDP, the levels of spending after 2000 were, on average, twice the level experienced during the peak of the domestic phase of the New Deal.[14]

The government's claim on GDP is the most commonly adopted indicator of the size of the government and it can be useful when drawing cross-national comparisons. But it has limitations. If economic growth is robust, the size of the government could expand in absolute terms but decline relative to the GDP. Similarly, if economic growth fails to outpace population growth, a state could claim a larger percentage of GDP while simultaneously spending less on a per capita basis. Inflation-adjusted spending per capita—that is, the amount of money the government spends per person expressed in constant dollars—

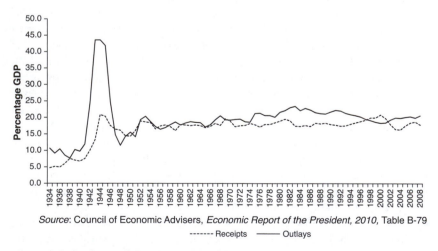

Source: Council of Economic Advisers, *Economic Report of the President, 2010,* Table B-79

------- Receipts ——— Outlays

Figure 1.2 Outlays and Receipts, 1934–2008.

would seem to address each of these issues. But let us be more precise. Since the trends in overall government spending can be affected by wars, let us consider the inflation-adjusted per capita non-defense spending.

In 1929, the federal government spent $294 per person (once again, all figures are expressed in 2005 dollars). Things would change dramatically over the course of the New Deal, and by 1940, the federal government spent $715 per person. Unsurprisingly, with the heavy demands of war production, the government was spending a total of $6,617 per capita in 1944. But subtracting defense spending, it spent a far more modest $880 per capita. With reconversion from World War II, there were significant reductions in federal spending between 1945 and 1948, before a new pattern of growth commenced. By 1960, federal non-defense spending was $1,332 per capita. The Kennedy and Johnson presidencies witnessed a dramatic expansion of the welfare state, and non-defense spending reached $2,286 per capita by 1968. In many ways, this year marked the apogee in the support for the Keynesian social welfare state.[15]

The 1970s, a period of economic stagnation and high inflation, led to a discrediting of Keynesian macroeconomic management and growing support for deregulation and welfare reform. Yet, by the time Ronald Reagan was elected president, the federal government's claim on GDP had actually risen slightly over the peak years of the Johnson administration and non-defense spending rose to $2,633 per capita. Reagan called for a reduction in the size and scope of the federal government. But by the last year of his two-term presidency, non-defense spending had risen to $4,827 per person—more than twice the level of the Great Society. There would be some reductions in the size of government relative to GDP in subsequent years. But once again, because of strong economic growth, by 2001 per capita spending increased to $6,171 and reached $7,263 by the end of George W. Bush's presidency. In sum, by 2008, although the size of the government relative to GDP was approximately what it was four decades earlier, inflation-adjusted nondefense spending per capita reached unprecedented levels. Comparable growth occurred at the state and local levels during the period such that by 2008, total government nondefense spending as a percentage of GDP approached 29 percent, or $12,561 per capita.

The long-term growth in the size of the American state is striking. One should not be surprised that per capita nondefense spending increased by some 240 percent between 1929 and 1940, given the introduction of so many new government programs during the depression. But during the two decades separating the end of World War II reconversion and the end of the Johnson presidency, per capita spending increased by 220 percent, with a comparable rate of growth in the decades separating the peak of the Great Society and the end of the so-called Reagan revolution. Regardless of party or ideology, growth in the government has been an ongoing trend for much of the past century.

Ironically, although the government was spending unprecedented amounts per capita, it never had less discretionary authority. In 1962, mandatory programs constituted approximately 27 percent of government spending. By 2008, they had grown to 63.7 percent, leaving elected officials with discretionary

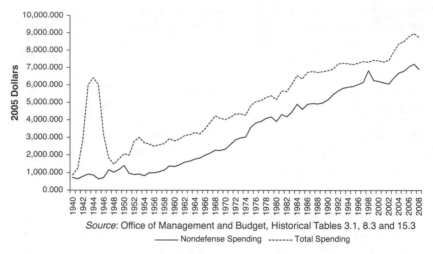

Source: Office of Management and Budget, Historical Tables 3.1, 8.3 and 15.3
——— Nondefense Spending   ------- Total Spending

Figure 1.3 Real Per Capita Federal Spending, 1940–2008.

authority over a mere 36.3 percent of the budget. In 1935, the New Deal introduced Social Security old age pensions; three decades later, the Johnson administration expanded entitlements with Medicare and Medicaid. As of 2008, Social Security and healthcare entitlements constituted some 42 percent of total government spending. Given the high levels of deficit spending in recent decades, interest on the national debt has grown to claim another 15.5 percent of spending. With an aging population and unprecedented deficits, the claims on the budget imposed by these commitments are projected to exceed 70 percent of the budget by 2014. As noted in the early pages of this chapter, the growing demands of entitlements constitute one of the great challenges that may be difficult to address given the financial collapse.[16]

The figures on per capita spending are useful, but they cannot capture changes in the emphasis accorded various governmental activities. Consider regulation. Between 1960 and 2008, real federal nondefense spending increased by some 519 percent. During that same period, total inflation-adjusted regulatory spending (expressed in 2000 dollars) increased from $2.53 billion to $42.7 billion, an increase of 1686 percent. The real engine of growth in regulatory spending came in the area of social regulation (e.g., environmental and occupational safety and health). Inflation-adjusted social regulatory spending increased by 2161 percent during this period, and currently constitutes approximately 85 percent of all regulatory spending.[17] The number of pages in the *Federal Register* has often been used as a rough indicator of regulatory growth insofar as it is devoted primarily to the publication of regulations. During the period 1960 to 2008, the *Federal Register* grew from 14,479 to 80,0700 pages. Regulations can mandate changes in occupational safety practices, pollution control technologies, or bank underwriting standards; they can redefine property rights, prohibit various forms of inter-corporate relations, or demand that businesses recognize the right of workers to engage in collective bargaining. None of these activities will have a significant impact on the size of the budget, even if they have a substantial aggregate effect on the organization of production and the economy.

Conclusion

Rather than viewing the market and state as constituting two separate realms of human activity, this chapter has argued that political economy must be grounded in an understanding of the role of public policy and institutions in constituting the economy and shaping economic performance. But state policies and institutions are not static. As shown above, there has been ongoing expansion in the size of the state. But we must go beyond long-term expansion to consider qualitative changes in the state's role. This requires that we examine, first, the path dependent process of development that exhibits relative stability for prolonged periods of time, and second, the ways in which crises have punctuated this stability. These crises create an opportunity for significant and rapid change that alters the trajectory of development. In each period of rapid change, new policies and institutions have shared common features that were grounded in a distinctive understanding of the economy, the role of the state, and the most appropriate policy instruments and patterns of state-civil society relations. As such, it is useful to refer to the combination of policies and institutions introduced in a given period as constituting distinctive "regimes." Yet, post crisis, many of the policies and institutions inherited from the past continue to exist. New policies and institutions are layered upon the old, contributing to institutional thickening, policy incoherence, and contradictions that may well set the stage for subsequent crises.

In the following chapters, we will explore this process of change as it has unfolded over the course of the past century, giving rise to successive regimes. We will also investigate a host of contemporary problems, some of which were introduced in the early pages of this chapter, as a means of better understanding the contradictions inherent in the current regime. We may well be on the brink of another period of rapid and substantial change that will culminate in a new distinctive policy regime. Before we can embark on this exploration, we must examine in greater detail both the key institutions of the political economy and the process of change introduced briefly above. We turn to this examination in Chapter 2.

2 Making Sense of Institutions and Institutional Change

Much of our thinking about public policy and the economy has been shaped by a simple contrast between the market and the state, as noted in Chapter 1. Yet, it is difficult to conceive of large, functioning markets absent state institutions. They are central to the creation of functional property rights. Moreover, key actors in the economy (corporations, labor unions, financial institutions) and the permissible relationships between them, are a product of public policy. Laws shape economic development by favoring certain methods of coordination and control while rendering others illegal. The key lesson thus far is that simple lines of demarcation between the market and the state do not provide a descriptively accurate or analytically useful means of understanding the political economy. Rather than comprising two potentially opposing forces, the market and the state are institutionally intertwined.

This chapter explores the key institutions of the political economy, starting with an examination of the state, before moving to consider corporations, labor and finance. As will be argued below, these actors are constituted by the law and thus cannot be understood apart from public policy decisions. As Douglass North notes, institutions are important because they "provide the incentive structure of an economy." But institutions are not static, formal or constitutional entities. They evolve over time and, as North continues, "as that structure evolves, it shapes the directions of economic change towards growth, stagnation or decline."[1] Thus, the chapter concludes with a discussion of the logic of institutional development and the theoretical assumptions that will frame subsequent chapters in this book.

The State

Drawing on Max Weber, one can begin by defining the state as a constellation of complex organizations that claim monopoly over the legitimate use of coercive force within the boundaries of a nation. Institutions comprise the rules, roles, and decision-making procedures that both define the inner workings of the state organizations and shape the relationships between the state and civil society.[2] With respect to the state, institutions determine how authoritative decision-makers are to be selected, the scope of their authority, the processes by which they can make legally binding decisions, and the ways in which various societal interests are integrated into the policy process. Along each of these dimensions there can be great variation across the state. Different agencies, for example, may have very different grants of authority, resource flows, and patterns of interest group relations; they may vary significantly in their analytical and administrative resources and the kinds of policy instruments they can bring to bear in formulating and executing policy. To the extent that different agencies with overlapping jurisdictions vary along these dimensions, there may be significant problems of coordination.[3] There is a rich body of scholarship on the state grounded in varied theoretical perspectives. Although this book will employ primarily an institutional perspective, a brief discussion of two alternative frameworks—public choice and class theory—is quite useful. Each provides a unique understanding of internal dynamics and inherent tensions that can provide a richer understanding of the state, even for institutionalists.

The first perspective under consideration is public choice. It is grounded in methodological individualism, the assumption that for purposes of analysis, "the basic units are choosing, acting, behaving persons rather than organic units such as parties, provinces, or nations."[4] As James Buchanan explains: "Only individuals choose; only individuals act. An understanding of any social interaction process must be based on an analysis of the choice behavior of persons who participate in that process."[5] Public choice theorists argue that self-interested actors engage in rational, utility maximizing behavior in political life, much as they do in their economic activities. In the market, individuals can pursue their self-interest by engaging in bilateral exchanges. In politics, in contrast, collective action is necessary. The government "is seen as nothing more than the set of processes, the machine, which allows such collective action to take place. This approach makes the State into something that is constructed by men, an artifact."[6] Indeed, the state is understood quite explicitly as a set of constraints created by self-interested actors to bring stability to their exchanges.

As Mancur Olson argues in *The Logic of Collective Action*, it is inherently difficult to mobilize in support of public goods.[7] Because individuals will receive the benefits associated with public goods regardless of the costs they incur, they have no incentives to invest in their attainment. It is far more rational to allow others to bear the costs and engage in free riding behavior. Policies that provide selective goods, in contrast, can exclude those who fail to make the requisite investment. Groups are most successful when they mobilize to secure narrowly focused benefits like government subsidies, tax exemptions, or regulatory barriers to entry. These benefits usually take the form of transfers: benefits for group members are funded through costs that are widely dispersed throughout society either through taxation or through higher costs borne by consumers. For such rent-seeking to be rational, it is only necessary that the net benefits enjoyed by the group (that is, the group benefits minus the group costs, divided by group members) are greater than the overall social costs divided among members of the entire society. In practical terms, this means that members of a group will impose social costs that are far greater than the benefits enjoyed by group members.[8] These transfers, once secured, rarely disappear. In the end, as policy commitments accumulate, they claim an increasing proportion of national income and a greater share of private sector resources are devoted to securing and preserving transfers. As a result, governments can become sclerotic, losing their ability to respond to new challenges.[9]

While public choice views the state as a set of rules structuring political exchanges of rational actors, class theory situates the state in a larger dynamic of capitalist production and the conflicts inherent in a state that is both capitalist and democratic. The class theory of the state is grounded in Karl Marx's observation that relationships of production—the struggle between classes over the control of the means of production and the resulting wealth—is the central dynamic in a capitalist economy. In capitalism, the state is not a neutral entity but, by necessity, represents capital in its efforts to manage the class struggle and promote the capital accumulation process. The state must promote capital accumulation because it is structurally dependent on it for revenues. Regardless of the partisan affiliations of office holders, the need for revenues places hard limits on what can be accomplished.

There is a further complication. As James O'Connor argued in *The Fiscal Crisis of the State*, there is an inherent tension between capital accumulation and legitimation. In O'Connor's words: "A capitalist state that openly uses its coercive forces to help one class accumulate capital at the expense of other classes loses its legitimacy and hence undermines the basis of its loyalty and support. But a state that ignores the necessity of assisting the process of capital accumulation risks drying up the source of its own power, the economy's surplus production capacity and the taxes drawn from this surplus."[10] To meet the demands of voters, state officials must provide social spending, but this requires tax rates that undermine profitability and may precipitate a capital strike (i.e., a refusal to invest). In the short term, state managers may avoid the "structural gap" between expenditures and revenues through deficit spending, but this only defers the inevitable. The difficulties of managing these competing pressures can be exacerbated, moreover, by fluctuations in the business cycle, long-term industrial cycles, and changes in the relative power of nations in the international economy.

Contemporary class theorists recognize that capital is not monolithic. Different industries with diverse interests compete over "the private appropriation of state power for particularistic ends."[11] Different blocs of capital may secure power bases within different parts of the state, making the state, when taken as a whole, the embodiment of intra-class conflicts.[12] State managers, as a result, must not only manage the struggle between capitalists and labor, but the divisions within capital. In the words of Jill Quadagno: "The contradictions between the dominant fractions imbedded in the state make it necessary for the state to perform an organizing function. The state thus becomes a mediating body, weighing priorities, filtering information, and integrating contradictory measures into state policy."[13] The state does not simply translate the demands of capital into public policy. Rather, the divisions within capital provide the political space for state managers to exercise some autonomy. This autonomy is arguably the greatest during periods of crisis (e.g., war, depression). The threat of a capital strike loses its power during a depression; businesses are already failing to invest. During times of war, demand is high but state managers can use their control of resources, transportation, and labor to starve firms that fail to accede to the requirements of war production. As Fred Block notes:

> It is hardly surprising ... that such periods have seen the most dramatic qualitative growth in state activity and the most serious efforts to rationalise capitalism. State managers take advantage of the changes in the structural context to expand their own power and to pursue policies that they perceive as necessary to strengthen the nation's position in the world system and to preserve internal order.[14]

Public choice is a world of rational individuals designing institutions to structure mutually beneficial exchanges. Class theorists, in contrast, work at a far higher level of aggregation and see the state as structurally dependent on capital accumulation and forced to mediate struggles between classes and class factions. Yet, they also tell complementary stories. Public choice, for example, can provide a compelling explanation for why transfer seeking is so ubiquitous in democratic systems, thereby providing insights that are useful in seeking to understand how competing blocs of capital become embedded in the state and why managing the resulting incoherence is so difficult for elected officials and bureaucrats. The logic of collective action can help understand why narrowly focused business interests are so successful in achieving selective benefits whereas the kinds of policies that would provide greater support for labor (e.g., universal programs) are so difficult to secure. Rather than viewing competing theoretical perspectives as mutually exclusive, it may be far more prudent to seek out those components that can provide us with a greater explanatory power.

As noted above, this analysis will be grounded primarily in an institutional perspective on the state (and the economy, more generally). There has been a proliferation of "institutionalisms" in the past several decades. Richard Swedberg provides a useful definition of institutions that would satisfy institutionalists from multiple disciplines. Institutions are "distinct configurations of interests and social relations, which are typically of such importance that they are enforced by the law."[15] The state, in this perspective, is a set of complex public organizations and rules that structure the relationships between public authority and private interests and among private interests.

As with public choice accounts, there is clear recognition that institutions constitute the rules and procedures that structure exchanges and collective action. However, rather than assuming that state institutions are designed by rational actors seeking to maximize joint gains, it is commonly argued that institutions actually shape preferences. James G. March and Johan P. Olsen, for example, contrast the "logic of consequentiality" employed by public choice with a "logic of appropriateness" which prevails in institutions. They explain: "Political institutions ... define appropriate actions in terms of relations between roles and situations. The process involves determining what the situation is, what role is being fulfilled, and what the obligations of that role in that situation are."[16] Although one cannot deny self-interested behavior, actors are embedded within a specific set of institutional arrangements, norms, and commitments that shape their preferences and govern their behavior.

Institutions are critical, moreover, because they provide policymakers with a set of administrative capacities, analytical and budgetary resources, statutory authority, and patterns of interest group relations that constrain and enable their activities. Much of the institutionalist work on the state focuses on the historical conditions that gave rise to institutions in the formative moment and the ways in which institutions successfully reproduce themselves over time. The overarching focus on stability may result from the fact that for most political scientists and many sociologists, "the massively reinforced and embedded array of the state exemplifies the concept of institution."[17] Institutional structures inherited from the past constrain the actions of political actors and the avenues open for future action, thereby creating a pattern of path dependency.[18] This raises an important question: if institutions are inherently conservative, how can one explain periods of significant change? We will turn to the logic of institutional change later in this chapter.

Beyond the State

In *The Great Transformation*, Karl Polyani offered an important corrective for the belief that markets emerge spontaneously as self-regulating entities. He carefully documented both the creation of national markets through changes in public policy, and in what he describes as the "corrective counter-movement," the introduction of policies to compensate for the effects of market competition and past policies that had disembedded labor. "Social history in the nineteenth century history," in Polyani's words, "was the result of a double movement," first "the extension of market organization," and second, the counter-movement "which blunted the action of this self-destructive mechanism."[19] As Fred Block notes, the Polyanian perspective is grounded in "the insight that the economy is never fully autonomous. It suggests that what we generally call 'the economy' is always the product of a combination of state action and the logic of individual or institutional economic actors." Rather than privileging the market and economic forces, it recognizes that "those economic logics have never—by themselves—produced a coherently functioning whole."[20]

In this section, we turn to a brief exploration of the non-state economic actors. The examination is grounded in an understanding of the role of the law in constituting the very building blocks of the economy and governing their interaction. Following Lauren B. Edelman and Mark C. Suchman, one can observe the law creates a *constitutive* environment, a *facilitative* environment, and a *regulatory* environment within which economic organizations function.[21] In the constitutive environment, law "constructs and empowers various classes or organizational actors and delineates the relationships between them."[22] Corporations, financial institutions, trade associations, and labor unions and legal entities. As Richard Swedberg notes: "Law, in modern society, is *constitutive* for most economic phenomena, meaning by this that it is an indispensable as well as an organic part of them ... they are inseparable."[23] In its facilitative capacity, the law establishes the means by which organizations can defend their property rights, forge commercial relations, and resolve disputes. In the regulatory environment, the law imposes rules that govern acceptable forms of conduct and coordination (e.g., antitrust, regulatory rate-setting, and information disclosure) and imposes penalties and incentives that shape corporate decisions regarding product design, production processes, and capital investments (e.g., environmental regulations, debt and tort law). Drawing on Polyani, rather than assuming some autonomous logic of economic activity, it is far more accurate to view the economy as being embedded in a dense network of laws and institutions.

The Corporation

In 1937, Ronald Coase asked a fundamental question: Why do firms exist? According to Coase, although the many functions assumed by the corporation could, in theory, be executed through market exchanges, this would impose significant costs. Prices need to be discovered, contracts have to be negotiated, deliveries must be inspected, and contractual conflicts between parties must be resolved and all of these functions create "transaction costs." These activities can be internalized in the firm. There are limits, however. In Coase's formulation, firms will cease expanding when the administrative costs associated with internalizing these functions exceed the transaction costs of conducting them in the market.[24] Rather than modeling the corporation as a simple production function, it is more fruitful to recognize that corporations are complex organizations that coordinate the behavior of actors.

Corporations are legal entities. In the early years of the republic, corporate charters were awarded by state legislatures. But the rapid dissemination of general incorporation laws in the early nineteenth century made the corporate charter widely available to entrepreneurs. The corporate charter carries a number of benefits. Because the corporation is a legal entity separate from those who own and manage it, all parties have limited liability. Shareholders may lose their investments; managers may lose their jobs. But they cannot be held personally liable. Limited liability creates greater incentives for individuals to invest in corporations and this access to capital was particularly important as companies grew in size. Corporations, moreover, have a separate legal personality that provides them with the right to own property, for example, or sue to enforce contracts. In the United States, corporations *qua* legal entities were guaranteed certain constitutional protections afforded to real flesh-and-blood citizens. For example, they possess freedom of expression under the First Amendment; they cannot be deprived of property without due process of law nor can they be denied just compensation under the Fifth Amendment. As John Micklethwait and Adrian Wooldridge note: "Companies have proved enormously powerful not just because they improve productivity, but because they possess most of the legal rights of a human being, without the attendant disadvantages of biology; they are not condemned to die of old age and they can create progeny pretty much at will."[25]

Corporations as organizations evolved over the course of US history. As Alfred D. Chandler, Jr., has shown, the multi-divisional corporation emerged initially in the railroads during the nineteenth century and was subsequently disseminated to manufacturing firms seeking to manage the complexity of functioning in expanding markets.[26] Some firms adopted functional divisions, organizing employees by function or processes. Others adopted product divisions with different product lines assigned to different divisions. Geographical divisions were created in some cases for firms serving multiple markets, and various hybrids were employed to combine two or more forms of organization. The movement from relatively simple corporate forms to multi-divisional organizations was, in part, a product of organizational isomorphism. That is, corporate managers adopted the kinds of innovations that were being employed by other firms. The dissemination of the multi-divisional firm cannot be separated from three other larger changes in the American economy. First, as the nation's rail system expanded over the course of the late nineteenth century, it allowed for the integration of previously separate, local markets, to create regional and even national markets. Second, the development of new mass production technologies (e.g., large-batch production, continuous-process production, standardized and interchangeable parts) allowed corporations to achieve new economies of scale and service the vast markets opened by the rails. Finally, the expansion of capital markets allowed corporations to finance growth well beyond what might have been possible if firms had been forced to rely on retained profits or the personal wealth of their founders.

The development of the corporate economy during the late nineteenth and early twentieth century occurred, in part, through consolidation. During the merger wave of 1897–1904, horizontal mergers eliminated more than 3,000 companies, thereby creating oligopolies or monopolies in a number of industries and giving rise to some of the giant enterprises that became synonymous with American industry. A second merger wave, from 1916 to 1929, was once again dominated by horizontal mergers, eliminating some 12,000 additional firms.[27] In some four decades, the levels of industrial concentration increased dramatically, and large consolidated firms came to dominate mining, manu-facturing, and utilities despite the fact—or because of the fact—that Congress had passed a series of important antitrust statutes to govern corporate organ-ization and conduct. By prohibiting conspiracies in restraint of trade (e.g., cartels), the Sherman Act of 1890 may have increased the incentives to pursue other forms of coordination such as actual corporate consolidation.

The complexity of the functions integrated in the large multi-divisional firms demanded professionalized management, thereby displacing the family management that had been prevalent in earlier generations. Increasingly, cor-porate mangers had specialized training and new professions such as engineer-ing and finance became ever more important in controlling and coordinating the corporation's multiple functions. This professionalization was combined with a diffusion of corporate ownership. As corporations sought to produce and distribute their goods in regional or national markets, the financial demands exceeded what could be accomplished through family fortunes or retained profits. It became necessary to enter capital markets and rely on the sale of stocks and bonds to fund industrial expansion. These two trends—the pro-fessionalization of management and the diffusion of ownership—marked a significant change in the organization of corporations. As Adolf A. Berle and Gardiner C. Means observed in their 1932 book, *The Modern Corporation and Private Property*, one now witnessed "two new groups created out of a former single group—the owners without appreciable control and the control without appreciable ownership."[28] Whereas the former sought to maximize profits, the diffusion of ownership limited their capacity to shape corporate policies.

The separation of ownership and control—and the diffusion of ownership more generally—would become far more significant over the course of the twentieth century. During the first great merger wave, investment bankers like J.P. Morgan used their control over finance to engineer large consolidations. But over the course of the next century, the major players were increasingly large institutional investors like mutual funds, pension funds, and insurance companies that pooled the savings of many small investors and used them to purchase large blocks of corporate stock. In theory, these institutional inves-tors could exercise greater control over corporate policy. However, given the development of secondary markets, it was less expensive for investors to sell their shares than to seek to exercise voice over corporate decisions. Thus, institutional investors adjusted their portfolios on a regular basis in response to poor management decisions or downturns in corporate profitability. Their fiduciary responsibility to investors did not involve shaping the long-term stra-tegic decisions of corporate managers. According to Robert B. Reich, by the 1970s, under conditions of stagflation and growing foreign competition, this created a bias toward "paper entrepreneurialism."[29] That is, rather than invest-ing in the kinds of technologies that could generate long-term competitiveness and exploit new economic niches, many managers focused on the acquisition of under-valued firms, selling the components, and claiming paper profits. This was certainly a means of promoting short-term profitability and thus meeting the demands of institutional investors and raising the value of stock, but unlike real entrepreneurship, it did nothing to create wealth.

Finance

The evolution of the corporate economy cannot be understood without devoting attention to the role of finance. Financial institutions (or intermediaries) play vital roles in any capitalist economy. They aggregate the savings of individuals and make it available for commercial transactions and investment. Most of what we understand as money does not take the form of currency but transfers between individuals and/or institutions. Through the practice of fractional reserve banking (i.e., when banks retain a fraction of their deposits and lend the remainder out), financial intermediaries expand the money supply thereby facilitating a higher level of commercial activity than might otherwise occur. Finally, finance provides a key lever for policy makers seeking to shape macroeconomic performance (e.g., by controlling what fraction of deposits banks must retain as reserves).

Corporations can fund expansion through three basic means, each of which has different implications for organizational autonomy. First, corporations can draw on retained profits, an option that provides a maximum level of autonomy. Second, they can rely on bank loans. Because banks are providing long-term capital, they have a direct stake in major corporate decisions and may demand some representation on corporate boards, thereby severely restricting autonomy. Third, corporations can rely on commercial paper markets—stocks and bonds. The United States has a capital-market based system wherein firms rely primarily (although not solely) on stocks and bonds. Although major investment banks are responsible for the initial issuance of stocks, they quickly enter the secondary market and ownership is dispersed, thereby providing corporations with greater autonomy than would exist if funding came through bank loans. However, as noted earlier, this can carry a large cost insofar as institutional investors routinely adjust their portfolios in response to minor fluctuations in corporate profitability, and, as a result, they create disincentives to pursue long-term strategies at the cost of short-term profitability.[30]

As noted earlier, law is particularly important because it constitutes the very building blocks of the economy. Arguably, there is no clearer example than finance. The divisions between investment and commercial banking, and the distinctions between commercial banks, savings and loans, and credit unions, are the product of public policy. In essence, a series of statutes created distinct financial sub-industries, each with its own set of regulatory institutions controlling entry and exit and governing what kinds of products and services could be offered and the extent of price competition. In response to the financial panic of 1907, Congress created the Federal Reserve in 1913, which was given the responsibility of setting reserve requirements and serving some lender of last resort functions. Two decades later, during the cataclysm of the Great Depression, Congress forced the separation of commercial and investment banking. The regulation of investment banking and the exchanges was assigned to a new Securities and Exchange Commission. The regulation for commercial banking was assigned to a number of agencies with overlapping responsibilities and new agencies were created to regulate various segments of the commercial banking industry (e.g., the National Credit Union Administration, the Federal Home Loan Bank Board) and to insure deposits (e.g., the Federal Deposit Insurance Corporation, the Federal Savings and Loan Insurance Corporation). In short, regulatory legislation and institutions literally created the various financial industries and defined the relationships between them.

Finance has been one of the most regulated parts of the US economy. Nonetheless, there has been ongoing innovation in the financial industry often in response to new technologies and efforts to circumvent regulatory restrictions that impeded attempts to manage the pressures imposed by larger macroeconomic forces. During the 1970s, when the United States suffered under abnormally high rates of inflation, for example, regulations limiting the interest rates that banks could pay led to a host of novel innovations and disintermediation—the flow of funds out of regulated financial intermediaries. Subsequently, a wave of deregulations increasingly eroded the regulatory structure created during the New Deal. Ongoing innovations involving the securitization of mortgage debt and the issuance of credit-default swaps resulted in the emergence of a shadow system of finance free from regulatory oversight. The vulnerability of this system became painfully apparent in 2007–8, when the collapse of the real estate bubble created a financial crisis second in magnitude only to the collapse during the Great Depression.

Organized Labor

The position of labor in the political economy is in many ways determined by decisions made by corporations. In the words of Claus Offe, "unions are associations of members who, before they can become members of unions, are already members of other organizations, namely employees of capitalist enterprises. Thus, unions are 'secondary' organizers, and capital itself functions as a primary organizer."[31] Historically, key corporate decisions have had significant implications for workers. For example, the decision to adopt mass production technologies (so called "Fordism") in the early twentieth century depressed the demand for skilled labor, exacerbating divisions between skilled workers in craft-based unions and unskilled workers in industrial unions. Decades later, the decision to respond to competitive pressures by outsourcing production to nations with less expensive labor accelerated the decline of unionized manufacturing industries, while leaving fewer opportunities for unskilled workers outside of low-paid service sector occupations. In large part, the fluctuating fortunes of organized labor in the United States were a product of corporate strategies over which labor had little or no voice. But the history of organized labor, like the history of corporations and finance, is impossible to tell without engaging the history of public policies and institutions.

During the early twentieth century, corporations and labor literally engaged in industrial warfare. Key features of American political institutions (e.g., federalism and the Constitution's commerce clause) frustrated efforts to regulate industrial relations in the early decades of the twentieth century, such that by the 1920s, as David Robertson notes, "American labor regulation remained a patchwork of limited protections, uneven laws, and poor enforcement, lacking basic national standards even for child labor."[32] To be certain, some firms sought to manage the so-called "labor problem" through welfare capitalism and human relations, limiting the appeal of unions by providing company unions and giving workers a stake in corporate profitability through the provision of pensions, stock ownership programs, and health care. These efforts came to a halt in the 1930s, with the passage of the National Labor Relations Act of 1935 and the creation of the National Labor Relations Board (NLRB). Although a more sustained discussion of New Deal labor policy is reserved for Chapter 4, it is important to note that with the passage of the National Labor Relations Act, the government provided federal protection for workers' right to form unions and the NLRB was given the responsibility for supervising union elections, determining the appropriate labor organization, and adjudicating industrial relations disputes. However, the NLRB also determined what kinds of questions could be addressed in industrial relations, insulating managerial prerogatives and frustrating cooperative strategies.

After the passage of New Deal labor legislation and World War II mobilization, unionization levels peaked in 1945 at some 35.5 percent of the nonagricultural workforce before entering a period of long-term decline.[33] Between 1980 and 2008, union membership fell from 19.5 to 12.4 percent, and this latter figure veils the magnitude of the changes insofar as the high level of membership among public sector workers (36.8 percent) offsets the low level of membership in the private sector (7.6 percent).[34] The decline in union membership is a product of several factors, including long-term changes in the structure of the US economy. But policy changes played a significant role. Following the passage of the Taft-Hartley Act in 1947, twenty-two states passed "right-to-work" laws prohibiting union shops (i.e., businesses that require employees to belong to unions), thereby suppressing union membership rates. Moreover, beginning in the 1980s, the NLRB, beset by significant budget constraints, assumed a more passive role in the regulation of industrial relations. To the extent that union growth in earlier decades was a product of government promotion of union membership, one should not be surprised that changes in governing philosophies, policies, and resource flows had important implications for unionization.

Governance

In the past several decades, scholars have devoted much attention to exploring the different ways in which economic organizations coordinate their behavior and the ways in which law has shaped the evolution of economic governance in different industries and societies.[35] Governance structures, as Neil Fligstein notes, are "the general rules in a society that define relations of competition, cooperation, and market-specific definitions of how firms should be organized. These rules define the legal and illegal forms of how firms can control competition."[36] They can take the form of laws or informal institutional practices that coordinate the behavior of discrete organizations. States must develop rules about property rights and governance structures—the legal and institutional architecture of the economy—if they want to promote growth and stability, and this process is inherently political: "There are political contests over the content of laws, their applicability to given firms and markets and the extent and direction of state intervention into the economy. Such laws are never neutral. They favor certain groups of firms."[37] Once in place, they structure subsequent economic development by favoring certain methods of coordination and control and rendering others illegal. State making and economic development are necessarily intertwined.

In the research on governance, rather than presenting *the market* as being synonymous with the economy, *a market* is one of many potential governance mechanisms available to economic actors. In its purest form, a market is a decentralized system of exchange linking formally autonomous actors engaged in self-liquidating transactions. It is the most appropriate means of coordinating behavior when transactions involve standardized goods or commodities.[38] But a market does not support long-term coordination nor can it support transactions that involve higher levels of complexity or asset specificity, both of which increase uncertainty and the vulnerability to miscommunication, shirking, or various forms of opportunism.

Much of the research on governance has drawn on transaction cost economics. Oliver Williamson argues that transaction costs incurred in markets drive the search for nonmarket governance mechanisms. One might object, first, that this argument continues to grant the market a privileged status; it is, after all, both the starting point in the analysis of governance and something of a benchmark for evaluating the efficacy of alternatives.[39] Second, and more important, critics have correctly recognized that through its focus on efficiency, transaction cost economics is under-socialized. As Mark Granovetter observes, it assumes that "social institutions and arrangements previously thought to be the adventitious result of legal, historical, social, or political forces are better viewed as the efficient solution to certain economic problems."[40] Finally, it ignores the role of power. Governance decisions involve important strategic implications for the relative power of firms. Governance structures may bring greater stability to the economic environment, but they also often entail asymmetrical distributions of power and reinforce and reproduce the power of key economic actors.[41]

When considering the history of the American economy, we can see a variety of means by which economic organizations have sought to coordinate their behavior. Long-term contracting, joint ventures, collective bargaining and formal integration provide means of coordinating bilateral relations, whereas trade associations, standard-setting organizations, research and development alliances, and interlocking directorates can be employed in multilateral relations. At the extreme, firms may consolidate through mergers as a means of fully coordinating their behavior. As noted above, the search for new governance mechanisms may be driven by the need to economize on transaction costs. It may reflect the efforts on the part of larger firms to exercise control over the supply chain and use this control to secure market share. However, public policies and institutions delimit the range of options open to economic organizations. The state both creates an institutional structure within which governance regimes evolve and is an actor in its own right.[42]

The evolution of public policy and institutions has had profound implications for governance decisions overtime. Consider the vagaries of competition policy. As noted above, there is much to suggest that the great merger wave at the turn of the twentieth century was a response to Sherman Act prohibitions on conspiracies in restraint of trade that threatened associations.[43] But the Clayton Act (1914) permitted the use of associations to coordinate some activities and, by the 1930s, key New Deal legislation promoted labor organizations and agricultural associations, subsidizing the latter. The state often went well beyond the promotion of associational governance. During the Progressive Era and the New Deal, a number of regulatory policies were created to coordinate the behavior of firms in various industries, controlling conditions of entry and exit, assigning markets, and setting prices. Many economic regulatory policies were eliminated via deregulation in the late 1970s and early 1980s, the claim being that the market—in contrast to the state— could promote greater efficiencies. And yet, when seen through the lens of governance theory, these policies often allowed industry actors to adopt non-market forms of governance, often developing mechanisms that replicated some of the coordinating functions of earlier regulatory policies.[44]

Our discussion, thus far, has focused on the policies of the national government. But in a federal system, individual states may arrive at very different decisions regarding what forms of governance are permissible, thereby giving rise to considerable variation across the nation. Consider finance. Although the Glass-Steagall Act of 1933 prohibited members of the Federal Reserve System from engaging in investment banking, state-chartered banks were under no such prohibitions. Moreover, there was great variation in branching practices. State governments created a "bewildering patchwork of interstate banking rules with various restrictions on who could enter their territory and under what conditions." Some states permitted national reciprocity, whereas others had regional reciprocity agreements that restricted entry to bank holding companies from a distinct geographical area and thus "protected[ed] the leadership positions of dominant regional banks."[45] A second example can be drawn from industrial relations. The Taft-Hartley Act created great regional variations in the governance mechanisms that could be used to coordinate the behavior of corporations and labor organizations. In states that permitted union shops, the formal relationship between corporations and unions took a different form than in states with "right-to-work" laws. In each of these examples, federal policies shaped governance decisions but their impact was mediated by state policies over which the federal government exercised little control.

Path Dependence and Institutional Change

"Path dependence" is central to our understanding of institutional change. Scholars in multiple disciplines have adopted various notions of path dependence and thus, it makes sense to note explicitly what is meant by this concept as applied here.[46] To present things in simplified terms, consider a point in time when actors seek to design institutions or introduce significant new policy initiatives. Several alternatives may be considered, but at a critical juncture, they must make a decision to adopt one alternative over the others. Once this decision is made, a path has been chosen that *may* shape the trajectory of future development. This has been stated conditionally for a reason: path dependence requires that once a choice has been made, there are factors that increase the costs of reversing course. The power of these forces may vary across policy areas and overtime. Ultimately, some decisions are, in effect, "locked in." As a result, even if actors discover at some future point that initial choices were suboptimal, this realization is often insufficient to permit movement to an alternative path.[47]

Several kinds of factors can increase the costs of reversing course and may, in some cases, be of sufficient force to make change impossible absent a significant shock. First, because institutions and public policies affect the power, resources, or investment decisions of social interests, these interests have an important stake in their preservation. Industries that enjoy subsidies or protection via regulatory barriers to entry, for example, have powerful incentives to mobilize electoral and financial resources to insulate their favored policies from change. Groups that benefit from transfers can readily form alliances with congressional committees and administrative agencies, creating what have been variously referred to as "iron triangles," "policy subsystems" and "policy monopolies." These arrangements create an institutionally induced equilibrium that can be remarkably stable for extended periods of time.[48] Second, bureaucratic agencies specialize in executing a limited set of functions that are embedded in organizational routines, decision-making procedures, staffing decisions, and patterns of interest group relations. When administrators encounter challenges, they address them within the constraints and capabilities of the agencies they occupy and this, necessarily, narrows their discretion. Third and related, there are cognitive constraints. Public policies embody a given understanding of policy problems and the underlying causal structures. They privilege certain theories and bodies of knowledge as being inherently applicable to the policy, and this, in turn, shapes organizational decisions (e.g., agency professionalization, the development of analytical resources) and the cognitive lens through which new policy problems are understood.

To make an argument that development is path dependent is not to make a far stronger claim that it results in stasis. Incremental change continues to occur, and overtime, the aggregate effects of these changes can be substantial. As B. Guy Peters, Jon Pierre, and Desmond S. King caution, political conflict "is not just a feature of formative moments but just as often occurs during path-dependent periods, whenever path dependency is sustained by a dominant political coalition successfully fending off all attempts by minorities to alter the political course."[49] But even if we stipulate that conflicts and change occur within a path dependent processes, the core point remains: decisions that are made at key moments begin a movement along a particular developmental trajectory that increasingly narrows the range of options open to policymakers.

If development occurs along a given trajectory, shaped by a host of endogenous factors, one may well witness overtime a growing disjunction between state capacities and the problems that emerge in the political economy. The state may become increasingly incapable of managing a variety of challenges. For example, Stephen Skowronek has documented how most governmental tasks in nineteenth century America were carried out by state and local governments, the national state being essentially a state of parties and courts. The stresses caused by the social and economic disruptions that accompanied industrialization led, gradually, from "state building as patchwork" to "state building as reconstruction."[50] But Skowronek's study of American state building is not one of rapid and decisive change. Rather, "administrative capacity expanded through the cracks in an edifice of rules of action and internal governmental controls articulated by courts and parties." It was an "incremental struggle simultaneously to break with the governing arrangements articulated over the course of a century and to build a whole new range of governmental capacities" which "ultimately produced a state in disarray."[51]

In many policy areas, long periods of stability are the norm. But, arguably, the most interesting features of institutional development involve the moments when the stable equilibrium that forms around policies breaks down, creating in Skowronek's words, "a state in disarray." Punctuated equilibrium arguments contend that institutions lock in a certain configuration of institutions and actors until it is upset by some exogenous shock. These shocks force new issues on to the policy agenda, mobilize new interests, or raise profound concerns about the adequacy of the prevailing approach to and understanding of policy.[52] This may occur on a policy-specific basis. However, shocks can also be of such a magnitude as to force rapid and dramatic changes in multiple policy areas, affecting broader institutional change and significant revisions in the governing philosophies regarding the role of the state in the economy. In the twentieth century, the Great Depression provides the most striking example of a shock that carried profound ramifications for the political economy, changing the trajectory of institutional development for generations.

Crises often result in an expansion of the bureaucracy and/or the creation of new administrative agencies. During such episodes, Congress may pass new statutes or presidents may issue executive orders, creating new agencies or placing demands on existing agencies that exceed their administrative capacities. Agencies, in turn, may seek to develop new and novel policy instruments in order to execute new functions. They may expand and professionalize their bureaucracies. They may develop new mechanisms for integrating new interests into the policy process. These changes, in turn, alter the trajectory of development. However, because the creation of new policies and administrative capacities rarely results in the wholesale elimination of what came before, the changes may introduce new forms of friction and incoherence. In some cases, there may be great contradictions between the changes initiated in response to crisis and the policies and institutions inherited from the past.

Although there may be a reduction in the size and scope of government immediately following a crisis, things never return to their pre-crisis level. Policies and practices embraced as a response to crisis are often retained because groups that have secured transfers from the policies (or businesses that have altered their investment, production and employment decisions in response to the policies) have substantial stakes in their perpetuation. Tight linkages between congressional committees, bureaucracies, and mobilized interests can prove remarkably resilient. Once a stable equilibrium forms around policies and agencies, they insulate policies from change, contributing to the directionality of path-dependent development. Even if conditions change substantially, policy commitments can be redefined to secure the support of new constituents. Thus, a system of agricultural subsidies introduced during the Great Depression, when 30 percent of the population was involved in the farm economy, served a very different purpose half-a-century later when large agribusiness dominated a sector that accounted for less than 2 percent of the workforce.

The directionality is also a product of changes in popular expectations or ideology that reinforce the expansion of the state and the relationships between the state and various social groups.[53] Consider the case of the Great Depression. On the eve of the New Deal, the federal government assumed very limited responsibility for social welfare. In contrast, by the end of the New Deal, citizens looked to the government for unemployment compensation, old-age pensions, agricultural subsidies, protection of the right to organize in the workplace, and a host of government services that had been introduced in the prior decade. Popular expectations changed in response to this expansion of state authority. The criteria for judging performance of governmental institutions—and one might argue, the legitimacy of the state—were permanently transformed.[54] Indeed, the changes in expectations were so great that even once Republicans regained control of the presidency and Congress during the Eisenhower administration, there was a clear recognition that success would be contingent on accepting the key changes that had occurred during the New Deal. Similarly, while the post-1980 period witnessed the growing prevalence of anti-statist rhetoric, it did not translate into retrenchment in the largest middle-class entitlement programs that have been an important driver of government growth.

Policy Regimes and American Political Economy

As a generalization, the history of the American state since the early years of the twentieth century is one of long-term institutional thickening. But let us go beyond the general institutional thickening to explore the qualitative changes in the role of the state in the economy. The thickening has been punctuated and directed by periods of rapid and substantial change in public policy and institutions, and the role of the state in the economy more generally. In such periods, new policies and institutions have common features such that one can view them as constituting more or less distinct regimes. Elsewhere, I have defined the term "regime" as "a historically specific configuration of policies and institutions which structures the relationship between social interests, the state, and economic actors in multiple sectors of the economy."[55] Regimes reflect a particular combination of interests, political-economic ideas, and administrative reform doctrines that provide broad coherence across multiple policies. The policies commonly display a related set of goals that transcend the particular features of the industry or actors they are designed to address. Regimes, once in place, are relatively durable. They structure the interaction of economic organizations and interests, thus linking the development of state structures with the development of governance and the economy more generally.

What precipitates these episodes of rapid and substantial change? In the years preceding the emergence of each of the regimes, there were significant economic crises: the depression of 1893, the Great Depression that began in 1929, and the stagflation of the 1970s. In each case, economic dislocations were followed by significant electoral change and the emergence of a new coalition capable of bringing about changes in economic policy and institutions. Political scientists have devoted much effort to the analysis of "realigning" or "critical" elections. Walter Dean Burnham observes that "eras of critical realignment are marked by short, sharp reorganizations of the mass coalitional bases of the major parties" that are "closely associated with abnormal stress in the socio-economic system" and have "durable consequences as constituent acts which determine the outer boundaries of policy, in general, though not necessarily policies in detail."[56] The electoral realignment that occurred in the 1890s gave rise to the "system of 1896," with unified Republican control of the Presidency and Congress that extended for some sixteen years. The Great Depression gave rise to the New Deal coalition and unified Democratic control for more than a decade, followed by Democratic dominance that would extend for almost half-a-century. The stagflation of the 1970s was followed by the 1980 election of Ronald Reagan and Republican control of the Senate. Although the 1980 election is rarely characterized as a realigning election, subsequent decades were characterized by split party control of the Presidency and Congress interrupted by brief periods of unified control—a sharp change from what had occurred in the decades following the rise of the New Deal coalition.

The economic dislocations that gave rise to regime change revealed the limitations of existing policies and institutions and confronted policymakers with extreme uncertainty. They were forced to make sense of a chaotic environment, identify the causes of key problems, and design remedies that often forced departures from existing patterns of state-economy relations. But it is essential to recognize that there is nothing inherent in a crisis that dictates the corresponding policy and institutional changes. To understand the shape that change assumes, one needs to look to ideas, interests, and existing policies and institutions. Let us address each in turn.

Ideas play a critical role in the formation of regimes. Crises are not self-interpreting. Rather, they are seen through the lens of prevailing political and economic theories. During significant crises, agents are confronted with high levels of uncertainty. As Mark Blyth explains:

> Cognitive mechanisms, *pace* ideas, are important because without having ideas as to how the world is put together, it would be cognitively impossible for agents to act in that world in any meaningful sense ... complex sets of ideas, such as ideas about the workings of the economy, allow agents to order and intervene in the world by aligning agents' beliefs, desires and goals. Only then can agents diagnose the crisis they are facing.[57]

Ideas are not abstract entities that are scrutinized by neutral and dispassionate actors. Rather, competing ideas or arguments are tightly bound with interests. They justify alternative policy proposals that can have very different implications for the core questions of politics: who gets what, when and how. Thus, it is necessary to discuss ideas and interests together.

Ideas were central to each of the regimes that emerged during the period since the beginning of the twentieth century. Consider the Progressive Era. New theoretical understandings of economic evolution, the role of the state in the economy, and institutional design played a central role in shaping innovations. However, divisions among Progressives over central questions about the relationship between the state and corporations created deep internal fissures. If the rise of the large-scale corporate economy was both inevitable and largely beneficial, perhaps the best response would take the form of corporatism. Following Theodore Roosevelt's New Nationalism, the state could respond to the growing concentration of economic power by negotiating the terms of economic change with large economic institutions. Alternatively, if the concentration of economic power was not inevitable—if it was a product of corporate decisions regarding organization and conduct—the state could play a far different role. As Woodrow Wilson's New Freedom suggested, neutral experts could identify with precision the practices that led to the creation of market power and prohibit them. While both of these strands of progressivism envisioned an expanded role for the state in the economy, the implications for policy and patterns of state-economy relations were radically different.

During the Great Depression, actors with competing interpretations of the economic collapse battled over what constituted the correct policy response.[58] The competing theoretical arguments had radically different implications for policy, institutional design, and the integration of economic interests in the state. Some argued that the depression was a product of administered pricing among large corporations, which collaborated to reduce levels of output and thus elevated unemployment. Harkening back to arguments that came to prominence in the Progressive Era, one response would be to create new administrative structures to coordinate pricing and output decisions in a manner that would support recovery. In contrast, others argued that the depression was the product of secular stagnation. As corporations engaged in more capital intensive production, the demand for labor would be permanently depressed, thereby creating persistent problems of underemployment. The correct response would be the creation of public works to employ those who could no longer be absorbed by a mature capitalist economy. These positions could be contrasted with Keynesian (or pre-Keynesian) arguments about under-consumption and aggregate demand failure that were used to justify redistribution and counter-cyclical demand management.[59]

Each of these intellectual arguments prevailed at one time or another, giving rise to a broad range of institutions and policies ranging from the corporatist experiment of the National Recovery Administration (NRA) to the universal welfare state programs created under the Social Security Act of 1935. The resulting policies had very different implications for economic actors. The NRA envisioned a role for government-supervised self-regulation, and thus could be potentially useful in integrating big business—and unions that were empowered by the NRA's codes—into the New Deal's coalition. The Agricultural Adjustment Administration (AAA) sought to raise farm incomes, thereby giving the agricultural economy a powerful stake in the New Deal, even if it created difficulties for the urban unemployed. The secular stagnation thesis envisioned the expansion of public employment, thereby providing support for the unemployed and gaining the allegiance of municipal party machines. The under-consumption thesis, insofar as it demanded a redistribution of income, would provide benefits for lower and middle-income Americans while forcing far greater burdens on the wealthy and large corporations. The battle over ideas during the New Deal was thus, simultaneously, a battle over interests.

The symbiosis of ideas and interests was perhaps nowhere more evident than during the 1970s. A series of political defeats (e.g., the expansion of social regulations) mobilized corporations and trade associations, which dramatically expanded their investment in organization, campaign spending, and policy advocacy. A number of scholars and policy analysts, often working within corporate-funded think tanks, argued that stagflation was a predictable consequence of the failed policies of the past. The correct response was a return to the market.[60] The debates of the period, largely dominated by the Right, found an expression in deregulation and regulatory reform, which gained momentum during the late 1970s and 1980s, a rejection of active Keynesian demand management and an embrace of supply side and monetarist policies, dramatic reductions in taxation (particularly among the wealthier tax payers), and significant changes in the means-tested income support policies for the non-elderly population.

Of course, interests and ideas are only part of the story. The policies and institutions inherited from the past play a central role in shaping the terms of regime change. First, and most obviously, past policies and institutions frame debates about the causes of current problems, as suggested in the above discussion of stagflation. Second and more importantly, the array of options open to policymakers is constrained by the forces identified above. To change the trajectory of political development is not to eliminate the legacy of the past. If governmental institutions lack the capacity to formulate and implement the new policies, if key interests are not integrated into the agencies in question in a way that is supportive of change, there may be significant difficulties. There is much to suggest, for example, that the success of the AAA relative to other New Deal initiatives was a product of these factors. It was placed in a highly professionalized department (the Department of Agriculture) with well-established relationships with agricultural organizations and the departments of agriculture and agricultural economics in the nation's land grant institutions.[61] On the other side of the equation, some explanations of the poor macroeconomic performance in the 1970s relative to many European nations focus on the incapacity in the United States to design and implement an effective wage-price policy. Unlike northern European nations, the United States had not developed the capacity to bargain effectively with peak business and labor associations, thereby allowing conflicts between capital and labor to be fought out in the market rather than resolved within government structures.[62]

Third, because new regimes are layered upon existing institutions and policies, each period of rapid change can give rise to new sources of friction, conflict and incoherence in the overall role of the state in the economy and its relationship to key constituent groups. Although popular periodization creates the impression that there is a sharp break between historical periods— that the introduction of the new brings the elimination of the old—new policies and agencies are, more usually, superimposed upon the old, creating a "path-dependent layering process." Preexisting policies representing disparate interests and models of state-economy relations give rise to a host of tensions and conflicts that compromise the extent, direction, and rapidity of institutional change.[63] The end result is not simply a general thickening of government, but growing complexity that exacerbates problems of policy incoherence. Consider the example of finance—a salient topic given the financial crisis that began in 2007–8. During the Progressive Era, the regulatory structure created under the Civil War banking laws was supplemented by a newly created regulatory agency, the Federal Reserve, which shared responsibilities with the Treasury. During the New Deal, the Banking Act of 1933 (the Glass-Steagall Act) forced the separation of investment and commercial banking and created deposit insurance via the Federal Deposit Insurance Corporation. A parallel regulatory system was created for the thrift industry while the Securities and Exchange Commission was created to regulate the exchanges and the over-the-counter market. New government-sponsored enterprises were created to add liquidity to the real estate markets. In the past three decades, many of the regulatory distinctions created during the New Deal were eliminated through deregulation, and financial innovations led to the emergence of new financial products, practices, and institutions that were outside of the existing regulatory structure. Although successive regimes brought significant changes in financial regulation, rather than eliminating old policies and institutions, new initiatives were layered upon the old, giving rise to a complex regulatory labyrinth that promoted patterns of economic activity that were difficult to anticipate and control. The collapse of 2008 was partially the production of the disjunction between the complex regulatory structure created over the past century and the tightly coupled financial system that had emerged in the shadow of the state.

Conclusion

When one surveys the development of the political economy since the turn of the twentieth century, there are several periods of rapid and substantial change in policies and institutions that have brought about qualitative changes in the role of the state in the economy. We can identify three distinct regimes: the Progressive Regime, the New Deal Regime, and the Neoliberal Regime. Let us discuss the key features of each regime and preview the chapters that constitute Part II of this book.

The first regime, the Progressive Regime, solidified in the early decades of the twentieth century. The emergence of the modern corporate economy in the late nineteenth century, the rise of organized labor, waves of immigration and urbanization forced a host of new policy problems on to the agenda. Following the depression of the 1890s and the realigning election of 1896, prolonged stability in the control of national institutions created the context for a series of reforms, most notably, new regulatory policies that embodied novel experiments in institutional design. Reflecting the internal divisions within Progressivism, the new policies and institutions reflected both New Nationalist and New Freedom arguments regarding the role of the state and patterns of state-economy relations. In some cases, most notably, the Federal Reserve, economic actors were integrated directly into state institutions. In other cases (i.e., antitrust), regulation was used to prohibit various forms of corporate conduct and coordination that could undermine market processes. This period is the subject of Chapter 3.

The New Deal regime emerged in response to the Great Depression. The policy and institutional initiatives introduced by the New Deal and expanded in subsequent decades dramatically changed the role of the state in the economy and society more generally. New regulatory institutions were created to govern multiple industries, most notably, finance and agriculture, and manage industrial relations. These regulations had profound implications for the economic governance and the role of the state in coordinating key corporate decisions. New social welfare policies were introduced to provide income maintenance for the elderly, the unemployed, and children. The Social Security Act was arguably the most significant legislation of the period, creating entitlements for the majority of citizens. By the end of the period, the federal government had also made a commitment to countercyclical fiscal policy as a means of managing the vicissitudes of the business cycle. The innovations of the New Deal will be explored in Chapter 4.

The dramatic expansion of the state and the introduction of new policies and institutions during the 1930s served to reinforce the New Deal coalition and gave the Democratic Party extended control over national institutions. Thus, the next several decades allowed for a consolidation and extension of the New Deal Regime. In the immediate postwar period, the subject of Chapter 5, a number of significant changes were introduced to prevent the recurrence of the carnage of the Great Depression and World War II. On the international side, the introduction of the Bretton Woods monetary system and the General Agreement in Tariffs and Trade facilitated a dramatic expansion of international commerce. Henceforth, trade would become an increasingly important source of growth and instability for the United States and other nations integrated into the world economy. On the domestic side, debates over a full employment act resulted in the creation of a new institutional structure for managing the macroeconomy. While greater stability in the international and domestic economies allowed for a period of prolonged growth, significant changes in industrial relations provided a mechanism by which the fruits of growth could be distributed to a much larger portion of the population.

During the 1960s, it appeared to many that the promise of the earlier reforms would find their ultimate expression in the rise of the Keynesian social welfare state. Fiscal policy devoted to the attainment of full employment and further expansions of the welfare state allowed for impressive growth and the highest level of income equality in the postwar period. However, by the 1970s, stagflation created a window of opportunity to challenge some of the core policies and institutions put into place since the New Deal. The seeming incapacity of policymakers to restrain inflation and induce growth raised serious concerns about the efficacy of macroeconomic management grounded in Keynesian theory. Simultaneously, there was growing skepticism regarding the welfare-regulatory state that had emerged out of the New Deal and evolved in the postwar period. While there were many competing explanations of stagflation, those that prevailed in this environment called for state retrenchment and a return to the market. This episode is the subject of Chapter 6.

Chapter 7 turns to the rise of the Neoliberal Regime. Ronald Reagan won the 1980 presidential election based, in part, in his success in associating the economic turmoil of the 1970s with the advent of the interventionist state. His program, which combined a rejection of Keynesianism, regulatory expansion and social welfare, with the promotion of significant tax cuts and an embrace of free markets, set the tone for subsequent administrations. The neoliberal agenda first articulated in the United States by Reagan found its clearest expression in subsequent administrations. The chapters that comprise Part III of this book will consider some of the ramifications of the policy decisions made during this critical period and will explore whether they have set the stage for a new period of rapid and substantial change that could precipitate the emergence of a new regime.

Part II

The Evolution of the American Political Economy

3 The Progressive Regime and the Regulatory State

The Progressive Era, spanning from the 1890s to the end of World War I, brought rapid and dramatic reforms that combined democratization, an expansive policy agenda, and a profound transformation in the understanding of the state and its role in the economy. By the end of the period, regulations had been extended to corporate organization, railroads, food and drugs, natural resources, and finance. Initiatives were combined with novel experiments in institutional design that departed from established constitutional principles and placed a heavy reliance on scientific and social scientific expertise. The new regulatory policies had significant consequences, both intended and unanticipated, on the organization and evolution of the modern corporate economy. Although there were other significant changes (e.g., the ratification of the 16th Amendment authorizing an income tax), this chapter focuses on the regulatory legacy. Before exploring the Progressive Regime in greater detail, we need to survey briefly the broad changes in the economy. The rise of the modern corporation and the emergence of national markets raised serious questions about the balance of public and private power.

The Transformation of the American Economy

The latter half of the nineteenth century brought a fundamental transformation of the U.S. economy. The railroads, which expanded from some 30,626 miles in 1860 to 166,703 miles three decades later, were central to this process.[1] In the words of Richard Bensel:

> the railroad in many ways transformed the United States from a disparate collection of self-sufficient local communities into an integrated national market .... By the turn of the century, these networks, themselves subjected to corporate consolidation and reorganization, amply provided the means through which organizational and technological advances in the major industrial processes might be harnessed.[2]

The rails created a demand for iron and coal and, by permitting an expansion of markets, promoted innovations in storage and distribution. The new scale of activity forced corporations to develop far more sophisticated managerial structures. Railroads employed operating divisions to manage lengths of rail, with subdivisions to supervise traffic, maintenance and investments; by the 1880s, the model had evolved into line-and-staff organizations with lines of communication and authority linking the general manager, the general superintendent, and the division superintendents, thereby integrating a complex set of tasks.[3] As corporations in industries such as chemicals, petroleum, food processing, primary metals and manufacturing employed high-volume, continuous production technologies and expanded into an ever-growing market, the multi-divisional corporate form evolved and spread through the economy.[4]

Federal and state governments heavily subsidized railroad expansion. Railroads were given special action franchises that allowed them to exercise eminent domain when laying tracks, and land grants that amounted to almost 7 percent of the continental United States and constituted more than one-fourth of the total railroad investment.[5] The demand for capital also stimulated financial markets. Railroads enlisted the assistance of investment bankers and traded their securities on the New York Stock Exchange. Investment banks like J.W. Seligman & Co. and Drexel, Morgan & Co. used overseas affiliates to raise funds for the expansion of the rails and US industry more generally. Wall Street became "the funnel whereby funds from all parts of the nation were gathered and then distributed to transportation, manufacturing, and mercantile establishments."[6]

Railroads also began to coordinate operating procedures and standardize rails and equipment through associations. But these associations could also be used to undermine competition. When the Supreme Court determined that traffic associations were a violation of the Sherman Antitrust Act,[7] the railroads turned to consolidations. Although the great merger wave of 1898–1902 brought some 270 railroad mergers, it spread well beyond transportation. Throughout the economy, firms replaced horizontal agreements with consolidation. The period witnessed 529 mergers in manufacturing.[8] Investment bankers, most notably, J. Pierpont Morgan, played a key role in managing consolidations to create some of the giant firms that would come to symbolize American capitalism. US Steel, the nation's first billion dollar company was the product of a 1901 consolidation engineered by Morgan that united the Carnegie Steel Company, the Federal Steel Company, and the National Steel Company, the latter two being themselves the products of earlier consolidations. US Steel controlled over two-thirds of the nation's steel production, a number of transportation and mining companies and firms producing finished goods.[9] The merger wave gave birth to a number of additional commercial leviathans, including General Electric, International Harvester, Dupont, Standard Oil, American Tobacco, and Eastman Kodak.

The period also witnessed a rapid growth of organized labor. The American Federation of Labor (AFL) was created in 1886, uniting some 150,000 craft workers from 25 different labor unions. By 1900, its membership exceeded half-a-million members, with an additional quarter million workers belonging to independent or unaffiliated unions.[10] The AFL's president Samuel Gompers promoted "business unionism," focusing on bread-and-butter issues like wages, hours, and working conditions. The founding of the AFL coincided with a significant increase in the number of strikes. In the five years preceding the AFL (1881–85), there was an average of 527.8 work stoppages a year, involving an average of 148.2 thousand workers. In the next fifteen years (1886–1900), the average number of strikes almost tripled to 1,410 per year, involving an average of 381.8 thousand workers per year.[11] Corporations employing mass production technologies created a demand for unskilled industrial workers, a demand that was met by waves of immigration that, in the last three decades of the nineteenth century, brought 11.7 million immigrants, less than 12 percent of whom could be classified as skilled workers.[12] Conflicts between the skilled craft workers of the AFL and the growing army of unskilled industrial labor would create a division in the labor movement that would continue for the next half-century.

For all of the long-term trends exhibited in the late nineteenth century, the most important event was the depression that began in January 1893 and reached its trough in June of 1894. The initial shock was a financial panic and a wave of bank failures. At the depth of the depression, the economy was operating at 20 to 25 percent below capacity. "Distress was evident in the knots of idle men clustered murmuring around plant or store entrances, whiling away time at home, or tramping the countryside … the look of want was common in the land."[13] Republicans attributed the depression to President Grover Cleveland and congressional Democrats who had lowered tariffs and, with the 1894 midterm elections, they gained 130 seats in the House to wrest control from the Democrats, and four seats in the Senate to strengthen their working majority. Most troubling for Democrats, Republicans gained even in urban areas that had previously supported the Democratic Party.

In the 1896 convention, the Democratic Party abandoned the incumbent and gravitated toward William Jennings Bryan. Bryan waged a populist campaign based on the expansion of the money supply through the issuance of dollars backed by silver, further reductions in the Republican tariff, and an expansion of business regulation. This populist appeal, aimed toward farmers and workers, was most salient in the South and the West. It created divisions in the party, however, repelling some Eastern Democrats (some of whom would make a third party challenge as a pro-gold National Democratic Party). The Republican candidate William McKinley responded to Bryan with claims that the Democrats' easy money policy would be inflationary; an assault on the tariff would worsen economic conditions. McKinley's broad appeal allowed him to create a coalition uniting business, labor, and farmers, particularly from the Midwest where Bryan's evangelicalism was anathema to Catholic and Lutheran immigrants. In the general election, McKinley won a decisive victory in the Electoral College and although the GOP lost 48 seats in the House, it retained control of both chambers of Congress. The 1894 and 1896 elections brought an expansion of the Republican coalition and forced a realignment, resulting in a sixteen year Republican dominance of the presidency. Democrats would work to forge an alliance of farmers and labor, but these efforts—frustrated by sectional and cultural factors—would bear little fruit until the next major economic dislocation and the rise of the New Deal coalition.[14]

Progressivism and Institutional Design

Progressivism was distinctive for a number of reasons. First, the Progressives placed a heavy emphasis on the role of scientific and social scientific expertise. The late nineteenth century witnessed the dissemination of the German model of higher education in the United States (which promoted research rather than the mastery of classic texts) and the rapid expansion of the nation's system of higher education. At the same time, the academic disciplines were becoming professionalized. Between 1884 and 1903, a number of academic associations were founded, including the American Historical Association, the American Economic Association, the American Political Science Association and the American Sociological Society. Increasingly, social scientists sought solutions to the social and economic problems that emerged from the changes discussed above. In the words of Dorothy Ross: "The new concentrations of economic power, the teeming, polyglot cities, and the expansion of urban, state, and federal governance created new worlds that required detailed knowledge."[15]

The emphasis on expertise was combined with a new understanding of progress. Following Charles Darwin (and Herbert Spencer who developed the social implications of Darwin), many viewed political economic development through the lens of evolutionary theory. Rather than embracing a transcendent and trans-historical set of values and ideal types, they believed that nations, institutions, and human nature evolved. Under the influence of Georg Hegel, many also held a faith in progress toward a rational end-state. The contrast with James Madison's famous *Federalist* 10 could not be greater. Madison's argument (and the original constitutional design) was premised on the belief that the causes of factions were permanent, grounded in a human nature that was fixed and flawed. One must design institutions to manage their effects. Progressives countered that historical progress would eliminate the causes of faction and give rise to a unity of will. As Ronald J. Pestritto notes of Woodrow Wilson:

> for him, the latent causes of faction are *not* sown in the nature of man, or if they are, historical progress will overcome this human nature. With the unity of national sentiment, political questions become less contentious and less important. We cease to concentrate on the question of what should be done, and more on the question of how we should do it.[16]

As Herbert Croly stated in his 1911 treatise, *The Promise of American Life*: "Democracy must stand or fall on a platform of possible human perfectibility. If human nature cannot be improved by institutions, democracy is at best a more than usually safe form of political organization."[17] For Progressives, science could offer the expertise to direct this evolution toward ends consistent with the public interest.

The emphasis placed on social engineering carried powerful elitist implications and raises an interesting puzzle insofar as a third, and at first glance, seemingly contradictory feature of Progressivism was the celebration of democracy. Many Progressives were at the forefront of electoral reforms, including the initiative, the referendum, and the direct primary. Political parties came under a particularly heavy assault and were increasingly regulated as public utilities.[18] Moreover, the Progressive Era brought the direct election of senators, following the 1913 ratification of the 17th amendment. How does one make sense of this democratic strand of Progressivism given the elitist embrace of specialized expertise? Following the realigning election of 1896, electoral competition declined markedly and the power of party machines constituted a considerable barrier to reform and to the advancement of reform-minded politicians. As Martin Shefter explains:

> The ideology that bound the movement together was formulated by a class of intellectuals and professionals who argued that a government that was dominated by a party machine, and that consequently enacted only those policies which served the interests that were tied to the machine, was both corrupt and irrational … . In lieu of such a regime, the Progressives proposed to create a set of institutions that would respond directly to the voice of the people, rather than filtering it through party, and that would pay heed to the dictates of science.[19]

As James A. Morone recognizes, this was a "political paradox: government would be simultaneously returned to the people and placed beyond them, in the hands of experts."[20]

One must note a fourth feature of Progressivism: the rejection of constitutional formalism. In the words of Wilson, government "falls, not under the theory of the universe, but under the theory of organic life. It is accountable to Darwin, not to Newton … Living political constitutions must be Darwinian in structure and in practice. Society is a living organism and must obey the laws of life, not of mechanics; it must develop." And thus, in Wilson's concise formulation:

> All that progressives ask or desire is permission—in an era when "development," "evolution," is the scientific word—to interpret the Constitution according to the Darwinian principle; all they ask is recognition of the fact that a nation is a living thing and not a machine.[21]

The rejection of constitutional formalism permitted experimentation with institutional design. The independent regulatory commission, for example, with its combination of legislative, executive and judicial functions, violated the separation of powers. Yet, Progressives believed that such institutions could provide administrators with the flexibility needed to direct the process of economic change.

Competing Visions of the State in the Economy

One can observe the existence of evolutionary processes and yet accept vastly different notions of the role the state should play. William Graham Sumner, the chief academic proponent of Spencer in the United States, was a staunch opponent of government interference with evolutionary processes. In contrast, Progressives, influenced by Hegelian teleology, promoted a far more ambitious vision of the state. Yet, even here there were significant differences. These differences were most pronounced in the debates surrounding the election of 1912. Taft, the Republican incumbent, was an orthodox constitutionalist who wanted to preserve the separation of powers and resisted the expansion of the administrative state. Despite Teddy Roosevelt's reputation as a "trust buster," in four years the Taft administration had filed ninety antitrust prosecutions—more than double that of his predecessor who had served nearly twice as long.[22] Taft doubted that antitrust was sufficient as a regulatory tool; he advocated federal charters for corporations engaged in interstate commerce, believing that this would allow for greater judicial oversight. Although he supported an active role for the judiciary, he nonetheless argued that the government should not "prevent reasonable concentrations of capital ... necessary to the economic development of manufacture, trade, and commerce."[23]

Roosevelt's vision of the state was an expansive one that he had held for decades. In 1894, for example, he observed that "the laissez-faire doctrine of the old school of political economists" found little support in history, which revealed "that every race, as it has grown to civilized greatness, has used the power of the State more and more." The state had a vital role: "to counterbalance the operation of that baleful law of natural selection."[24] The next year, he explained:

> the great prizes are battled for among the men who wage no war whatever for mere subsistence, while the fight for mere subsistence is keenest among precisely the classes which contribute very little indeed to the progress of the race.

Roosevelt continued:

> In civilized societies the rivalry of natural selection works against progress. Progress ... results not from the crowding out of the lower classes by the upper, but on the contrary from the steady rise of the lower classes to the level of the upper, as the latter tend to vanish, or at most barely hold their own. In progressive societies it is often the least fit who survive; but, on the other hand, they and their children often tend to grow more fit.[25]

With the approach of the 1912 election, Roosevelt's focus turned to the rise of the large-scale corporate economy. The state had a vital function: to define the terms of economic change to further the public interest. Rather than denouncing large corporations, he celebrated their contributions to efficiency. They were "the result of an imperative economic law which cannot be repealed by legislation." Since "the effort at prohibiting all combinations has substantially failed," he argued that "the way out lies, not in attempting to prevent such combinations but in completely controlling them in the interest of the public welfare."[26] To this end, Roosevelt envisioned the creation of an industrial commission to collect information on production and economic organization and use its expertise to facilitate agreements both within industries and between corporations and labor, while regulating access to capital markets. Roosevelt's corporatist system was premised on the belief that most economic organizations would voluntarily cooperate, and "the good trusts" could be rewarded with an antitrust exemption. The "bad trusts" that failed to participate should be exposed to prosecution under the antitrust law, and any corporation violating the orders of the commission should also at once become exposed to such prosecution.[27]

Taft rejected the distinctions between good and bad trusts and, more importantly, found the system proposed by Roosevelt to be one that would place far too much power in the hands of a single agency and vest the presidency with arbitrary powers.[28] Others arrived at a similar judgment. For example, a review of *The New Nationalism*, the collection of Roosevelt's speeches published in 1911, asked:

> "Upon what meat doth this our Caesar feed that he is grown so great?" Strong meat, no doubt, too strong for babies, for the average man and woman, for the student of politics and the lovers of freedom, beauty, and wisdom, whose faint pipings are drowned by the trumpet's blare. This may be *The New Nationalism*, but it is not democracy.[29]

Wilson offered a much different vision and challenge to Roosevelt's New Nationalism. In 1910, he described the recent changes in the economy that had resulted in "the submergence of the individual within the organization" and rendered workers "mere cogs in a machine which has men for its parts." Roosevelt viewed the large corporation and trusts as the beneficial products of economic evolution. Wilson dismissed this romantic notion:

> a corporation is merely a convenient instrument of business and we may regulate its use as we please and those who use it. Here is merely an artificial, a fictitious person, whom God did not make or endow, which we ourselves have made with our own hands and can alter as we will.[30]

Unfortunately, Wilson argued in 1911, the prevailing approach to regulation was mired in an antiquated understanding of the corporation as an individual.

Under contemporary conditions, commerce "is pursued by great companies, great corporations, which exist only by express license of law and for the convenience of society." Rather than continuing to live in a fictitious world in which law is designed to accommodate "the impulses and enterprises of individuals," policymakers must understand that the law is concerned with "the impulses of bodies of men, to the aggregate use of money drawn from a myriad of sources as if from the common savings of society at large." The implications for the law and regulation were clear: "As experience becomes more and more aggregate law must be more and more organic, institutional, constructive. It is a study in the correlation of forces."[31]

New Nationalism may well have been grounded in a belief in the "correlation of forces," but Wilson found Roosevelt's plan naïve. As he asked in 1912: "Is the government going to make Christians of these trusts? ... Is the government going to persuade them to be kind and benevolent to us in the use of their enormous and irresistible power?" Or is it "going to take us back a hundred years, nay 150 years, in our development and put us in tutelage again?"[32] Wilson was convinced that under New Nationalism, the trusts would ultimately assume the dominant role:

> If the government is to tell big business men how to run their business, then don't you see that big business men have to get closer to the government even than they are now? Don't you see that they must capture the government, in order not to be restrained too much by it?[33]

Rather than condoning Roosevelt's corporatist vision, Wilson argued that one should use the law to frustrate the creation of market power. In Wilson's words: "Everybody who has even read the newspapers knows the means by which these men build up their power and created these monopolies. Any decently equipped lawyer can suggest to you statutes by which the whole business can be stopped." Wilson elaborated: "there must be no squeezing out of the beginner, no crippling his credit; no discrimination against retailers who buy from a rival; no holding back of raw materials from him; no secret arrangements against him."[34] To this end, Wilson proposed a new commission, staffed with neutral experts, to analyze the practices and trends within industry and, with flexible procedures, design administrative rules to prohibit those forms of conduct and organization that created market power. Rather than cooperating with good trusts, Wilson wanted to prevent their emergence.

Constructing the Regulatory State

The 1912 debates were emblematic of a larger question about the nature of the economy and the role of the state. As Nathan B. Williams observed: "It is apparent to students of present-day economics that a very real conflict is on in this country between two alliteratively designated economic theories—competition—cooperation. The results of this contest no man can foresee."[35]

The promotion of competition found its clearest expression in antitrust: the Sherman Act of 1890 made illegal monopolization or attempts to monopolize and conspiracies in restraint of trade whereas the Clayton Act of 1914 declared price discrimination, exclusive dealing and tying contracts, the acquisition of competing companies, and corporate interlocks to be illegal where the effects "may be to substantially lessen competition or tend to create a monopoly in any line of commerce."

At the same time, there was also growing support for cooperation. Many argued that large businesses had developed the organizational capacity to manage the most disruptive effects of competition; industrial self-government would benefit the public. As Allen Ripley Foote argued in 1912, the high costs of market competition "forced the era of co-operation into existence, which commenced when men who intelligently studied the use, development, ineffectiveness and tendencies of unregulated competition, began to change their business methods to safeguard their business against wastage and destruction by adopting measures to restrain trade by regulating competition between themselves." Antitrust had done great damage to cooperation and its prohibition of conspiracies merely "compelled the organization of combines, trusts and abnormally large corporations." For Foote, and other advocates of cooperation, the implications were clear: "Governmental regulation of business will benefit the people to the degree in which it successfully aids economic efficiency. This can best be done by providing for and promoting co-operation."[36]

As Wilson and other critics would note, the support for cooperation and industrial self-governance rested on optimistic behavioral assumptions. If, indeed, businesses were simply seeking to manage production scientifically, there might be little to fear. But if they were seeking to create and exercise market power, then public policy would simply create more autocrats of trade. A closer examination of three of the key regulatory initiatives of the Progressive Regime reveals that the simple dichotomy—competition versus cooperation—veiled more complicated questions of institutional design and the challenges of extending regulatory authority within a governmental structure that was accountable to Newton, not Darwin.

The Interstate Commerce Commission

The dichotomy between competition and cooperation obscures the fact that it is often impossible to create the preconditions of market competition. In some industries, such as the railroads, a concentration of power was inevitable. Thus, regulatory attention turned to the practices of the railroads and their ratemaking activities. The Interstate Commerce Act of 1887 created the Interstate Commerce Commission (ICC), and imposed federal regulation over what previously had been an object of state regulation. Section 1 of the Act stated: "All charges made for any service rendered ... shall be reasonable and just." It then prohibited a host of practices that could be used to discriminate (e.g., special rates, rebates, and drawbacks, price discrimination against shipments over shorter distances) and pooling or market sharing arrangements. Railroads were now required to publish their rate and fare schedules and give at least ten days' advance notice for increases (although not for reductions). They were also required to provide these rate schedules, along with agreements and contracts made with other common carriers, to the ICC. Railroads were held financially liable for damages resulting from violations of the Interstate Commerce Act.[37]

The ICC's success was compromised by several factors. First, the provisions in the Interstate Commerce Act, when taken together, lacked coherence: they were products of coalition building, employed to enlist the support of interests ranging from radical agrarians to oil producers. In Stephen Skowronek's words,

> Congress capitulated to all concerned. In the end, this first national regulatory policy partook of the old distributive principle that the best measure was the one that every legislator could take back to his district with some evidence of dutiful service.[38]

If the Act was designed with competition in mind, its effects were ambiguous. For example, the prohibition on pooling—one means of managing excess capacity and rationalizing competition—would promote competition. But the rate differentials, prohibited by the long- and short-haul clause, were products of competition insofar as competition varied over different segments of track.

A second problem: Congress employed terms like "unjust and unreasonable charges" and "unjust discrimination," but failed to provide legislative guidance on how to make these determinations. Authority was simply delegated to the ICC. Following the examples set by state railroad commissions, the ICC allowed carriers to set rates and then, upon complaint, addressed issues of reasonableness, ultimately setting maximum rates and relying on the courts to force compliance. However, in 1897, the Supreme Court struck a serious blow to the ICC when it decided that its rate-fixing powers lacked a statutory foundation. It concluded: "The grant of such a power is never to be implied. The power itself is so vast and comprehensive, so largely affecting the rights of carrier and shipper, as well as indirectly all commercial transactions ... that no just rule of construction would tolerate a grant of such power by mere implication."[39] As a result of this, and other decisions narrowing the powers and duties of the ICC, it had become, in the words of Justice John Harlan, "a useless body for all practical purposes ... shorn, by judicial interpretation, of authority to do anything of an effective character."[40]

New legislation would specify and expand the powers of the ICC. Most importantly, the Hepburn Act of 1906, passed at the urging of President Roosevelt, granted the ICC the explicit power to set maximum rates and made the commission's orders effective upon promulgation, thereby reducing the role of the courts. It also expanded the size of the commission, extended its jurisdiction to cover sleeping cars, express companies, and oil pipeline companies, and prohibited railroads from owning the goods they shipped. Four years later, Congress passed the Mann Elkins Act, creating a new Commerce Court to review appeals of ICC orders, strengthening the long- and short-haul clause, and once again extending the commission's jurisdiction, this time to telegraph, telephone, and cable companies. Although the Commerce Court was eliminated in 1913—it proved overly accommodating to railroad interests—the ICC became a more effective regulator, and the independent regulatory commission became a model that reformers would drawn on again.[41]

The Federal Trade Commission

Wilson argued in the 1912 campaign that the antitrust laws had to be given greater specificity to address the causes of monopoly. In a January 1914 address to Congress, he returned to the theme and stated:

> Surely we are sufficiently familiar with the actual processes and methods of monopoly and of the many hurtful restraints of trade to make definition possible, at any rate up to the limits of what experience has disclosed. These practices, being now abundantly disclosed, can be explicitly and item by item forbidden by statute.[42]

That year, Congress passed the Clayton Act, prohibiting practices that contributed to the creation of monopoly. Wilson was unsatisfied, opining to Colonel Edward House that the Act was "so weak that you cannot tell it from water."[43]

Some members of Congress had become alarmed by the Court's interpretation of the Sherman Act after its 1911 *Standard Oil* decision, which established the "rule of reason." Most commercial transactions impose restraints on trade, and thus their legality must rest on their reasonableness—a determination to be made by the Court.[44] Congress began considering various proposals for new antitrust legislation and the creation of a new administrative body prior to the 1912 election. With Wilson's active support, Congress passed the Federal Trade Commission Act. During the legislative debates, Senator Francis Newlands (D-NV), one of the chief proponents of the FTC, carefully distinguished the proposed commission from New Nationalism, noting: "Some would found such a commission upon the theory that monopolistic industry is the ultimate result of economic evolution and that it should be so recognized and declared to be vested with a public interest." The FTC would be grounded in the belief that "private monopoly is intolerable, unscientific, and abnormal" and "a commission is a necessary adjust to the preservation of competition and to the practical enforcement of the law."[45]

But this begged the question of what, in fact, the law should be and what powers should be vested in the commission. Congress ultimately decided that rather than specifying practices with precision, it should instead prohibit "unfair methods of competition in commerce." For some critics, the statutory vagueness undermined the potential role of the new agency. Writing in 1914, Samuel Untermyer was highly critical of the legislation: it was "carefully stripped of all vitality" to become "a mere empty shell." He continued: "There is no attempt here to deal with the innumerable secret arrangements in the forms of pools fixing prices, limiting production, and otherwise restricting competition, 'gentlemen's agreements,' and other similar devices with which the country is honeycombed." In his judgment, the final product "pretends to regulate and accomplishes nothing."[46] The Act, in contrast, was premised on the belief that corporate practices could change rapidly, and thus, rather than defining the FTC's mandate with excessive precision, it should be delegated the authority to make detailed determinations of what, in fact, constituted "unfair methods of competition in commerce."

Reflecting the Progressive faith in neutral expertise and a belief in the fluidity of institutional forms, the new FTC would need to be an independent commission, comparable to the ICC, with five commissioners appointed by the president, with no more than a simple majority drawn from the same party. Staffed by experts, many of whom were transferred from the Commerce Department's Bureau of Corporations, the FTC would have the capacity to analyze industrial conditions and business practices, and write regulatory rules prohibiting forms of conduct that were deemed to constitute "unfair methods of competition." This was a legislative function. But the new FTC would also exercise executive functions in filing complaints against firms that violated its rules, and judicial functions insofar as complaints would be adjudicated within the confines of the agency.

The FTC ran into significant problems from the beginning. Staffing and resources were woefully inadequate given the large number of complaints filed with the FTC and the ongoing congressional demands for investigations. Moreover, when the FTC concluded investigations and made recommendation to Congress, it could easily run afoul of local interests. For example, when an investigation of the meatpacking industry (the so-called "beef trust") led to recommendations for the nationalization of rail cars, refrigerator cars, stockyards, and cold storage facilities, Congress responded by stripping the FTC of jurisdiction over the industry. The FTC also, predictably, ran afoul of the courts, which challenged its authority to prohibit activities that were not explicitly addressed by the Clayton Act or previous court decisions, or regulate what could be construed as intrastate rather than interstate commerce. Moreover, although the FTC had been granted broad investigative powers, the Court placed restrictions on the ability of the agency to open investigations at will, finding this power to be in conflict with the Fourth Amendment's prohibition of illegal search and seizure.[47] Progressives like Wilson may have been able to muster a powerful intellectual justification for an expansion of the administrative state, but this state—at least for the time being—would stand in tension with existing national institutions.

The Federal Reserve

The third great regulatory experiment of the Progressive Era, the Federal Reserve, was also created during the Wilson presidency. The debates over the creation of a new regulatory agency grew in intensity following the financial panic of 1907, "a violent financial panic" that "shook the United States from the Atlantic to the Pacific" and "ruined multitudes of worthy men by unmerited disaster." Hearings by the newly created National Monetary Commission and the investigations of the so-called "money trust" by the Pujo subcommittee of the House Banking Committee contributed to the salience of financial regulation, the latter providing, in the words of Senator Robert L. Owen (D-OK), "a most remarkable and startling report, showing a concentration of control of credits and of business properties, through three hundred and forty-one directors of one hundred and twelve corporations, of property exceeding twenty-two thousand millions of dollars."[48]

The debates focused on what kind of institutional arrangement would be necessary to collect and hold reserves (and what kinds of assets might count as reserves), determine the discount rate, buy and sell financial instruments in open market activities, and issue currency.[49] One proposal, drawn up by Nelson W. Aldrich (R-NY), would have divided the nation into fifteen districts and vested authority in a National Reserve Association, with a board of directors dominated by bankers. It was, in essence, a system of financial self-governance that made the federal government a junior partner, much to the dismay of then President Taft. Although the American Banker's Association endorsed the plan, Taft's opposition, combined with the objections of Democrats who viewed Aldrich as being too closely tied to Wall Street and (through marriage) to the Rockefellers, undermined support.[50]

In 1913, as control of the Senate passed to the Democrats, Aldrich retired and Congressman Carter Glass (D-VA) took up the issue of financial regulation. Under the Glass plan, the nation would be divided into at least fifteen districts, with regional banks controlled by bankers, and a national board with thirty-six members, six of whom would be presidential appointees. More importantly, the plan called for a nine-member executive board, comprised of six presidential appointees and three representatives elected by regional banks, thereby providing a greater centralization of control and vesting far greater power in the federal government. Ultimately, at Wilson's insistence, the executive board—now the Federal Reserve Board—would consist of seven members, all of whom would be presidential appointees, including the Treasury Secretary and the Comptroller of the Currency, who would serve in an *ex officio* capacity (the original plan also included the Secretary of Agriculture). To ensure that the new system would not be dominated by Eastern banking interests, no more than one member of the board could be appointed from any single reserve district. And in order to promote continuity and independence, board members would serve staggered ten-year terms. Bankers would receive formal representation through a Federal Advisory Council that would meet with the board on a quarterly basis.

The politics surrounding the legislative process were complex. Yet, in the end, a consensus emerged and the Federal Reserve Act of 1913 was signed into law. The Federal Reserve was created with the goals of providing an elastic currency, creating the means of rediscounting paper (i.e., increasing liquidity by lending banks money with existing loans as collateral), and providing a monetary policy and system of credit that would meet the needs of commerce, industry, and agriculture. The decentralization of authority in the regional banks and districts was envisioned as important because, in the words of O. M. W. Sprague, "a central bank would be far more likely to give rise to sectional antagonism."[51] Moreover, following the revelations of the Pujo investigations, decentralization could mitigate concerns over the power of Wall Street. Although the final bill mandated the creation of "at least eight, and not more than twelve" districts, there remained concerns that this would have the effect of preventing "the central reservoir for reserves which is essential."[52]

Much of the statutory language was ambiguous, reflecting once again, the Progressive faith in neutral expertise and institutional design. As John T. Woolley explains, the optimism of Congress

> flowed from a belief that organizational structure could solve problems of political power … . The "independent" governing board was intended to be a public coordinator of private regional banks but to remain separate from any larger system of public power. The System was conceived in the spirit of other Progressive reforms that stressed faith in expertise, faith in the effectiveness of tinkering with the machinery of government, and distrust of politicians.[53]

But while the belief in neutral expertise was clearly evident, the question of institutional design was hotly debated, particularly among those who feared the impact that the new Federal Reserve could have on the distribution of power between the state and finance.

As one might expect, the larger national banks, represented by the American Bankers' Association, found the bill wholly inadequate. It forced contributions of capital (in the form of reserves to be held by the reserve banks) without representation. In a resolution of October 8, 1913, the association objected to the coercive features of the bill, noting: "In return for the capital thus appropriated the banks receive a certificate … over which none of the usual rights of property can be exercised." Banks that "refuse to make a coerced investment" can have their charters revoked in a "summary manner." The resolution concluded:

> If the government can appropriate one-tenth of a bank's capital in the manner provided by this bill this year, it may appropriate one-tenth the next year, and so on until the capital is all transferred to the government

bank … . For those who do not believe in Socialism it is very hard to accept and ratify this proposed action on the part of the government.[54]

While the bankers used this argument to justify representation on the board, Wilson rejected such claims, and stated that control must be "vested in the government itself, so that the banks may be the instruments, not the masters, of business and of individual enterprise and initiative."[55] Senator Owen, co-sponsor of the Federal Reserve Act, found the demands of the bankers to be absurd: "There is no more reason for allowing the banks to exercise a part of this governing function than there would be to allow the railroads to name certain members of the Interstate Commerce Commission."[56]

The decision to constitute a Federal Reserve Board free of banker represen-tation appeared to establish public control. But this judgment rested on a misunderstanding of the institutional design. As economist J. Laurence Laughlin noted in 1914: "the Reserve Banks form the backbone of the whole system … Here is the crux of the whole matter. Upon the directors of these banks lies the heaviest responsibility arising from the new law." Under the Act, each reserve bank would have a board of nine directors, three of whom would be bankers chosen by member banks, another three to be individuals drawn from business within the district, again chosen by member banks, and an additional three members appointed by the Federal Reserve Board.

> In short, the constituent banks have the power to choose more than a majority (6) of the directors of each Reserve Bank … By this arrangement … the responsibility for good or bad management is placed on the banks themselves, on the men whom they have elected.[57]

Similarly, although former Assistant Treasury Secretary Frank Vanderlip preferred direct banker representation, his fears of the "baneful influence of politics" were mitigated by the institutional design: "when it is not lost sight of that the bankers themselves are responsible for the management of the Federal reserve banks, the fear of political domination by the Federal Reserve Board is robbed of much of its force."[58]

The Federal Reserve would evolve rapidly over the course of the next several decades, as it managed the financial impacts of war and depression. And while the New Deal banking legislation would strengthen the role of the Fed relative to the reserve banks and the banking community more generally (see Chapter 4), the larger institutional design would continue to be some-thing of an anomaly. Structurally integrated into the banking community, it would remain quasi-public in nature. Its formal independence—a product of design and the fact that it is self-funded—would be enhanced by the removal of the Treasury Secretary and the Comptroller of the Currency. Such an insti-tutional design seems difficult to reconcile with Wilson's rhetoric of 1912. The New Freedom promised to attack concentrations of power, and was premised on a belief that the kind of structural integration that Roosevelt proposed would lead, ultimately, to the capture of government and the preservation of economic power. And yet, critics would assert, this is precisely what occurred with the Federal Reserve Act.

World War and the Truimph of New Nationalism

Wilson won the 1912 election, bringing with him a larger Democratic majority in the House and a Democratic majority in the Senate for the first time since 1895. But events would soon prove that Roosevelt had won the debate.[59] As the war in Europe escalated, Eastern Republicans denounced Wilson's lack of preparedness. In 1915, Roosevelt presented Wilson as "the great apostle of pacifism," and the Democrats as "professional peace prattlers ... who, with the shrill clamor of eunuchs, preach the gospel of milk and the water of virtue."[60] Although there was a formidable antiwar bloc in Congress and Wilson took pride in US neutrality, he nonetheless responded. In 1916, the Army Reorganization Act more than doubled the size of the army, the Merchant Marine Act authorized the creation of a Shipping Board, and an Emergency Revenue Act funded these efforts with a doubling of the income tax (from one to two percent), a surcharge on the incomes of the wealthiest Americans, and an increase in inheritance and corporate taxes. Yet, there was no institutional apparatus to mobilize the economy. As Grosvenor B. Clarkson explained, the War Department "had no comprehension of the fact that in modern war the whole industrial activity of the Nation becomes the commissariat of the army. It had no affiliations with the complex and fecund industrial life of the Nation" and "knew nothing of the economic sequences of new demands, so vast as to exceed existing supplies."[61] Even if Wilson had recognized a need for preparedness, it is doubtful that the American state would have the requisite institutional capacity.

The Wilson administration would develop this mobilization apparatus. But given the immediacy of the demands, it had to compensate for the lack of administrative capacity by relying heavily on private economic organizations—large corporations, trade associations, agricultural commodity groups, labor unions—that would be integrated into the state. Much of what occurred would involve coordinating the behavior of large economic organizations. As Fredric L. Paxson noted in 1920, war mobilization marked "a genuine attempt at a complete transition from the doctrine of individualism and free competition to one of centralized national co-operation."[62] The agencies created under the exigencies of war—and their relationship to economic interests—looked no different than what one might have expected had the New Nationalism been employed as a blueprint for institutional design.

The central agency created to supply the war effort was the War Industries Board (WIB), established in July 1917. The WIB encountered significant problems. There was a dearth of current data on the industrial capacity of the economy and little reason to believe that the bureaucracy had the administrative capabilities to implement wartime controls. Also, it was unclear whether the WIB could withstand constitutional challenges if it sought to mandate war production. These constraints were negotiated through the personal leadership of Bernard Baruch, a Wall Street financier appointed by Wilson in January 1918 to run the WIB after the near collapse of the mobilization process in the prior months. Baruch's personal relationships with corporate leaders and his encyclopedic knowledge of American industry were indispensable in facilitating business participation.

The organization of the WIB was, arguably, as important as the personal leadership of Baruch. The WIB operated through a decentralized network of fifty-seven commodity sections each staffed by a WIB official ("dollar-a-year" men drawn from business) and representatives of the consuming agencies. Each section, in turn, interacted with a "war service committee," staffed by industry representatives, to negotiate with the government. The US Chamber of Commerce was given a central role in the process. Where a trade association existed, the chamber had it designate members of the war service committee; where there was none, the chamber organized an association and certified the war service committee as being representative of the industry. The heavy participation of business leaders and their staffs in the WIB compensated for the limited administrative capacities of the board insofar as associations could generate the detailed information that the WIB lacked.[63] And yet, this institutional design created predictable problems.

Although the heavy reliance on associations and dollar-a-year men provided the WIB with access to information, it simultaneously made the state highly vulnerable to opportunism. As Robert D. Cuff notes: "Technical skill was concentrated along the outer edges of the WIB, within the commodity sections," thereby creating problems of control and oversight for the board. As a result, "if the commodity chief became a lobbyist for his industry ... there was little the board could do about it."[64] Certainly, the mobilization agencies controlled the flow of key commodities and transportation; in theory, a failure to cooperate could carry significant consequences. But given the structure of the WIB and the heavy reliance on corporate voluntarism, it was clear that the capacity of the board (and other agencies) to coerce recalcitrant industrialists could undermine the mobilization process. As Paul Koistinen notes, the WIB was simply "a form of industrial self-regulation writ large."[65]

In the end, conflicts of interest should have been expected in any system in which industry representatives negotiated with other industry representatives, and government officials were beset by ongoing problems of information scarcity. These conflicts were exacerbated by the fact that the WIB, seeking to mobilize slack resources in the economy, often based contracts on the costs incurred by high-cost producers, thereby generating significant profits for more efficient firms. A Price-Fixing Committee, chaired by Robert Brookings and provided analytical support by the FTC, sought to prevent profiteering, but once again, informational asymmetries were unavoidable. As Jordan A. Schwartz notes, the meetings of the committee "were really bargaining sessions in which only one of the two parties knew the facts ... In the end, there was no price-fixing without the consent of the businessman whose price was fixed."[66]

The WIB was the most significant of the mobilization agencies. However, Wilson created a number of other agencies, including the US Food Administration (headed by Herbert Hoover), the National War Labor Board, the US Railroad Administration, the US Shipping Board, the US Fuel Administration, and the War Finance Corporation. In most cases, the agencies placed a high reliance on voluntarism, giving rise to problems comparable to those experienced by the WIB. Despite the problems, economic output during the the war was simply unprecedented. Between 1916 and 1918, real gross national product increase by some 13 percent.[67] And these gains came despite the brevity of US participation in the war. As John Maurice Clark observed:

> the Armistice came too soon for industry to reach peak production. A nation whose economy had been operating at near-capacity before April 6, 1917, needed months, if not years, to arrange contracts, build or convert plants, construct machine tools, accelerate munitions production, adapt weapons to changes demanded by people at the front, and deliver the instruments of war.[68]

Demobilization proved challenging. As the stimulation from large wartime deficits dissipated and the government shifted its focus to reducing the debt, the nation slid rapidly into recession. By the middle of 1921, industrial production had fallen by 35 percent. At the end of the war, 25 percent of the workforce was involved in war production; absent these contracts and levels of wartime spending, unemployment increased from 1.4 percent (1919) to 11.7 percent (1921). President Harding called an Unemployment Conference, chaired by the new Commerce Secretary Herbert Hoover to explore ways of reducing unemployment and managing future economic fluctuations. Yet, by the fall of 1921, the economy began to expand again. Between 1921 and 1929, real GNP would increase by some 48 percent, making the 1920s appear to be a decade of prosperity.[69]

Conclusion

In the wake of the depression of the 1890s, policymakers searched for some means of extending public control over the emerging industrial economy. The next two decades brought a number of novel experiments in public policy and institutional design grounded in competing visions of economic change and the role of the state in the economy. Despite the divisions intrinsic to the Progressive Regime, the core initiatives when combined, created the foundations for the modern regulatory state. The experience of World War I mobilization is commonly acknowledged as marking the end of the Progressive Era. But in many ways, this experience when combined with the debates of the period shaped the dramatic period of state-building and reform that would come in the 1930s. For some Progressive reformers, mobilization was, in the words of Ellis W. Hawley, "a stepping stone to the social order that a progressive era had envisioned but failed to achieve. A system of war management, they came to believe, could be adapted to the peacetime management of social programs."[70] For business, the effects were similarly significant. As Eric F Goldman observed:

> Many of the dollar-a-year men went back to their fifty-thousand-dollar-a-year jobs with an idea buzzing in their heads. Perhaps their decades-old battle for "free competition" and against government in business had not been wise ... . Why not give up the talk about competition and draw firms together in trade associations, which would standardize products, pool information, advertising, insurance, traffic, and purchases, and draw up codes of proper practices? Why not stop fighting the government and work with it in setting up these trade associations.[71]

During the war, fifty-four new national trade associations had been created to represent commercial interests in the mobilization process.[72] Over the course of the next decade, primarily under the influence of Commerce Secretary Herbert Hoover, the state would increasingly support an active role for associations in regulation. Agencies like the FTC would begin developing policy through close consultation with trade associations. Following the passage of the Transportation Act of 1920, the ICC would reverse its regulatory posture, setting minimum rates instead of maximum rates, with the goal of creating stability in the railroad industry. The arguments for cooperation, which found their clearest expression in Roosevelt's New Nationalism, would find a peacetime articulation in the practices of the regulatory agencies created as part of the Progressive Regime. The Great Depression, however, would reveal the weaknesses of cooperation and the limitations of the Progressive Regime. With the advent of the New Deal, a new regime would be created that would shape the trajectory of institutional and policy development for decades to come. We turn to this remarkable episode in Chapter 4.

4 The Rise of the New Deal Regime

On the eve of the Great Depression, the state remained relatively small, consuming some 3.67 percent of GDP. With the onset of the depression and the election of Franklin Roosevelt, the nation entered a prolonged period of state building. The federal government tripled in size in less than a decade. More importantly, new agencies and public policies were created to extend regulation to a number of sectors (most notably, agriculture and finance) and industrial relations. The Social Security Act of 1935 created the foundations for a new welfare state, and policymakers began to develop new fiscal policy tools to manage the vicissitudes of the business-cycle. In many ways, the boldest aspirations of the Progressive era were realized during the 1930s, as the New Deal established the foundations for a new regime that would endure, albeit with significant modifications, for almost half-a-century.[1]

Associationalism and the 1920s

The first two decades of the twentieth century witnessed rapid growth in trade associations and many argued that they could give rise to a new form of competition. In Edward N. Hurley's words, trade associations were "the machinery of cooperation" that could destroy "ignorant competition," and thus, government "must abandon the attitude of the policeman and become the sympathetic, constructive counselor of American business life."[2] The arguments, reinforced by the experiences of mobilization, were given a new theoretical justification by Herbert Hoover. In his 1922 book, *American Individualism*, he observed that the "road to future advance" will depend on "greater invention, greater elimination of waste, greater production and better distribution of commodities and services." The state could promote such activities but one needed to exercise great care because "a bureaucracy over the entire population" could also "obliterate the economic stimulation of each member."[3] To avoid this problem, Hoover argued that a system of associations "held out the promise of a form of private government in which the economy was essentially self-regulatory."[4] It could allow for "self-government outside of formal government."[5] The state would assume the role of coordinating and facilitating associational action.

Hoover was appointed Commerce Secretary and in 1921, as chair of the President's Conference on Unemployment, he promoted a novel system of counter-cyclical spending for managing the business cycle. Public works projects could serve this purpose if they were planned in advance and deferred until the Commerce Department released statistical indicators of recession. But the federal government was relatively small, responsible for some $125 million in public works construction, compared with $675 million at the state and municipal levels. Thus, it was necessary to convince states and municipalities to create their own reserve funds for construction. During the heights of the business cycle, government should work with trade associations to advocate the "advantages of withholding postponable projects"—particularly those that were labor-intensive—and create reserve funds that could be expended during economic downturns.[6] Hoover concluded that management of the business cycle "will depend greatly upon the coordination and cooperation that we can figure from industries and civil bodies of the United States. That this is a problem for voluntary organization is consonant with the American spirit and American institutions."[7] Over the 1920s, Hoover sought to convince business leaders and associations to accept greater responsibility for employment and develop reserve-fund strategies consistent with the conference's broader recommendations.[8]

Associationalism also found an expression in several regulatory agencies. Consider the Federal Trade Commission. A decade after it had been created as an embodiment of Wilson's New Freedom, it began using trade practice conferences to identify and prohibit practices that violated the antitrust statutes, and to develop rules against unethical or unfair practices—"expressions of the trade"—that associations could use to govern their members.[9] The FTC, in its 1927 *Annual Report,* described its practices as furthering "the idea of self-regulation" and "helping business to help itself."[10] The US Chamber of Commerce celebrated these efforts and urged members to form joint trade relations committees. Similar experiments emerged in multiple policy areas, integrating organized economic interests into the formation and implementation of policy. Although popular accounts of the 1920s portray it as an era of *laissez faire*, in fact, state agencies were actively promoting associational governance grounded in a new theory of competition and the experiences of war.

Associationalism exhibited some of the same weaknesses as wartime mobilization. Lacking the administrative capacity to engage in war planning, the state depended heavily on the voluntary participation of businesses and trade associations. Business participation, in turn, was contingent on the expectation of profitability. Hoover could provide a theoretical justification for associationalism as a means of claiming the benefits of planning without state expansion. But once again, there was a significant delegation of authority to businesses and trade associations. Because the state lacked the administrative capacity to assume a leading role, the ends of associationalism would have to be compatible with corporate profitability if there was to be an expectation of success.

The Depression and the Limits of Associationalism

Over the course of the 1920s, the stock market had reached unprecedented heights, giving rise to a speculative bubble. With the average price of common stocks at some 300 percent of their 1925 values, many expected a correction. But few imagined that between September 3 and November 13, 1929, the *Times* industrial average would fall from 452 to 224, essentially losing half its value. And despite the efforts of large investment banks to stabilize markets with a pool of some $240 million, by the summer of 1932, the market would hit bottom at 58.[11] What might have been a simple market correction was undoubtedly exacerbated by a number of factors. Concerned about market speculation, the Federal Reserve pursued a restrictive policy in 1928–29. Following the 1928 death of Benjamin Strong, the powerful head of the New York Fed, the reserve banks failed to pursue a coherent policy. As Milton Friedman and Anna Jacobson Schwartz note: "In the absence of vigorous intellectual leadership by the Board or a consensus on the correct policy ... the tendencies of drift and indecision had full scope."[12] Then there was trade policy. The Smoot-Hawley Act of 1930 dramatically increased tariffs. Contemporary analysts have discounted its impact, noting that its effects were limited to about one-third of US import markets, and where it raised barriers, it diverted demand from imports to domestically produced goods. Moreover, it did not lead to immediate waves of retaliatory tariffs as has been so often claimed.[13]

Now president, Hoover was forced to put associationalism to the test. In November of 1929, he held conferences with representatives of industry, finance, construction, public utilities, and railroads hoping to deploy the strategy delineated by the Unemployment Conference. Having received an agreement that wages would be stabilized, he met with labor leaders to secure a commitment to cooperate and exercise restraint in wage demands. Hoover asked the US Chamber of Commerce to create the National Business Survey Conference, an executive committee representing business. He met with the conference and called on business and trade association representatives to continue construction, maintenance, and purchases, and retain employees. As the US Chamber of Commerce declared, government and business "stand together ... working hand in hand, as in wartime."[14]

Hoover's response may have been based in a philosophical aversion to planning. But in reality, the size of the federal government relative to the economy was quite small. Although Hoover was committed to balanced budgets, he nonetheless sought to use the limited fiscal tools at his disposal to promote recovery, including a reduction of personal and corporate income taxes, and an acceleration of federal construction spending. By the fall of 1930, Hoover created the President's Committee for Unemployment Relief to coordinate state and local efforts. But when faced with congressional demands for federal relief spending in February 1931, he responded by praising "charity and mutual self help through voluntary giving and the responsibility of local government as distinguished ... from appropriations." He warned that federal assumption of responsibility would impair "something infinitely valuable in the life of the American people," strike "at the roots of self-government," and force the nation into "the abyss of reliance ... upon Government charity."[15]

As conditions worsened throughout 1931, those who had pledged to work "hand in hand" with government were cutting payrolls and production. Attention turned to the resurrection of wartime models. In September 1931, General Electric president Gerald Swope proposed a recovery plan grounded in the experience of the WIB. All companies with fifty or more employees engaged in interstate commerce would be required to join trade associations and coordinate their decisions under government supervision, with an antitrust exemption.[16] Following the release of the Swope Plan, the Chamber of Commerce called for a National Economic Council and the National Progressive Conference proposed a National Economic Board. Stuart Chase promoted a "Peace Industries Board" and Bernard Baruch, Herbert Bayard Swope, and Federal Reserve governor Owen Young called for a national planning board. Most ambitiously, Charles Beard proposed a national council that would formulate five-year plans, "repeal the antitrust acts and declare all industries affiliated with the national economic council public service enterprises subject to principles of prudent investment and fair returns."[17] These proposals met with Hoover's disdain as flirting with fascism or socialism, neither of which was compatible with American individualism. Yet, as one contemporary critic responded: "If rugged individualism results in ragged individuals, it may be time to reconsider our concept of individualism." He warned:

> There is a growing army of the victims of economic insecurity that could well be recruited by an American Stalin or an American Mussolini if ... political and business leadership should remain persistently recreant to the duty of stabilizing the American economic order.[18]

Hoover's rejection of a return to wartime planning was uneven. In the autumn of 1931, New York bankers offered to extend $500 million of credit to stabilize financial markets if Hoover would reconstitute the War Finance Corporation. In a December 1931 address to Congress, Hoover complied, calling for "an emergency reconstruction corporation of the nature of the former War Finance Corporation." The next month, Congress passed legislation creating the Reconstruction Finance Corporation (RFC), capitalized at $500 million with authorization to borrow an additional $1.5 billion. Critics objected that the RFC would support banks that had precipitated the depression while rejecting direct relief. Hoover attempted to placate critics by guaranteeing that the RFC would focus its resources on smaller banks to create the liquidity necessary for small businesses and agriculture.[19] As concerns mounted over the RFC's effectiveness, WIB veterans Bernard Baruch, General Hugh Johnson, and Newton Baker suggested that the RFC support relief indirectly by making loans to states to fund self-liquidating public works that could generate revenues to repay the loans. Hoover accepted the proposal and requested that Congress authorize the RFC to lend $300 million to states and place an additional $3 billion in securities. Congress passed the Emergency Relief and Construction Act of 1932, thereby extending the role of the RFC without forcing it to engage in direct relief.[20] According to Jordan Schwartz, in so doing, Hoover had "admitted that the means of reconstruction was less important than the objective."[21]

The New Deal

Given Hoover's concessions in 1932, one suspects that a second term may have brought further expansions of the state's role. But with a record number of bank failures and unemployment approaching 25 percent, Roosevelt won an easy victory, claiming 57.4 percent of the vote and 472 electoral votes to Hoover's 59.[22] The Democrats gained ninety-seven seats in the House and thirteen seats in the Senate, creating a strong Democratic majority. The New Deal would introduce the most significant changes in the history of the American political economy; the key initiatives in industrial relations, regulation, and social welfare would prove instrumental in reinforcing a powerful coalition that would dominate American politics for decades.

In one of Roosevelt's most enduring campaign speeches of 1932, he argued that the nation was "steering a steady course toward economic oligarchy" and "equality of opportunity as we have known it no longer exists." Roosevelt concluded that this demands "a re-appraisal of values" and a qualitatively different role for the state.

> A mere builder of more industrial plants, a creator of more railroad systems, and organizer of more corporations, is as likely to be a danger as a help. The day of the great promoter or the financial Titan, to whom we granted anything if only he would build, or develop, is over. Our task now is not discovery or exploitation of natural resources, or necessarily producing more goods. It is the soberer, less dramatic business of administering resources and plants already in hand, of seeking to reestablish foreign markets for our surplus production, of meeting the problem of under consumption, of adjusting production to consumption, of distributing wealth and products more equitably, of adapting existing economic organizations to the service of the people. The day of enlightened administration has come.

Roosevelt promised "to assist the development of an economic declaration of rights, an economic constitutional order."[23]

Roosevelt returned to some of these themes during his first inaugural address. He framed the speech with military metaphors, noting the "larger purposes" that demanded "unity of duty hitherto evoked only in time of armed strife." He pledged to "assume unhesitatingly the leadership of this great army of our people dedicated to a disciplined attack upon our common problems." FDR exhibited a disdain for constitutional formalism, noting that the constitution "is so simple and practical that it is possible always to meet extraordinary needs by changes in emphasis and arrangement without loss of essential form." The normal balance of powers may be insufficient given the "unprecedented task before us" and thus he announced his plan to request "broad Executive power to wage a war against the emergency, as great as the power that would be given to me if we were in fact invaded by a foreign foe."[24] War had been declared, but was there a coherent strategy? There was great uncertainty as to how to pursue recovery and Roosevelt lacked an overarching theoretical vision. In the words of one advisor, he "had a general indifference to systems of all sorts" and was "not committed to any methods." The only strand of consistency was Progressivism. It was "the furniture of his mind" and thus, "Roosevelt could be persuaded to depart from the old progressive line only in the direst of circumstances and then only temporarily."[25] Under these conditions, one should not be surprised that Roosevelt deferred to his Brain Trust. But even here, there were competing explanations of the depression and thus uncertainty over the best means of addressing its root causes.

Some of the arguments focused on the problem of administered prices. Corporations in oligopolistic industries responded to falling demand by cutting production rather than prices, thereby exacerbating the decline and forestalling recovery. But what was the best response? Some would advocate more vigorous antitrust enforcement, whereas others would seek further cartelization and the introduction of state agencies to oversee output and pricing decisions.[26] Other explanations emphasized consumption. Additional fiscal stimulus would be necessary to promote sufficient levels of demand, a position that would ultimately find its classical formulation in the work of John Maynard Keynes. Alternatively, some accounts presented the depression as a product of secular stagnation. With the growing capital intensity, the corporate economy could not generate full employment. The correct remedy was the promotion of full employment through public works. Conservative critics, in contrast, simply called for a return to sound finance. By failing to balance budgets, the government could only prolong the depression by competing with the private sector for capital.[27]

The National Recovery Administration

The New Deal's initial response to the depression was largely informed by the administered pricing thesis. The single best example was the National Industrial Recovery Act of 1933. When Roosevelt signed the Act, he declared: "It is a challenge to industry which has long insisted that given the right to act in unison, it could do much for the general good, which has hitherto been unlawful. From today, it has that right."[28] The Act created the National Recovery Administration (NRA) that borrowed its institutional design from the WIB and was placed—at Baruch's suggestion—under the direction of the WIB's Army representative General Hugh Johnson. The NRA organized businesses on an industry-specific basis under an antitrust exemption to develop codes governing levels of output, prices, and flow to market. Under Title I, Section 7(a) of the Act, workers were guaranteed

> the right to organize and bargain collectively through representatives of their own choosing ... free from the interference, restraint or coercion of employers of labor, or their agents, in the designation of such representatives or in self-organization or in other activities for the purpose of collective bargaining or other mutual aid or protection.

Section 7(b) mandated that codes include maximum hours and minimum wages. If industries operating under codes could maintain higher levels of production and labor could claim higher wages, it was believed that recovery would be forthcoming.

For some participants, the NRA constituted a permanent movement toward planning. Labor leader Sidney Hillman argued that the NRA "aims at the reorganization of our economic life, at the substitution of plan and system for chaos, disorder, and social irresponsibility." It is a "democratic instrumentality for planning and administering our economic life."[29] But the NRA's Dudley Cates rejected talk of planning. The codes were "charters of self-government, with broad discretionary powers vested in the representative code authority in each case." As part of this system of "industrial self-government ... hundreds of the Nation's leading business men have thrown themselves whole-heartedly into these groups' efforts to prove their capacity to direct their own affairs with due regard to their public responsibilities." But Cates also observed that the Act had become "like St. Paul, all things to all men," used to promote "the purposes of conservatives and radicals alike."[30] Walter C. Teagle of the NRA's Industrial Advisory Board recognized the ambiguity inherent in the NRA but claimed one thing was certain: "We are on a new road, a one-way street by which we can never return ... to the positions we abandoned under the New Deal."[31]

In the end, the NRA floundered badly. While it aggressively enacted economy-wide regulations, approving some 557 basic codes and 189 supplemental codes in less than two years, the codes were the source of significant controversy. The NRA, like the WIB before it, lacked the capacities to execute its functions, and thus delegated tremendous authority to the business-dominated code committees. The codes, as one might expect, often reflected the interests of the larger enterprises seeking to cartelize their industries to the disadvantage of smaller firms. The costs imposed by the codes spread through the economy, raising concerns over prices that could depress aggregate demand. Roosevelt responded to the criticisms by creating a review board chaired by Clarence Darrow, but it only fueled the controversies when it reported: "in virtually all the codes we have examined, one condition has been persistent ... the code has offered an opportunity for the more powerful ... interests to seize control of an industry or to augment and extend a control already obtained."[32]

As the NRA came under scrutiny, business support evaporated. In September 1934, Roosevelt accepted Johnson's resignation, whose erratic behavior had become a liability (in his farewell speech, he invoked the "shining name" of Mussolini, whose model of fascism had inspired him).[33] The NRA was placed under the leadership of a seven-person board representing business, labor, and consumers, directed to conduct a review in preparation for the upcoming legislative reauthorization. However, the NRA experiment came to an abrupt end in 1935, at the hands of the Supreme Court. In *A.L.A. Schechter Poultry Corp. v. United States* the Court found that the NRA codes constituted an extra-constitutional delegation of legislative authority to the executive branch and exceeded the powers granted in the commerce clause of the Constitution.[34] Given the improbability of reauthorization, this may have been a fortunate *coup de grace*.

The Agricultural Adjustment Administration

The depression was particularly devastating in agriculture. The farm economy suffered from a classical collective action problem: when faced with declining prices, farmers planted more crops, creating surpluses that depressed prices. Since the war, the farm economy had suffered with problems of excess capacity and Congress and the USDA had been incapable of developing an effective response. Thus, between 1929 and 1933, farm commodity prices fell by 63 percent, compared with a 15 percent decline in industrial prices. With some 30 percent of the workforce in the farm economy, the decline in purchasing power arguably threatened recovery.[35]

One of the most important accomplishments of FDR's first hundred days was the Agricultural Adjustment Act of 1933 to be administered by a newly created Agricultural Adjustment Administration (AAA). Section 2 of the Act stated that it was the policy of Congress

> to establish and maintain such balance between the production and consumption of agricultural commodities, and such marketing conditions therefore, as will re-establish prices to farmers at a level that will give agricultural commodities a purchasing power with respect to articles that farmers buy, equivalent to the purchasing power of agricultural commodities in the base period [i.e., 1901–14].

Under the Act, the Agriculture Secretary was authorized to enter into agreements with farmers for acreage reduction in exchange for benefit payments, and to enter into marketing agreements with processors and producers who could control production levels under an antitrust exemption. The plan was funded through a tax placed on processors. The Act also authorized loans to farmers, using crops-on-hand as collateral, as a means of keeping commodities off of the market.[36]

The AAA increased farm incomes, although it is difficult to separate the effects of policy from the impact of the 1934 draught. By 1936, farm incomes had grown by more than 50 percent over 1932 levels.[37] Yet, there were concerns that the AAA was largely an exercise in redistribution. Joseph S. Davis, for example, noted in 1935 that its impact on recovery depended on the assumption that the transfer of resources to the farm economy would increase overall purchasing power (presumably, farmers would spend money that would otherwise lie inert). Yet, "most of the consumers' burden of these taxes ... has fallen on what are mainly necessaries of life for the mass of the people." Rather than tapping "appreciable reservoirs of immobilized purchasing power," Davis concluded, "the transfer of purchasing power from taxbearer to benefit receiver has ... decrease[d] the amount of purchasing power put to active current use."[38]

Moreover, there were concerns that the AAA was contributing to unemployment. Large Southern farms reduced acreage by evicting tenant farmers—largely African American. As one contemporary observer noted: "Obviously, the most economical method of reducing the acreage of cotton on a great many of the farms and plantations would be to reduce the number of tenants." Farmers, it was hoped, would compensate displaced tenants with support payments, but landlords were "in opposition to governmental aid to the cropper because it upsets the status quo in landlord tenant relations."[39] As Jonathan M. Wiener explains, as the AAA "took 53 percent of the South's cotton acreage out of production ... sharecroppers joined the general pool of unemployed wage workers." Displaced from the agricultural economy, many migrated north in search of work. Between 1930 and 1940, net migration of African Americans to the North was some 400,000, compared with fewer than 1,000 for whites.[40]

In 1936, the AAA ran afoul of the Supreme Court. In *United States v. Butler* the Court upheld a challenge to the processor tax and found:

> The act invades the reserved rights of the states. It is a statutory plan to regulate and control agricultural production, a matter beyond the powers delegated to the federal government. The tax, the appropriation of the funds raised, and the direction for their disbursement are but parts of the plan. They are but means to an unconstitutional end.[41]

While Congress and the administration had been willing to let the NRA die, they viewed the AAA as an overwhelming success and thus preserved it first under the guise of conservation (under the Soil Conservation and Domestic Allotment Act of 1935) and then through a second Agricultural Adjustment Act of 1937 that drew on general revenues.

The success of the AAA can be contrasted with the poor performance of the NRA. Theda Skocpol and Kenneth Finegold have offered a cogent explanation. The AAA was placed in the Department of Agriculture, "an island of state strength in an ocean of weakness." Historically, Congress had heavily funded the USDA and it had developed policy-relevant expertise through institutional connections with agriculture departments in land grant colleges. This expertise was enhanced dramatically in 1922, when the USDA created a Bureau of Agricultural Economics with the government's largest concentration of economists. It also had cooperative relations with commodity associations and an extension service that connected the agency to individual farmers. Thus, in agricultural policy, "the New Deal was indeed able to draw on a well-established governmentally centered tradition of political learning about what needed to be and could be done through government intervention in agriculture."[42] In stark contrast, consider the relationship of the state with the corporate economy. After the war, corporations coordinated their behavior through trade associations and Hoover's associationalism placed the state in the role of facilitating coordination and ratifying their decisions. As a result, the Commerce Department—the obvious analog to the USDA—never developed the capacity to direct the NRA and engage in the kinds of tasks Roosevelt envisioned.

A New Deal for Finance

The wave of bank failures following the market crash devoured some 9,000 banks and $2.5 billion worth of deposits and bank stocks.[43] A number of states declared bank holidays in the fall of 1932 and, the day after his inauguration, FDR declared a four-day national bank holiday. Under the authority of the Emergency Banking Act of 1933, the Treasury examined banks and reopened those deemed solvent. Other banks could be opened on a restricted basis under the supervision of the Comptroller of the Currency.

> With the general closing of all banks ... came a profound sense of relief. A change, of great suddenness and intensity, occurred in public sentiment—the shattered confidence in banks gave way to a buoyant hope that emergency remedial measures would permit most banks to reopen and render their deposits safe.[44]

The next several years marked a period of remarkable change in the regulation of finance.

The Banking Act of 1933 (Glass-Steagall) forced the separation of commercial and investment banking, on the theory that the comingling of the two activities had magnified the crash. It also prohibited the payment of interest on demand deposits (i.e., checking accounts) on the belief that banks engaged in potentially destabilizing activities to pay higher interest rates and attract funds. Most importantly, Glass-Steagall created the Federal Deposit Insurance Corporation (FDIC) to guarantee deposits. All members of the Federal Reserve System were required to carry FDIC insurance (nonmembers were insured at the FDIC's discretion). Thereafter, commercial bank suspensions fell dramatically (from an annual average of 632.6 during the period 1921–29, to an average of 49 a year for the decade following the creation of the FDIC). As Friedman and Schwartz note, deposit insurance "succeeded in achieving what had been a major objective of banking reform for at least a century, namely, the prevention of banking panics."[45] Indeed, they conclude that the FDIC did more to promote monetary stability than the creation of the Federal Reserve two decades earlier.

The Banking Act of 1935 concentrated greater authority in the Federal Reserve's Board of Governors, first, by reconstituting the Federal Open Market Committee to consist of the seven governors and five representatives of the Federal Reserve Banks—previously, all twelve Bank presidents served on the Committee. It also enhanced the Fed's independence by removing the Comptroller of the Currency and the Treasury Secretary as *ex officio* members of the Board and extending members' terms from twelve to fourteen years. Finally, it authorized the Fed to change reserve requirements without presidential approval and reaffirmed its authority to regulate the interest rates on member banks' time deposits (the FDIC was allowed to exercise this function for non-member banks with insurance).[46]

Changes in investment banking were equally dramatic. The Securities Act of 1933 required that issuers register securities with the FTC and mandated financial information disclosure. The Securities Exchange Act of 1934 created a new regulatory agency, the Securities and Exchange Commission (SEC) to regulate the industry. The Act mandated that national exchanges register with the SEC, which was also given the responsibility of registering all stocks sold on the exchanges. The SEC's regulatory model was one of government supervised self-regulation.[47] That is, it would oversee private associations, which in turn served as surrogate regulators to govern their members. Indeed, the SEC would use its authority to force a reorganization and professionalization of the New York Stock Exchange and to promote the self-regulation of the over-the-counter market through the National Association of Securities Dealers, which "assumed the functions and structure of a regulatory agency."[48]

A New Deal for Labor

The NRA provided formal recognition of the right to organize. John L. Lewis, president of the United Mine Workers, viewed Section 7(a) as a major accomplishment, proclaiming: "there has been no legal instrument comparable with it since President Lincoln's Emancipation Proclamation."[49] The efforts to create a stable system of industrial relations under the NRA were difficult for a number of reasons. First, Section 7(a) did nothing to mandate that employers engage in collective bargaining nor did it provide much in the way of mechanisms for managing industrial conflicts. As one critic explained in 1934, collective bargaining often reaches an impasse.

The trouble with Section 7(a) is that, at just this critical point, it calmly walks out on the turmoil it has stirred up. It doesn't suggest, even by implication, what government is going to do when the "collective bargainers" shall have failed to agree.[50]

Emboldened by Section 7(a) and frustrated by the corporate intransigence, the number of strikes more than doubled between 1932 and 1933, when there were 1,695 strikes involving some 1.2 million workers—the highest level of worker militancy since 1921 when unions were attempting to preserve wartime gains. The number of strikes would continue to increase in each successive year until they peaked at 4,740 in 1937.[51]

Roosevelt responded to the high level of strike activity by creating a National Labor Board with representatives of business and labor (including GE's Gerald Swope and the AFL's William Green), under the direction of Senator Robert Wagner (D-NY). Although the board had tenuous authority and no enforcement powers, it established several important principles. It found that the right to organize imposed an obligation on employers to negotiate regarding the terms of the codes. Most important, under the so-called "Reading formula," the board established that elections to certify unions would occur via secret ballot, with a single union being recognized as the sole organizational representative of the workers. The issue of representation was an important one. NRA Administrator Johnson, for example, condoned proportional representation, and Roosevelt was quite willing to defer to Johnson on this point. However, the board was convinced that divisions between blocs of workers in a single enterprise would undermine labor's negotiating power.

Following the *Schechter* decision, Congress moved quickly to pass the National Labor Relations Act creating a new National Labor Relations Board (NLRB) and placing the labor provisions of the 1933 Act on new statutory foundations. In 1933, some critics had viewed the NRA as being overly conciliatory to businesses that controlled the code committees; labor was but a junior partner. However, it was clear to some analysts what the future would hold. As David J. Saposs presciently observed in 1935:

> Big business ... wants self-regulation with government sanction. To the extent that the Roosevelt administration has consented, big business has gone along. However, the day of reckoning is not far distant. The consumers, the farmers, and the workers will press for more genuine intervention on their behalf. Roosevelt will probably yield, and the big business interests having steadied themselves somewhat in the meantime will resist. If Roosevelt should then decide to hold to his course, he will need the support of organized labor and other elements. Throughout the world in their attempt to check the power of capitalism the middle class groups have found it necessary to strengthen organized labor and to court it as an ally.[52]

With the passage of the Wagner Act, the Roosevelt administration effectively integrated labor into its coalition. This alliance would prove critical as the New Deal's relationship with business deteriorated.

With the advocacy of the NLRB, organized labor made extraordinary gains. In 1932, some 3 million workers were unionized—12.9 percent of the nonagricultural workforce. By 1940, the number of unionized workers had almost tripled, constituting 26.9 percent of the workforce. The growth in unionization, however, exacerbated problems of dual unionism. The AFL, which represented skilled craft unions, stood at tension with industrial unions that represented mass production workers and, after 1935, found representation in the Congress of Industrial Organizations. The CIO's support for the New Deal was rewarded as the NLRB made decisions as to where to assign newly certified unions. Its membership grew rapidly in the next several years, doubling from some 2 million members in 1937 to approximately 4 million by the end of the war. The AFL would have consistently more members, but the CIO could claim to represent almost one-third of the unionized workforce.[53]

For all the benefits, the new labor regulations also imposed costs. Prior to the New Deal, labor gains were products of worker militancy. Under the new regime, its fortunes were a function of the NLRB's policies. Following the New Deal, the state would never again prove to be as supportive of organized labor. Moreover, while many in the labor movement envisioned a more expansive role in addressing what had historically been managerial prerogatives, the Roosevelt administration was committed to limiting the scope of industrial relations to issues of hours, wages, and working conditions, reaffirming business unionism. Because the NLRB's legitimacy was seen to rest on its perceived neutrality, the board was placed outside of the Labor Department and industrial relations disputes were cast in legal terms by an agency dominated by attorneys, and resolved in quasi-judicial hearings. Labor contracts would increasingly take the form of complex legal documents inaccessible to the rank-and-file, further concentrating authority at the apex of union bureaucracies.[54]

The New Deal and the Birth of the Welfare State

In 1933, the crisis of the depression was exacerbated by the fact that, for most Americans, there was no social safety net other than a collapsing patchwork of state and local relief. Roosevelt and Congress moved quickly and, in the first hundred days, created the Federal Emergency Relief Administration (FERA) which was placed under the direction of Harry Hopkins. Between 1933 and 1935, FERA and its Civil Works Administration provided $3.1 billion to states to support the unemployed and fund public work. Similarly, the Civilian Conservation Corps was created in 1933 to provide employment in conservation projects. By 1934, the spending of these agencies was reaching 28 million people, over 22 percent of the population. In 1935 alone, government at all levels was spending some $3 billion in public aid, fifteen times the amount that had been spent in the last year of the Hoover administration.[55] Yet there was growing uneasiness over potential problems of dependency. Hopkins famously noted: "Give a man a dole, and you save his body and destroy his spirit."[56] As Paul H. Landis noted in 1935, the old question "Will the crops fail?" had been replaced by a new query: "Will the government relief revenues fail?" Although the provision of assistance fostered greater loyalty, he feared it would "turn traitor when benefits are exhausted."[57]

In the 1935 State of the Union address, Roosevelt unveiled a change in policy. In words that would be echoed by advocated of welfare reform half-a-century later, he noted "continued dependence upon relief induces a spiritual and moral disintegration fundamentally destructive to the national fibre. To dole out relief in this way is to administer a narcotic, a subtle destroyer of the human spirit." He announced: "The Federal Government must and shall quit this business of relief." The president explained that of the 5 million currently on relief, two-thirds were unemployed because of "a nation-wide depression caused by conditions which were not local but national." For these individuals there would still be public employment, but henceforth, it would have to be "useful" and "self-liquidating," with wages that were "not so large as to encourage the rejection of opportunities for private employment." Moreover, projects would be "selected and planned so as to compete as little as possible with private enterprise." This shift in emphasis would find one expression in a newly created Works Progress Administration (WPA) that replaced FERA. In contrast, approximately 1.5 million were "unable for one reason or another to maintain themselves independently." Roosevelt promised a legislative proposal to address "the broad subjects of unemployment insurance and old age insurance, of benefits for children, for mothers, for the handicapped, for maternity care and for other aspects of dependency and illness where a beginning can now be made."[58]

The Social Security Act of 1935 provided the statutory foundations for the US welfare state. It established old age pensions, funded through a payroll tax of 2 percent divided equally between employers and employees, with payment of benefits scheduled to begin in 1942. In the interim, it allocated funds to the states for the needy aged. It also established unemployment compensation, providing funds to states that had unemployment compensation programs approved by the Social Security Board. The Act also created Aid for Dependent Children, allocating funds for states that had Board approved plans. Additional provisions covered support for maternal and child welfare, "crippled" children, and the blind. With the exception of old age pensions, each of the programs relied on joint federal-state funding.

Although the Act covered an unprecedented number of citizens, it explicitly excluded agricultural labor, domestic servants, and "casual labor," with profound implications for African Americans who were concentrated in these categories. As Mary Poole notes: "African Americans were ghettoized into public assistance programs that stigmatized them as society's dependents. Their unemployment was perceived as a different condition ... from the majority of white men." Although unemployment compensation treated "unemployed white industrial workers as if their unemployment was the fault of an imperfect economy," most unemployed African Americans "received assistance only on the basis of their poverty, not their status as workers, the implication being that they, not the system, had failed."[59] While no one could provide a normative justification for these exclusions, they were necessary to retain the support of Southern Democrats who would reject federal interference with legal white supremacy.

In the end, the Social Security Act was one of the most important legacies of the New Deal. While public work was a short-term expedient, the Social Security Act proved far more enduring. Although the first Social Security old age check was paid in January 1940 (one time lump sum payments were made between 1937 and 1940), millions of Americans left the Roosevelt era with expectations of future benefits and, thus, a powerful stake in regime stability. The number of beneficiaries would grow exponentially, from some 222,488 in 1940 to more than 45 million six decades later, with total expenditures in excess of $407 billion.[60] For more than half a century, Aid for Families with Dependent Children would be the main source of means-tested income for the non-elderly population, and major expansions of the welfare state—most notably, Medicare and Medicaid—would be created through amendments to the Social Security Act.

The End of Recovery

Although recovery was slow to come, by 1936, unemployment had fallen to 16.9 percent with a further decline to 14.3 percent in 1937.[61] But the economy entered freefall near the end of 1937. According to one contemporary account, the year began with "superficial indication of prosperity and perhaps approaching boom" followed by a contraction "at a pace for which scarcely any precedent can be found."[62] The economic decline between September 1937 and June of 1938 is broadly acknowledged as the most severe in US history. Industrial production fell by one-third, with a 50 percent reduction in durable goods production. National income fell by 13 percent and employment in manufacturing by 23 percent. Corporate profits plummeted by 78 percent.[63]

A number of factors came together to produce this dramatic reversal. First, there was a reduction in stimulus. In 1936, Congress passed the Adjusted Compensation Payment Act over a presidential veto, which provided World War I veterans advance cash bonuses promised for 1945. The distribution of some $1.5 billion provided a source of stimulus that was absent a year later. At the same time, the newly authorized Social Security taxes further reduced purchasing power. Second, there were miscues in monetary policy. As the economy began to expand, the Fed harbored new concerns about inflation and speculation and announced a 50 percent increase in reserve requirements, effective August 1936, with additional increases to be phased in during the spring.[64]

A third factor was uncertainty created by recent policy changes that dramatically undermined incentive to invest. In the 1935 State of the Union address, Roosevelt admitted: "In spite of our efforts and in spite of our talk, we have not weeded out the over privileged and we have not effectively lifted up the underprivileged."[65] That year, he sent to Congress the Revenue Act of 1935 that increased the marginal tax on the wealthiest taxpayers, corporations, and estates, justified as a means to address "an unjust concentration of wealth and economic power."[66] In 1936, the administration introduced an undistributed profits tax at the urging of Treasury Secretary Morgenthau. The new tax, which subjected corporate profits to higher rates if not paid out in dividends, "posed the greatest threat to the autonomy of corporate finance since the passage of the excess-profits tax during World War I."[67]

The most important result of the downturn was the effect it had on Roosevelt's fiscal policy. Many of Roosevelt's key advisors—most notably, Morgenthau, Vice-President John Garner, and budget director Lewis W. Douglas—presented balanced budgets as the hallmark of responsible government. In contrast, the "spenders," including Hopkins, Interior Secretary Harold Ickes, Labor Secretary Frances Perkins, and members of the Brain Trust made proto-Keynesian arguments about the need for stimulus. Despite the arguments made by the spenders, in 1937 Roosevelt announced his intention of balancing the budget in 1938. Once the economy began its precipitous decline, Roosevelt cast the blame on business and continued to rely on the counsel of Morgenthau, discounting the advice of the spenders and even correspondence from Keynes advising higher levels of spending and warning of trying to tread a middle path.[68]

Although Roosevelt blamed the recession on business, it was not monolithic. In 1933, the Commerce Department had created a Business Advisory Council (BAC), under the chairmanship of Gerald Swope. The BAC was "a bastion of those who dreamed of a business commonwealth—a system involving national planning and regulation of industry, with government cooperation but without government control."[69] In 1935, charter members of the BAC initiated a study that concluded that compensatory fiscal policy was essential. In 1938, they issued a volume entitled *Toward Full Employment* that made the case for a Keynesian program. In the words of Robert M. Collins:

> The authors brandished modern analytical devices, such as the multiplier concept, and argued, as had Keynes, that there existed under capitalism no self-correcting mechanism to deal with the problem of excessive savings. The interest rate, that old standby of the classical formulation, was simply not up to the job; capitalism did not enjoy a built-in tendency towards equilibrium at a high level of employment. Their basic policy prescription was similarly Keynesian: government spending in excess of receipts was required to shift money from the savings stream to the consumption stream. In short, the need was for a compensatory fiscal policy that would "operate at times with an unbalanced budget and at other times with an overbalanced budget."[70]

New Dealers who supported a more expansive fiscal policy were impressed by the work and provided Roosevelt with an advanced copy of the manuscript.

The critical turning point came in March 1938, as Roosevelt vacationed in Warm Springs, Georgia. Hopkins met FDR and proceeded to make the case for a Keynesian plan. He had ensconced WPA deputy administrator Aubrey Williams, economist Leon Henderson, and the New York Fed's Beardsley Ruml nearby to provide technical briefs. A memo written by Ruml and Henderson argued that historically, the government played a central role in stimulating economic growth. Gold was mined from public lands and turned into money; land was given to homesteaders and railroads; corporations were provided with special franchises. Borrowing from future income to stimulate the economy was fully consistent with past practices. In Herbert Stein's words, the argument "made the whole thing seem very elemental" and "put the President in the picture as an agent of a long historical process, and appealed to his pleasure in the role of prudent manager of the national domain—a role which he himself had said he enjoyed."[71] When the vacation ended, the "Warm Springs conversion" was complete and FDR was committed to compensatory fiscal policy.

Within two weeks, Roosevelt called for $1.2 billion in additional funds for public works and $300 million in housing, $1.5 billion in additional appropriations for 1939, and an expansion of the money supply. In his fireside chat of April 14, 1938, he justified his requests in terms that reflect the imprint of Warm Springs, observing "from our earliest days we have had a tradition of substantial government help to our system of private enterprise … . It is following tradition as well as necessity, if Government strives to put idle money and idle men to work, to increase our public wealth and to build up the health and strength of the people—to help our system of private enterprise to function again." He then quoted his words to the Senate in introducing his new program: "Let us unanimously recognize the fact that the Federal debt, whether it be twenty-five billions or forty billions, can only be paid if the Nation obtains a vastly increased citizen income … . The higher the national income goes the faster will we be able to reduce the total of Federal and state and local debts. Viewed from every angle, today's purchasing power—the citizens' income of today—is not at this time sufficient to drive the economic system of America at higher speed."[72] Congress approved the president's spending program, but in response to business lobbying, it also cut capital gains taxes and reduced the undistributed profits tax, which it slated for revocation at the end of 1939.[73]

The New Deal paid a heavy price for the recession in the 1938 midterm elections. Although the Democrats retained majorities, the Republicans added an additional 81 seats in the House and 6 seats in the Senate. Roosevelt maintained the anti-business rhetoric of the past several years, and combined it with a new emphasis on antitrust. He appointed Yale law professor Thurman Arnold to the Justice Department's Antitrust Division. Arnold was a critic of past antitrust enforcement: it had "made business less ruthless and more polite."[74] Trust busting, the Division reported, "is not an end in itself … its objective is not an attack on the efficient side but the freeing of the channels of commerce."[75] With significant increases in budgetary resources, the Division under Arnold's tenure filed almost one-half of the antitrust cases prosecuted since the passage of the Sherman Act, and the prosecutions drew so much attention that the press began to refer to the antitrust statute as the "Thurman Act."[76]

The war on monopoly also found another expression in the work of the Temporary National Economic Committee (TNEC), created in 1938. In transmitting the recommendations for the TNEC, Roosevelt explained: "One of the primary causes of our present difficulties lies in the disappearance of price competition … . Managed industrial prices mean fewer jobs." The president predicted: "action by the Government to eliminate these artificial restraints will be welcomed by industry throughout the Nation."[77] After a three-year investigation of 95 industries that produced a 37-volume report and some 43 monographs, the results were less than compelling. The TNEC recommended a strengthening of antitrust, national incorporation, the promotion of small business investment, and changes in the patent laws, among other things. In the words of Robert A. Brady, the final report revealed "considerable confusion as to the implications of the facts uncovered" and merely "glossed over very nearly every basic implication—economic, political, and social." But Brady clearly understood that the context had changed. The United States was now at war: "In such a national emergency many of the critical peace-time problems associated directly or indirectly with this amazing concentration movement seemed relatively unimportant."[78]

A Return to War Planning

The war's first political victim was the antimonopoly campaign. Arnold was removed from the Justice Department via judicial appointment; the TNEC reports were safely stored in government repositories. Even with the administrative expansion of the past decade, the state was forced, once again, to rely on corporate voluntarism and the placement of business executives throughout the mobilization apparatus. And while World War II demanded a far greater investment in resources than the previous war to end all wars, the high levels of deficit spending accomplished what Roosevelt's New Deal could not: an elimination of the depression. In the year following the Warm Springs conversion, federal spending as a percentage of GDP increased from 7.7 percent to 10.3 percent. By way of comparison, during the peak years of World War II (1943–44), federal spending reached an unprecedented 43.6 percent of GDP, with deficits exceeding 30.3 percent of GDP (1943).[79] Unemployment levels, which rose to depression levels following the downturn of 1937–38, fell to between 1.2 and 1.9 percent (1943–45).[80]

Mobilization began prior to Pearl Harbor, with the creation of the Advisory Commission of the Council of National Defense and the Office of Production Management. Following US entry into the war, their functions were consolidated in a new War Production Board (WPB), placed under the direction of

Sears Roebuck's Donald Nelson. As with the WIB, the WPB delegated authority to functional divisions that were placed under the direction of business executives on leave from their corporations. Business had additional points of access through advisory committees that supported the WPB's 24 industrial divisions. Once again, mobilization was assigned to businessmen whose "outlook and background were identical with those who remained within their firms, which were now subject to the controls they established ... businessmen controlled other businessmen."[81] Although the Senate's Truman Committee objected to potential conflicts of interest, Nelson argued that mobilization depended on the expertise, connections, and cooperation of business.

In addition to the WPB, agencies were created to manage the labor supply. Initially, the administration relied on the WPB's Labor Division. But in 1942, Roosevelt created a new War Manpower Commission (WMC). Working with the US Employment Service, the WMC identified labor shortages and imposed hiring ceilings on nonessential industries. Industrial relations, initially addressed by a National Defense Mediation Board, were regulated by a new National War Labor Board (NWLB) once the United States entered the war. The NWLB facilitated labor organization through a "maintenance of membership" principle, prohibiting contracts from addressing the existence of an opened or closed shop.[82] With the protection of the NWLB and the NLRB, unionization of the nonagricultural workforce would increase from 27.9 percent to 35.5 percent between 1941 and 1945.[83] Applying a formula it developed in the steel industry, the NWLB based wage increases on inflation, a practice that was statutorily mandated with the passage of the Economic Stabilization Act of 1942.[84]

With the passage of the Emergency Price Control Act of 1942, the Office of Price Administration (OPA) was authorized to promote price stability by imposing maximum prices on key commodities. The OPA's mandate was limited, however. Labor had been successful in restricting its control over wages. And the American Farm Bureau Federation, along with the USDA and the farm bloc in Congress, won provisions limiting the OPA's control over agricultural prices until they exceeded 110 percent of parity. With these exclusions, the OPA encountered ongoing difficulties in controlling prices. However, the Economic Stabilization Act of 1942 granted the president the authority to stabilize prices, wages and salaries at levels prevailing on September 15, 1942, and Roosevelt created a new Office of Economic Stabilization, to coordinate price controls from the White House. Ultimately, he issued an executive order in April 1943 demanding that all agencies "hold the line," through the continued application of price ceilings, the Little Steel formula, and rationing.[85]

While wartime inflation claimed much attention, the primary focus was on production, and here the WPB was strongly influenced by Nelson, who was committed to business voluntarism. As he explained in *Arsenal of Democracy*,

we had to get our nation's tremendous productive machine harnessed to do its utmost in the way of war production; but we had to do it within the framework of the American tradition ... . We had to prove, once and for all, that our system of political and economic freedom was in fact more efficient, more productive, more able to respond to the demands of a great emergency than the dictatorial system of our enemies.[86]

As mobilization progressed, Nelson became far less deferential to the armed forces over procurement, creating a Production Executive Committee to evaluate requests. Roosevelt responded to the WPB's growing power by creating a new Office of War Mobilization (OWM), under the direction of Supreme Court Associate Justice James F. Byrnes, to oversee the entire mobilization process from the White House.

Tensions between the WPB and the OWM and Joint Chiefs of Staff were the sharpest over reconversion. Reconversion planning began in 1943, in hopes of avoiding dislocations comparable to those that followed World War I. The greatest beneficiaries from mobilization were the largest firms: the largest 100 corporations received two-thirds of all the war contracts by value; small companies were integrated into mobilization through subcontracting relationships.[87] As war production declined, it was feared that large corporations would cancel subcontracting relations and smaller firms would fail. Nelson and the Smaller Defense Plants Corporation—with the support of the small business committees in Congress—called for early reconversion, allowing small plants to gain market share while larger firms were still engaged in war production. This would be in keeping with the New Deal's anti-monopoly position, as articulated only a few years earlier. To this end, the WPB announced in November 1943 that it would release materials and labor for civilian production where it would not interfere with war production, although Nelson subsequently settled for a less ambitious system of "spot authorizations."[88]

Early reconversion was strongly opposed by the OWM, the WMC, the Joint Chiefs and representatives of the largest corporations. The Joint Chiefs argued that it could endanger the war; the WMC argued that the unemployment resulting from contract cancellation would free labor for other defense-related production. Representatives of large corporations appealed to norms of fairness: no one should be allowed to enter civilian production until all producers had fulfilled their contracts. As Brian Waddell remarks: "Fairness, it seems, dictated that smaller producers not gain any advantages over the industrial giants who dominated prime contracts—and who, in contrast, suffered no moral or political qualms over the oligopolization of the economy occasioned by war."[89] In August 1944, Roosevelt removed Nelson from the WPB, sending him on a diplomatic mission to China. In his absence, and with the Battle of the Bulge, attention returned to maximum production.

With the end of the war, the government cancelled more than 300,000 war contracts worth in excess of $65 billion. It compensated contractors for between 75 and 90 percent of incurred costs, 100 percent for goods that had been completed, and 90 percent for raw materials.[90] A newly created Surplus

War Property Administration was directed to sell surplus materials at market prices, if possible, and through competitive bidding if not. Ultimately, the government disposed of some $21.5 billion of surpluses for $310 million, providing a subsidy for the largest corporations involved in wartime production that only added to the $16 billion that had been spent to expand private production facilities.[91] As John Morton Blum notes, big business "had a first claim to the facilities the government had financed." Although "Congress had tried to legislate a vision of society, a vision in which small enterprises would compete fairly against large in a market uncontrolled by government," Blum concludes, the "postwar hopes of small business shrank before the wartime gains of industrial giants."[92]

In the late 1930s, Roosevelt's hostility toward big business was palpable and he was intent on attacking the structural constraints that were presumably impeding growth. Ironically, the war forced the New Deal into retreat, once again delegating authority to the same corporations that had been the target of such severe criticism. The war may have provided the stimulus necessary to bring the economy to full employment, but it also led to an abandonment of the goals of addressing industrial structure. By all accounts, the US economy at the end of the war had greater concentrations of economic power than at anytime in recent history. As noted earlier, Roosevelt had announced in 1932 that the "day of the great promoter or the financial Titan, to whom we granted anything if only he would build, or develop, is over." The war had tested that proposition.

Conclusion

Even if the war forced retreat in Roosevelt's attack on the monopolies, the accomplishments of the New Deal were nonetheless impressive. It dramatically expanded the regulation of banking and extended regulations to securities, agriculture and industrial relations (and a number of additional industries, ranging from communications to commercial aviation and trucking). The experience of depression and the need to stabilize the economy shaped the goals associated with regulation and marked a departure from the earlier Progressive Regime. In social policy, the public works programs of the early New Deal gave way to the Social Security Act, which created a number of enduring welfare policies (most notably, old age pensions) and would provide a foundation for welfare state expansion in the 1960s, with the introduction of Medicare and Medicaid. In economic policy, the Warm Springs conversion and the embrace of Keynesian countercyclical demand management would be institutionalized in 1946, with the passage of the Employment Act, which created a new institutional structure for macroeconomic policymaking. Through these New Deal initiatives and subsequent extensions, the role of the state in the economy had never been greater.

There were significant political changes as well, many of which are beyond the scope of this chapter. The power of the executive relative to the legislative branch, which had been growing since the turn of the century, accelerated under conditions of depression and war. The Court, which overturned the NRA and the AAA in the mid-1930s, became far more compliant by the late 1930s, in response to Roosevelt's proposed Judicial Reorganization Act that would have empowered him to appoint additional justices and thus reduce the independence of the judiciary. By 1937, the Court's expansive view of the interstate commerce clause and the "necessary and proper" clause of the Constitution would reduce the barriers to government expansion and the extension of social policy and regulations.[93] There were great changes in popular expectations and the prevailing understanding of legitimacy that would increasingly turn on whether the government had successfully provided an expansive set of services.[94] The popularity of the New Deal programs and Roosevelt's success in locking in various constituency groups with new policies were so great that postwar Republican presidents would be hesitant to promote significant reforms. As Eisenhower observed when president: "Should any political party attempt to abolish social security, unemployment insurance, and eliminate labor laws and farm programs, you would not hear of that party again in our political history."[95] Following the New Deal, George H. Mayer noted, "the pressure groups had multiplied to the point where Eisenhower could reduce neither expenditures nor services without risking organized retaliation."[96] The New Deal Regime would be challenged in the last decades of the twentieth century, but only after it had undergone considerable expansion. We turn to this topic in the next two chapters.

5 The Postwar Consolidation of the New Deal Regime

World War II, in many ways, constituted a sharp line of demarcation in the history of the American political economy and the global political economy more generally. The depression created a window of opportunity for introducing new policies and institutions that one can refer to as a distinctive New Deal Regime. Yet the new policies were insufficient to end the depression and there is much to suggest that the rapidity and inconsistency of change created uncertainty that impeded investment. But World War II forced levels of production that would have been unimaginable from the perspective of the 1930s and the unemployment rate fell to 1.9 percent in 1943, and 1.2 percent in 1944. For those who had experienced a 25 percent unemployment rate a decade earlier and the sharp decline of 1937, the contrast could not be greater.[1]

There remained several important questions. Would peace mark a return of depression? What might be done to prevent a recurrence of depression and the carnage of a future world war? The first question was answered rather quickly, as the nation entered a period of prolonged growth. The second question found a response in the creation of new institutions that strengthened the New Deal Regime and would play a central role in shaping the economic performance of subsequent decades. In this chapter, we examine the new system of macroeconomic management established under the Employment Act of 1946, the international institutions created for exchange rates and trade, and the system of industrial relations that evolved out of the experiences of the New Deal and World War II.

Managing the Macroeconomy

John Maynard Keynes' *General Theory of Employment, Interest and Money* set the theoretical foundations for a revolution in macroeconomics that would endure for decades. The most important argument in the *General Theory* was that markets would not necessarily return to full employment equilibrium. Rather, the system

> seems capable of remaining in a chronic condition of sub-normal activity for a considerable period without any marked tendency towards recovery

or towards complete collapse. Moreover, the evidence indicates that full, or even approximately full, employment is of rare and short-termed occurrence.[2]

Under conditions of aggregate demand failure, Keynes argued that there was an ignition problem. Levels of spending were simply insufficient to create incentives to invest or expand production. The state had an indispensable role in stimulating the economy. Although the *General Theory* provided a theoretical foundation for an active fiscal policy, support for some form of countercyclical spending predated Keynes. Even if Roosevelt embraced deficit spending in 1938, it would be difficult to attribute this decision to the intellectual impact of Keynes. As Herbert Stein explains: "The assimilation of the *General Theory* into American thinking and the formation of a Keynesian school came too late to be of much influence on that decision. Of course, there was in this period a considerable group of 'spenders' in Washington" but "[t]heir ideas were of pre-Keynesian origin and did not respond quickly, if ever, to what was in the *General Theory*."[3]

In the 1944 State of the Union address, Roosevelt announced an economic bill of rights, which included "the right to a useful and remunerative job in the industries or shops or farms or mines of the Nation."[4] Even 1944 Republican presidential candidate Thomas Dewey embraced an expanded role for government, proclaiming: "If at any time there are not sufficient jobs in private employment to go around, the Government can and must create job opportunities, because there must be jobs for all in this country of ours."[5] There were profound concerns about the impact of peace on employment. As a 1944 Senate report on reconversion, coauthored by then Senator Harry Truman (D-MO) and Senator James E. Murray (D-MT) warned:

> Almost half of the framework supporting this giant structure consists of war contracts ... . Unless an economic substitute is found for war contracts, mass unemployment will become a serious threat and the number of unemployed men and women in this country might easily surpass anything that was dreamed of during the last depression.[6]

In January 1945, the Senate considered a proposed "Full Employment Act" sponsored by Senator Murray. Following FDR's economic bill of rights, section 2(b) of the bill declared:

> All Americans able to work and seeking work have the right to useful, remunerative, regular, and full-time employment, and it is the policy of the United States to assure the existence at all times of sufficient employment opportunities to enable all Americans who have finished their schooling and do not have full-time housekeeping responsibilities freely to exercise this right.[7]

The bill proposed an institutional mechanism for providing full employment. It required the president, with the assistance of the Bureau of the Budget, to submit annually a National Production and Employment Budget that would, in Murray's words, make

> known to Congress and the country (1) the total number of job opportunities needed for all persons willing and able to work; (2) the total amount of goods and services that our economy must provide if we are to have full employment; (3) the total power of the country to buy goods and services, i.e., the total purchasing power of business, consumers and the government; and (4) an appraisal as to whether this purchasing power is adequate to create a demand for enough goods and services to provide full employment.[8]

The bill also proposed a Joint Congressional Committee on the National Production and Employment Budget, to integrate the legislative branch in to the fiscal policy process.

The full-employment bill was significant on several counts. First, it gave full employment a privileged status relative to competing macroeconomic object-ives. Second, by proposing to create an entitlement to employment, it could permanently enshrine the more activist features of the New Deal—public works and planning. Third, as Mark Blyth explains: "by establishing *as mandatory* a consumption gap analysis as the centerpiece of a national full-employment budget, the Act enshrined a stagnationist analysis that *by definition* deemed private initiative and investment inadequate and necessitated permanent compensatory spending."[9] Indeed, Murray claimed the bill addressed "the remarkable increase in our productive capacity in the last few years" that created "the threat of so-called 'over-production'" and made clear that "business cannot by itself keep the wheels of industry turning at a rate that will provide sustained employment opportunities for all who are willing and able to work."[10] Finally, the bill proposed a set of institutions that, in the words of J. Bradford De Long, "would have solidly entrenched a strong bias toward active countercyclical fiscal policy in the core of the American exe-cutive branch."[11] As Seymour Harris explained in 1945, "Congress now is fractionized into a large number of committees; and this fractionization may be contrasted with the unity required of our economic policies." The proposed institutions could "go a long way toward correcting the weaknesses of our present legislative set-up."[12]

There were sources of concern. Full employment was never defined in the bill and the "right" to employment seemed both overly broad and incompatible with liberty. As Sumner H. Slichter asked in 1945:

> what duties go with the right? Does the man who claims the "right" to employment have the duty of making himself employable? If his skills become obsolete, does he have an obligation to acquire new skills? If

industries decline in some places, are workers under obligation to move to places where employment is expanding?[13]

The political problems were potentially even greater. Political scientist E. E. Schattschneider predicted that the odds in favor of the bill were not good. "In fact, a major political-conflict over these policies can probably be avoided only by the abandonment of the whole project." Full employment policy depends on the support of the majority—a group inherently difficult to mobilize. In contrast,

> it is easy to organize minorities as pressure groups ... . The conservative groups long opposed to social experiments of this sort have ready-made an array of organizations able to make a great display of strength before the congressional committees. Under these circumstances, the proponents of full-employment legislation are likely to be swamped by the opposition.

Schattschneider correctly observed that full employment would require the coordination of multiple public policies. However, "a regime of pressure politics is unsuited to the needs of the new legislation ... adequate political means for the execution of the policies in question can be found only in the use of the party system." Unfortunately, the party system seemed in disarray. Southern Democrats had formed a conservative coalition with Republicans, and "this coalition is likely to be ruinous, because it is designed to defeat the policy altogether or to cripple it by the adoption of 'states' rights' amendments and by cutting appropriations unreasonably."[14]

Organized labor and the National Farmers Union supported the Senate bill, as did now President Harry Truman. But the New Deal coalition was already starting to show stress and, as the legislation moved to the House, a legislative coalition comprised of Southern Democrats and Midwestern Republicans proved an insurmountable obstacle. The US Chamber of Commerce, the National Association of Manufacturers, and the American Farm Bureau Federation mobilized in opposition, raising concerns about planning and the inflationary consequences of deficit spending. Representative Will Whittington (D-MS) played a decisive role as the swing vote in the subcommittee, and used this position to introduce a substitute version largely written by the Chamber of Commerce and the business-dominated Council for Economic Development. It passed the House and prevailed in the joint conference committee.[15] Perhaps the fatal blow to the original full employment bill was the economy itself. As Margaret Weir notes: "As unemployment dissolved on its own, legislation seemed less pressing to most Americans."[16]

In the end, Congress passed the Employment Act of 1946. The change in the title of the legislation was more than symbolic. The entitlement to employment was stripped away, replaced with a responsibility "to promote maximum employment, production, and purchasing power." The commitment to provide "such volume of Federal investment and expenditures as may be needed" to assure full employment disappeared in the final version, and was replaced by "all practicable means consistent with its needs and obligations and other considerations of national policy."[17] Yet, the Act created an institutional framework for macroeconomic policymaking. It established the Council of Economic Advisers (CEA), to assist the president, and established the *Economic Report of the President* as an annual statement of administration policy. It also created a Joint Economic Committee in Congress to strengthen oversight of economic policymaking. Yet, there was nothing in the Act that bound policymakers to Keynesianism. Although some argued that it marked a sea-change in economic management, economist Jacob Viner had his doubts. Writing in 1947, he explained:

> In recent decades at least, Congress has usually been willing upon request to acknowledge its obligations to promote national prosperity "consistent with ... other essential considerations of national policy." Herbert Hoover himself would have subscribed to this, and to more than this. The preambles to hundreds of Acts of the last generation say as much. The fact that no Senator felt hostile enough to the Act to vote against it at least suggests that it would be a mistake to read too much into the declaration of policy as marking a change of economic philosophy.

Viner noted that the act embodied "no economic doctrine except the proposition that any program for promoting maximum production and employment shall be of a kind 'calculated to foster and promote free competitive enterprise' " and the legislative history "reveals that the Act won its way to the statute books only on the basis of its avoidance in its final form of specific doctrinal content."[18]

As the new Council of Economic Advisers began to execute its functions, critics saw little evidence of a credible commitment to full employment. Alvin H. Hansen, a chief advocate of the secular stagnation thesis, found the first report of the Council to be a "public relations" document, while the second report issued in 1947 "could not pass muster as a serious economic document," containing "highly dubious comments about the nature of the business cycle which would not command the assent of competent specialists in this field." Of even greater concern, the CEA misrepresented the government's role under the Employment Act:

> It is sometimes alleged (several phrases in the report of the Council are not altogether free from this implication) that the Act places primary responsibility upon private business for the maintenance of prosperity. This is not correct. In the Act, Congress declared that it is the responsibility of the Federal Government to use all practicable means, with the assistance and cooperation of private industry and local governments to achieve the goals set forth with respect to employment, production, and purchasing power.[19]

Viner joined in the critique, observing that the CEA's "main hope ... lies in the possibility of guiding and educating business to stabilize itself." After reviewing the CEA's proposals, he noted: "it is not clear that they do not represent a revival of Herbert Hoover's reliance on exhortation."[20]

From Statute to Practice

The Employment Act recognized a plurality of goals and the tension between these goals would find a concrete expression in the postwar period. During the 1950s, Keynesians focused greater attention on the trade-off between unemployment and inflation, two goals embodied in the Employment Act. This relationship was given a systematic expression in the Phillips Curve, developed by economist A.W. Phillips. There is an inverse relationship between inflation and unemployment. When unemployment falls, tighter labor markets place upward pressure on wages that will have inflationary consequences unless they are offset by comparable productivity gains. While policymakers would prefer full employment *and* price stability, both cannot be achieved simultaneously and thus attention turns to the optimal mix of inflation and unemployment. Of course, this decision is politically and ideologically charged; one should expect parties to support a mix of unemployment and inflation that meets the demands of their underlying political coalitions.[21]

Keynesianism proposed a solution to aggregate demand failure, but the precise policy instruments varied cross-nationally. In the closing pages of the *General Theory*, Keynes observed: "The outstanding faults of the economic society in which we live are its failure to provide for full employment and its arbitrary and inequitable distribution of wealth and income."[22] One approach to addressing these faults would be through an active labor market policy, public employment, and an extensive welfare state. One of the great attributes of this variant—known as social Keynesianism—is that it allows policymakers to meet their larger macroeconomic goals while addressing pressing social problems. This vision of Keynesianism, one that informed the original Full Employment bill, would be embraced by many northern European nations in the postwar period. But in the United States, the internal complexities of the New Deal coalition and the opposition of organized business constituted significant obstacles. Instead, there would be a heavy reliance on commercial Keynesianism that would rely heavily on automatic stabilizers. That is, during periods of economic downturn, reductions in revenues would have an automatic stimulative effect. When needed, tax cuts could be used, moreover, to provide businesses and consumers with additional income that could be spent in the market. The reliance on automatic stabilizers was so great that "looking back at the budget since World War II," De Long notes, "it is difficult to argue that on balance 'discretionary' fiscal policy has played any stabilizing role."[23]

The argument for automatic stabilizers found its strongest presentation in a 1947 volume entitled *Taxes and the Budget: A Program for Prosperity in a Free Economy*, produced by the business-dominated Committee for Economic

Development (CED).[24] The CED argued that the budget should not be balanced on an annual basis. Rather, tax levels should be set to produce a moderate surplus at high employment. During downturns in the business cycle, automatic stabilizers—combined with discretionary monetary policy—would have a stimulative effect. The deficits generated during downturns would be paid for by surpluses created during cyclical upswings. The CED argued that forecasting, beset by technical limitations, could become politicized by elected officials who promoted low taxation and high expenditures for their political utility. Managed compensatory policy could be far more destabilizing than automatic stabilizers. Moreover, as Herbert Stein notes, "while the committee was in general opposed to discretionary changes in budget policy, it expected and welcomed discretionary flexibility in monetary policy ... . It was willing to accept discretion in monetary policy which it would not accept in budget policy because it considered monetary policy the quicker-acting instrument ... and because it had more faith in the objectivity of the Federal Reserve than in the administration and Congress."[25]

The central role of automatic stabilizers was possible, in part, because of the growing size of the federal budget relative to the economy. Recall that at its 1930s peak, the federal budget claimed some 10 percent of GDP. In the postwar period, levels of spending would never come close to these levels. In the 1950s, federal expenditures were, on average, 17.6 percent of GDP, increasing to an average of 18.7 percent in the 1960s, and 20 percent in the 1970s. During the 1980s, a decade dominated by the Reagan "revolution" and discussions of the merits of the free market relative to the state, the federal government spent an average of 22.2 percent of GDP—twice the peak level of spending during the 1930s.[26] The greater the size of the state relative to the economy, the greater the potential impact of the automatic stabilizers.

Making Economic Policy: The Institutional Context

The Employment Act created a new institutional framework for macroeconomic policymaking. Nonetheless, responsibility for economic policy would remain fragmented, creating ongoing problems of coordination. Presidents could draw on the advice and technical support of three executive branch agencies (informally called "the Troika") in formulating policy. The CEA would provide economic forecasts and the projected impact of various policy options on key indicators. The Treasury could provide estimates of revenues under competing scenarios. The Bureau of the Budget (reorganized as the Office of Management and Budget in 1970) could work with the administration in setting spending targets, reviewing agency needs, and developing the budget. The *Economic Report of the President* would provide a detailed presentation of economic conditions and policy objectives; the president's budget would provide the chief means of translating fiscal policy goals into expenditures.

Even if we can assume a relatively coherent executive policy process, things become far more complicated when we recall that the Constitution, in the words of Richard E. Neustadt, created a system of "separated institutions sharing powers."[27] The success of the president's program will be a product, in part, of congressional action. Every dollar spent by the federal government must be authorized and appropriated by Congress and all revenue bills must originate in the House Ways and Means Committee. Congress' decentralized committee system provides high levels of interest group access, exacerbated by the localism of elected officials and the vagaries of campaign finance, and engenders coordination problems. During the postwar period, moreover, Congress developed a far greater capacity to engage in economic policy-making. The Congressional Budget and Impoundment Act of 1974 created the Congressional Budget Office (CBO) to provide legislators with an independent source of economic expertise. Moreover it established new budget committees in the House and Senate, responsible for setting overall spending and tax levels and to serve a coordinative function, and a new budget process, which mandated passage of a budget resolution establishing fiscal policy goals. While the 1974 Act strengthened the economic policy-making capacity of Congress, it did not affect the larger institutional dynamic. The budget remained the product of a system "organized to make incremental distributive decisions in favor of strong interests groups, agencies, and congressional committees."[28]

Fiscal policy is developed in a fragmented, permeable institutional setting with high levels of interest group mobilization. Monetary policy, in sharp contrast, is tightly controlled by the Federal Reserve. Key deliberations over monetary policy are conducted in secret, free from open meeting requirements. The president and Congress might have a great stake in these decisions, but their influence is constrained by problems of information scarcity and a dearth of mechanisms to force political control (e.g., Congress cannot use the power of the purse because the Fed generates its own resources). These factors, combined with the inherent complexity of monetary policy and the Fed's reputation for expertise, have allowed it to function relatively free from political pressures. This is not to say that the Fed does not serve a representational function. The Federal Reserve is directly integrated into the financial community. The twelve district Federal Reserve Banks are private, for-profit, corporations owned by member banks and governed by a board of directors, the majority of whom are selected by member banks, and a president appointed by the board of directors. The Federal Open Market Committee—the entity responsible for the sale and purchase of govern-ment securities, and thus determining the money supply—is comprised of the members of the Board of Governors and five district bank presidents (including the president of the New York Fed), thereby providing additional representation. Thus, the banking community is given a seat at the table in the most important decisions made by the Federal Reserve.

What are the implications for public policy? As noted above, the Employ-ment Act recognized "maximum employment" and "purchasing power" as coequal policy objectives and the United States, as a generalization, placed a heavy reliance on automatic stabilizers. Even if Congress—dominated for much of the period in question by Democratic majorities—preferred to use its control over the budget to pursue an expansionary fiscal policy, it would encounter a potential obstacle from the Fed. Low unemployment carries inflationary consequences and banks, with large holdings of fixed-interest-rate loans, have a powerful stake in maintaining low and stable rates of inflation. Their preferences are imported into the Fed's policies via the structural integration of the Fed and the financial community.[29] As a generalization, one can expect the policy mix promoted by the CED—automatic stabilizers and discretionary monetary policy—to create a bias in favor of price stability. However, the capacity of the Fed to exercise true independence can be overstated given that the Treasury can counter monetary policy through the issuance of securities. Despite norms of coordination, at various points in the immediate postwar period, the Fed used its powers to pressure presidents to exercise greater restraint.[30]

Building a New International Order

From the perspective of the 1940s, the past three decades had witnessed unprecedented carnage of two world wars and a global depression. Many hoped that new international institutions could prevent the recurrence of such events. For present purposes, the most important components of the postwar order included the new international monetary system developed at Bretton Woods and the liberalized trade regime under the General Agreement on Tariffs and Trade (GATT). The combination of growing trade and monetary stability facilitated postwar growth, making subsequent decades the most prosperous in the world's history. Europe and Japan exited World War II with their capital stock damaged or destroyed, often without the capacity to meet the basic needs of citizens. The United States, in sharp contrast, had made significant investments during the war and was prepared to take advantage of the new system of trade and monetary relations.

The United States also played an important role in stimulating demand globally through the Marshall Plan. In 1947, Secretary of State George Marshall initiated what would become assistance worth some $13 billion to European nations that joined the Organization for European Economic Cooperation. The rejection of the Marshall Plan by the Soviet Union and the Eastern Bloc nations invested the European Recovery Program with a geopolitical and symbolic importance that was likely greater than its economic importance. Although Marshall Plan money was never greater than 5 percent of the GNP of recipient nations, rapidly increasing Cold War defense spending undoubtedly stimulated growth in recovering economies of Western Europe.[31]

The Bretton Woods System

The lack of a stable international monetary system was one of the products of World War I and the Great Depression. The gold standard began to fray during World War I, as nations expanded their money supplies to cover wartime expenses, stimulating inflation and problems of convertibility. With the Armistice, efforts to reestablish a stable monetary system were frustrated by high levels of war debt. The United States was the world's largest creditor and nations could manage their debts through the provision of gold. But during the 1920s, US tariff policies frustrated efforts of debtor nations hoping to raise specie to service their debts. With the depression, the attempts to reestablish a stable gold-based payments system were officially abandoned as the United States and Britain rejected the gold standard.

The United States and Britain began negotiations over a postwar monetary system in 1941. Competing plans were circulated, most importantly, a British plan written by Keynes and an American plan authored by Harry Dexter White. There were significant differences between the plans, but where the two differed, White's plan largely prevailed. As James M. Boughton explains, the success of White's plan was only partially attributable to the economic power of the United States. "White understood that American ascendency depended on a multilateral and multinational regime of open trade and finance. British aspirations, in contrast, depended on perpetuation of the system of Empire preferences and—despite American opposition to that system— development of a bilateral economic partnership with the United States."[32] Despite these differences, a consensus emerged on the key features of the postwar regime, and the architecture of the new system was finalized at the United Nations Monetary and Financial Conference held at Bretton Woods, New Hampshire, in the summer of 1944.

The experience of depression and war shaped the debates; many participants believed that a stable monetary system must be a cornerstone of the postwar order. As Henry Morgenthau Jr., Roosevelt's Treasury Secretary and chair of the US delegation explained, the 1930s witnessed "the spread of depression from country to country" and "the growth of the twin evils of international economic aggression and monetary disorder." Exchange rate controls were used as tools of "international economic aggression, and they were the logical concomitant of a policy directed toward war and conquest. The postwar international economic problems may well be more difficult than those of the 1930's, and unless we cooperate to solve these problems, we may be faced with a resumption and intensification of monetary disorder and economic aggression in the postwar period."[33] Mabel Newcomer, a US delegate to Bretton Woods, framed the alternatives in stark terms: "The real alternative to acceptance of the Bretton Woods agreement is no international agreement at all. This means return to the economic warfare that prevailed between wars—intensified by the greater trade and monetary dislocations resulting from this war."[34]

What would henceforth be referred to as the Bretton Woods system created a new system for international monetary affairs. Most importantly for the United States, the system made the dollar the *de facto* world currency, thereby locking in the nation's role as the world's leading economy. Under Bretton Woods, all currencies could be converted into dollars at a fixed exchange rate and the dollar, in turn, could be converted into gold at $35 an ounce. The dollar, in essence, could serve as the world's currency. Corporations based in the United States could conduct global business in dollars, thereby reducing transaction costs that might otherwise exist. Bretton Woods also created two new institutions, the International Monetary Fund (IMF) and the International Bank for Reconstruction and Development (or World Bank). The IMF was created to manage the system of fixed exchange rates and provide loans to nations with persistent balance-of-payments problems. Member nations could revaluate their currencies only after consultation with the IMF, and then only within a band of 10 percent. Bretton Woods required "unqualified adherence to specified exchange practices." A nation that made changes in parity without IMF authorization would become "ineligible to use the resources of the Fund" and if it persisted in its practices, it would be "subject to expulsion from both the Fund and the International Bank."[35] The World Bank, in contrast to the IMF, was given a limited mandate to make or underwrite loans for postwar reconstruction. Initially, it was believed that such an institution, capitalized at $10 billion through national subscriptions, would be self-liquidating with the completion of reconstruction. Ultimately, the World Bank's mission evolved, from promoting postwar recovery to encouraging development more generally.

Opposition to Bretton Woods was greatest in the New York financial community, that found the World Banks to be "a 'novel and untried' departure from sound banking principles" insofar as it gave debtors a voice in determining the policies of creditors. As one critic noted, the concerns of the banking community were comparable to "the earlier opposition of many bankers to such great improvements as the Federal Reserve System and the Federal Deposit Insurance system, which they would probably not now want to do without."[36] Other opposition arose from those who supported a return to the gold standard, arguing that its automatic adjustments were far more stabilizing. Yet, as Newcomer correctly observed, the gold standard was not "the venerable institution" often assumed and its brief success was "attributable to conditions that can never be restored." Thus, the operative choice was not "between the automatic gold standard and a managed currency."[37]

The Bretton Woods discussions raised important questions regarding the relationship between domestic policy decisions and the international accord. Valdemar Carlson, writing in 1944, recognized that in the wake of the depression, governments across the world would seek to "inflate the domestic money in order to overcome a depression" thereby affecting "the external value of the currency" and undermining the stable exchange rates envisioned by Bretton Woods."[38] B.H. Beckhart argued that IMF intervention would be inevitable under these conditions. "If the members of the Fund are free to follow domestic policies which they deem important from the point of view of their own interests and which are immune from criticism by the Fund, currency depreciation will become an accepted policy and international monetary arrangements are made impossible." Beckhart found this a source of some concern and suggested that it be "thoroughly explored before Congressional action on the Fund takes place."[39]

Here, the debates over the full employment bill and Bretton Woods merged. Bretton Woods was presented by some as "the application of the Keynesian economics to the international level … . No nation can maintain full employment and full use of its productive resources unless it finds an outlet for all its potential savings."[40] Alvin Hansen, who had served as one of the technical experts at the meeting, argued that Bretton Woods, taken by itself, would be insufficient. "If the fundamental structure of a country's imports and exports is seriously out of balance, enormous changes in the exchange rate would be required to bring about equilibrium." He concluded: "a solution must be found by a direct attack upon the problem of full employment and parallel programs of economic stability in the leading industrial countries, and not by juggling the foreign exchange rate." This would require a "thorough survey of the potential resources of the country, both human and material, the possibility of diversification of its agriculture and its industries in a broad developmental program" rather than relying on "the weak reed of a change in the exchange rate."[41] Economist William Fellner went further, arguing that Bretton Woods be supplemented with new institutions to "co-ordinate the full employment policies of the participating nations … . There is no logic in depriving countries of the right to alter exchange rates and at the same time leaving them free to adopt commercial policies that would create or perpetuate disequilibrium."[42] Indeed, a broad agreement on trade practices would come in the next few years, a point to be explored in greater detail below.

Ironically, as the IMF evolved as an institution, it tended to adopt a path that was the polar opposite of that envisioned by Hansen and Fellner. The IMF would often make loans contingent on a nation's willingness to implement stabilization policies (e.g., restrictive monetary and fiscal policy), trade liberalization, privatization, and deregulation rather than full employment. Because the United States exercised great influence over the Washington-based IMF, these practices raised persistent concerns that the United States was using the institution to impose the American model on other nations, a critique that was extended to the World Bank.[43] And the success of the Bretton Woods system would be severely tested in subsequent decades. Harry Dexter White, who assumed directorship of the IMF, warned a year into its operations that once "keen competition for world markets again characterizes world trade" and "when the course of exports is largely determined by price considerations rather than by availability of supply," the "exchange adjustment problems, and problems of financial assistance … will subject the Fund to the severest of tests."[44] Indeed, after a quarter century concerns over inflation and the balance-of-payments deficits led President Nixon to close the gold window unilaterally, bringing an end to the Bretton Woods system. Henceforth, exchange rates would be determined largely through market forces, creating at times new sources of instability and the need for periodic coordination of finance ministers attempting to realign currencies.

The General Agreement on Tariffs and Trade

During the interwar period, high tariff rates, import quotas, and a maze of bilateral agreements reinforced economic nationalism and thus, there was a strong belief in the postwar period that future growth and peace would depend on significant reforms. As with monetary relations, the United States and Britain were intent on developing a new institutional architecture to govern trade. By 1947, a draft agreement was written to establish a new International Trade Organization that would be devoted to trade liberalization, with exceptions where necessary to promote economic development, and a General Agreement on Tariffs and Trade (GATT) was negotiated in Geneva and signed by 23 nations to coordinate their behavior until the agreement for a new trade organization could be ratified.

In 1948, the United Nations' Economic and Social Council met in Havana, Cuba, and produced a charter to create a new International Trade Organization. The negotiations, as Leicester Webb remarked, degenerated into "a nightmarish complexity." The US negotiators were forced "either to abandon the hope of universality or to accept a wide variety of exceptions and escape clauses, some of which sanctioned practices that were deeply repugnant to them." Although they fought to minimize "the derogations from liberal trade," in the end, the Havana Charter's complexity—some 106 clauses, 16 annexes, and 50 interpretive notes, were a "witness to their failure."[45] In the words of John W. Evans: "At Havana the forces of opposition on more than one occasion came close to winning control of the Conference and to writing not a Charter for freer world trade but an international endorsement of permanent and chronic economic warfare."[46] As one analyst explained in 1949, while the charter established a general principle that "members shall not employ quantitative restrictions on either imports from or exports to other members," the exceptions were "so extensive that it is not easy to weigh the significance of the general commitment." One could question whether the "continued widespread use of import quotas (and/or exchange restrictions)" would "render valueless many of the tariff concessions which have been concluded or may be negotiated in the future."[47] Moreover, there were provisions that again delved into domestic politics. Australia, for example, was successful in introducing into the charter "a pledge, binding on individual members, to promote within their territories full employment and 'a large and steadily growing volume of real income and effective demand'."[48]

Although fifty-six nations signed the Charter, ratification proved elusive. In the United States, domestic opposition grew in the Congress, as business and farm interests mobilized in opposition and others stood opposed to the myriad exemptions. As Barry Eichengreen notes: "The agreement was squeezed between protectionists who opposed its liberal thrust and perfectionists who criticized the myriad exceptions from open trade extended to countries seeking to establish full employment, accelerate their economic development, or stabilize the prices of commodity exports."[49] Given the proximity of the 1948 election, President Truman was hesitant to submit the charter for ratification and refused to resubmit it in 1950. Absent the ratification by the world's largest economy, the Havana Charter was doomed and the commercial policy portions of GATT—designed as a temporary measure—became the foundation for the postwar trade system.[50]

The primary goal was to liberalize trade. To this end, GATT applied the "most-favored nation" principle, whereby each member could export to other members on equal terms, thereby preventing the recourse to discriminatory duties. Of course, nations that were not members of GATT had no reason to believe that most-favored-nation status would be extended to them. The fear of discrimination by GATT members created strong incentives for the expansion of membership. Because member nations would have strong incentives to bow to domestic political pressure and use trade to protect key industries or constituent groups, GATT created grievance and dispute resolution procedures to resolve these issues as they arose.

One of the most important exemptions came in the area of agriculture. The New Deal system of agricultural regulation would fail if agricultural imports were allowed to enter the market freely. In Geneva, the United States secured exemptions for import restrictions of nations that limited domestic production or disposed of surpluses through free distribution or below-market price sales in domestic markets. Congress, in turn, amended the Agricultural Adjustment Act in 1951 to state that the nation's farm policy would supersede any international commitments. As George Bronz observed, the agricultural exception in GATT illustrated "the tendency of international agreements to be a formulation of the least common denominator of existing national policies, rather than an agreement by governments to change economic policies."[51] But the restrictions on trade liberalization extended beyond agriculture. In 1951, when Congress passed the Trade Agreements Extension Act, it stated that tariff reductions would not be continued if increases in imports "cause or threaten serious injury to the domestic industry producing like or directly competitive products."[52] The next year, Truman issued Executive Order 10401, requiring trade agreements to include an "escape clause." As we will see in Chapters 6 and 7, the departures from liberal trade in the United States would become ever more frequent as the nation encountered growing competitive challenges in the 1970s and 1980s.

The new trade system also had implications for the role of the presidency relative to Congress. During the nineteenth and early twentieth centuries, Congress dominated trade policy and used tariff provisions to maintain larger political coalitions. Yet, beginning in the 1920s, there were ongoing struggles between the executive branch and Congress over control of trade policy. The

Fordney-McCumber Tariff Act of 1922 raised tariff rates, but it also provided for a flexible tariff and authorized the president, working through the Tariff Commission, to adjust tariff rates by 50 percent, thereby transferring power to the executive. Indeed, there is much to suggest that the provisions in the Smoot-Hawley Act further empowering the president led Hoover to sign the legislation. In this context, GATT was important insofar as it dramatically changed trade policy. By placing constraints on the tariff policies of member nations, it diminished the power of Congress. Increasingly, authority of trade policy rested with the president.[53]

From an international perspective, the greatest accomplishment of GATT was the creation of an institutional context for negotiating multilateral tariff reductions through international meetings or rounds. Following Geneva, progress toward additional reductions was slow to come. The Annecy (1949) and Torquay (1950–51) rounds expanded participation in GATT, but made modest gains in tariff reductions. The most important accomplishment was preventing the erosion of the 1947 tariff reductions. Things would change greatly during the Kennedy Round of the 1960s. Concerns over the European Economic Community emerging as a separate trading bloc led Congress to authorize the president to negotiate for reductions of up to 50 percent on tariffs, thereby leading to significant progress. Between 1947 and 1967, average tariff levels fell from an average of 40 percent to an average of 9.9 percent in the United States, and between 8.6 and 10.8 percent among major trading partners.[54]

Trade issues became far more complicated after the Kennedy round, as they moved to address non-tariff barriers, including domestic regulations and subsidies, raising once again important questions about the extent to which a commitment to free trade should be subordinated to domestic policies. New issues like trade in services and intellectual property rights raised a host of novel and complex questions. As the issues confronted by trade negotiators moved beyond the relatively simple issue of tariffs, trade rounds became increasingly protracted and the kinds of significant gains realized in the earlier rounds became elusive. In 1994, in part out of recognition of the complexity of emerging trade issues and the need for a more robust system of dispute resolution, the members of GATT created a new World Trade Organization, in part, fulfilling the aspirations of the original Havana Charter. Whether the WTO will be more successful that its predecessor in achieving the ultimate aims of trade liberalization remains an open question.

Some advocates of GATT made the argument that it was the primary engine of postwar growth. Yet, as Douglas A. Irwin observed, this claim has a difficult time accounting for timing, given that GATT was "largely inactive during the 1950's, and the Kennedy Round was not concluded until 1967, and implemented thereafter. To say that this first negotiating round stimulated two decades of rapidly expanding international trade stretches the imagination."[55] Even if the causal connections are more complex, there has been a powerful correlation between postwar growth and trade expansion. After five decades, world merchandise trade had increased sixteen fold and the original agreement governing 23 nations had expanded to include 128 nations.[56] The United States benefitted greatly from GATT, particularly in the early decades when it was the world's greatest exporter. But as the postwar recovery took hold and major trading partners began to expand their exports, the United States experienced growing trade deficits. Between 1948 and 2006, merchandise exports grew by over 81 times, while imports grew by 261 times. Trade deficits, which exceeded $100 billion in 1984, continued to grow significantly in subsequent years.[57] By 2008, the United States exported $1.83 trillion in goods and services, but imported $2.52 trillion, creating a trade deficit of $696 billion, approximately 3.7 percent of GDP (See Figure 5.1).[58] Many analysts attributed the decline of manufacturing industries to the growth in trade. Presidents would seek to pressure trading partners to accept voluntary export restraints as a means of providing relief to domestic industries while simultaneously deploying the rhetoric of free trade.

Postwar Industrial Relations

Between 1935—the year Congress passed the National Labor Relations Act —and 1945, the number of union members had increased from 3.8 million to 12.6 million. In 1946, the year the Employment Act was passed, the nation experienced a wave of strikes, some 4,990 work stoppages involving 10.5 percent of the labor force.[59] The most important of these strikes involved key industries, including automobiles, coal, meatpacking, and steel. Congress responded by passing legislation, strongly backed by a business coalition led by the National Association of Manufacturers, to create a federal mediation board, impose a mandatory "cooling off" period before strikes could be

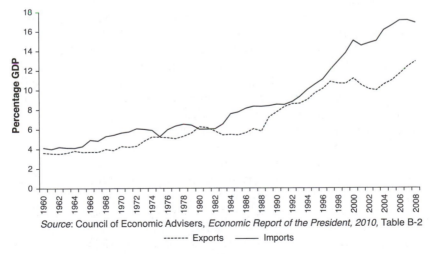

Source: Council of Economic Advisers, *Economic Report of the President, 2010*, Table B-2

------- Exports ——— Imports

Figure 5.1 Imports and Exports, 1960–2008.

initiated, and ban secondary boycotts. Truman responded with a veto. The next year, as control of the House passed to the Republicans, Congress passed the Labor–Management Relations Act or Taft-Hartley Act of 1947, and this time the president's veto was overridden.

The Taft-Hartley Act was designed, in part, to reign in the National Labor Relations Board, which was seen by critics as advocating organized labor rather than maintaining neutrality. Senator Robert Taft (R-OH) claimed that the NLRB "had a strong Communist tinge" and embraced "a public mission to place a union of the Congress of Industrial Organizations in every plant in America." Under its original design, the NLRB had a combination of functions, often determining whether a prosecution should occur, controlling the assignment of investigators, and ultimately judging the case. Taft-Hartley separated these powers by creating an independent General Counsel to decide whether to file complaints. In Taft's words, "It attempted to make the Board a truly judicial body ... concerned only with holding the scales of power and justice even between labor and management."[60] William Green, AFL president, dismissed talk of impartiality: "While professing to 'balance the scales' between unions and employers, the authors of the act added the weight of the government to the advantage already enjoyed by the antiunion employer and gave him new power, without responsibility."[61] Without question, the Act changed the role of the NLRB. As John Judis explains, it completed "the transformation of the NLRB from a tribunal of social justice to a dispute settlement board" and "put the class struggle between labor and business in the hands of Washington lawyers and lobbyists."[62]

The Act also placed new restrictions on labor unions. They were prohibited from using jurisdictional strikes, secondary boycotts, or refusing to bargain collectively. Unions were required to give a 60-day notice before terminating or changing agreements, and could be held liable for damages in the federal courts for violations. The president was given new power to impose an 80-day injunction against strikes that "imperiled the national health or safety." Taft-Hartley also sought to address the political influence of unions. They were prohibited from making direct donations to federal campaigns (henceforth they would work through political action committees) and, reflecting the growing Cold War concerns, union officials were required to submit affidavits that they were not members of the Communist Party. Most important, Southern Democrats secured provisions that banned the closed shop and permitted states to pass so-called "right-to-work" laws prohibiting union shops (i.e., shops imposing contractual obligations for new employees to join unions and pay dues).[63]

Law plays a central role in constituting unions and regulating the relationship between corporations and organized labor. As a result of Taft-Hartley, there were different institutional structures in place across the states, and this would have significant implications for patterns of unionization. Within a year of the passage of Taft-Hartley, fourteen states passed right-to-work laws; the number would ultimately rise to twenty-two, primarily in the South and

Mountain regions. There is conclusive evidence that levels of unionization are far lower in these states. By 2004, for example, only 3.8 percent of the private workforce was unionized in right-to-work states, compared with 14.4 percent in states without restrictions on union shops.[64] Moreover, one might argue, the existence of different systems of industrial relations had long-term consequences for patterns of economic development. During the latter decades of the twentieth century, businesses that migrated from the old industrial regions of the Northeast and Midwest to the Sunbelt found low levels of unionization and, consequently, lower wage levels, attractive.

Although Taft-Hartley was clearly a defeat for organized labor, the initial postwar decades nonetheless proved to be something of a golden age in industrial relations. The sharp conflicts between craft and industrial unions constituted a deep division in organized labor that became particularly pronounced during the New Deal. Writing in 1946, Aaron Levenstein described "interfederation warfare" and found the prospects for unity quite limited.

> The only remaining possibility for an early peace between the two labor federations is the development of a sharp attack on labor which would threaten its very survival ... . No such large-scale elemental attack on labor's existence seems probable. And even if it does come, there is nothing to indicate that American labor leaders will be any wiser than their European brethren who continued their political and economic disunity even after the fascist threat became imminent. We must therefore be prepared for a continuing war of attrition between the AFL and the CIO.

In Levenstein's judgment, "only when they face a genuine issue of life or death will the AFL and the CIO be willing to grapple with the real mechanical difficulties which lie in the way of unity."[65] A year after these comments, Congress passed Taft-Harley, and in 1955, after decades of discord, the AFL and CIO merged. This merger also allowed for a more unified voice in politics, as the CIO's Political Action Committee and the AFL's Labor League for Political Education were consolidated to create the AFL-CIO Committee on Political Education or COPE.[66]

The period also witnessed a growth in industrial wages and an increasing prevalence of multi-year labor contracts. The agreement between General Motors and the United Auto Workers in 1948 marked a significant change. The new multi-year contract guaranteed cost-of-living adjustments (tied to the Bureau of Labor Statistics cost of living index) and an annual "Improvement Factor" of between 2 and 4 percent for productivity gains, along with an expansive benefit package including health care, insurance, and pensions. As John Harris Howell notes: "GM workers were put on an elevator which was much more ready to move up than down, while GM secured a measure of downward flexibility in its labor costs ... . More important, it won the union's endorsement of management efforts to raise productivity; and the long-term goal of stability and predictability in labor relations was brought closer."[67] Contracts increasingly followed this model and specified elaborate internal grievance procedures. Alan Wolfe has referred to the capital-labor relations of this period as constituting a growth coalition: "Productivity would generate economic growth, and economic growth would keep labor relations peaceful."[68]

The union gains during the immediate postwar period brought a greater conservatism to the political agenda of organized labor. Under the direction of George Meany, the AFL-CIO embraced business unionism and pursued greater benefits for union members with little concern over larger social policy issues. As Howell notes, union leaders "were not subject to very great rank-and-file pressures, so they were free to build the centralized 'apolitical' bureaucracies needed to conduct businesslike labor relations. They could discipline workers and discourage local union militancy, where outbreaks of it occurred."[69] Critics were concerned that the United States had developed a clear division between the unionized workforce with high wages, benefits, and job security, and the nonunionized population that relied, instead, on low wages and a relatively under-developed welfare state while paying premiums for union-made products. Moreover, there was a growing belief that the union movement was more intent on capturing benefits for members than in extending unionization more generally.

While growing incomes were clearly exhibited in the immediate postwar period, things would change significantly by the late 1960s. Under conditions of price stability and steady economic growth, industrial relations were relatively peaceful and, as noted above, much of organized labor could depend on cost-of-living adjustments and productivity-based gains. But the changing economic conditions had significant implications. With high inflation and low growth punctuated by recessions, contractual negotiations became more confrontational. Businesses had growing incentives to restrain costs by exploiting the wage differential between union and non-union labor.[70] Under the pressures of inflation, growing international competition, and long-term economic structural changes—most notably, the decline of manufacturing relative to service industries—the peak levels of union membership in the immediate postwar period would become, at best, a distant memory. From a postwar peak of some 33 percent of the workforce (1953), private sector unionization rates would fall to levels comparable to what had existed before the advent of the New Deal Regime.[71]

Conclusion

During the initial postwar decades, the economy functioned with relatively low levels of unemployment and inflation, excluding the dislocations associated with the Korean War (1950–53). Yet, the macroeconomic policy mixes of the Truman and, in particular, the Eisenhower administrations created problems of fiscal drag. Fear of deficits often led policymakers to accept higher levels of unemployment than many thought possible. Much of this changed following the election of 1960. By the end of the Kennedy and Johnson presidencies, the United States had experienced several years of robust economic perform-ance and, with a more expansive welfare state, it appeared that the social Keynesian vision that informed the original full employment debates had been realized. But by the 1970s, inflationary consequences of spending were combined with economic stagnation. This created a window of opportunity for opponents of the regulatory-welfare state to initiate a new period of political change that created the foundations for a new regime. We turn now to an examination of this period.

6 The Rise and Pause of the Keynesian Welfare State

The Kennedy-Johnson years marked a clear departure from the economic policies of earlier postwar presidents. Johnson, in particular, advocated a far more aggressive brand of Keynesianism designed to achieve full employment and support the pursuit of an ambitious reform agenda. He was committed to the proposition that racial equality and the elimination of poverty were contingent on the achievement of full employment. The combination of full employment policy and expanded social spending was an extension of the New Deal Regime, albeit one that embodied the vision of its most progressive advocates. But this embrace of social Keynesianism was brief, undermined ultimately by the stagflation of the 1970s. The combination of high inflation and high unemployment—and the seeming inability of policymakers to find a solution—created a critical window of opportunity for policy changes designed to force a retreat from Keynesianism and the regulatory-welfare state. A period that began with a faith in Keynesian fine tuning and an optimistic belief in the capacity of social policy to address a host of vexing social problems ended with a new faith in unfettered markets and growing skepticism regarding the role of the state.

Toward the Keynesian Social Welfare State

The 1960 Democratic Platform identified the slow economic growth of the Eisenhower administration as a failure of political leadership, and made a clear promise: "We Democrats believe that our economy can and must grow at an average rate of 5% annually, almost twice as fast as our average annual rate since 1953. We pledge ourselves to policies that will achieve this goal without inflation."[1] Kennedy was an avid consumer of economics and Walter Heller, Chairman of the Council of Economic Advisers (CEA), tutored the president in the theoretical justifications for policy. Kennedy favored a more expansionary fiscal policy to achieve full employment, and Heller made the case that a large tax cut was the best instrument for fulfilling the promise of 1960. Initially, the promotion of tax cuts found a rather modest expression in the form of an investment tax credit in the Revenue Act of 1962. But by 1963, the administration proposed large tax reductions, claiming that there were two overriding justifications:

First, for the sustained lift it will give to the economy's demand for goods and services, and thus to the expansion of its productive capacity; second, for the added incentive to productive investment, risk-taking, and efficient use of resources that will come from lowering the corporate tax rate and the unrealistic top rates on personal income and eliminating unwarranted tax preferences that undermine the tax base and misdirect energy and resources.

Congress proved hesitant, despite the CEA's assurance that tax reductions "can not only provide stimulus for growth and prosperity, but can even, as a result, balance the budget or produce surpluses."[2]

The Kennedy administration introduced its tax proposals in January 1963, calling for a combination of individual and corporate tax reductions of $11.3 billion for fiscal years 1964 and 1965. Congressional resistance evaporated following the assassination of President Kennedy. Three months later, Johnson and Congress produced what would be the largest tax cut thus far in US history. Passed under conditions of relative prosperity, its stimulative effects were rapidly exhibited: Gross National Product increased by 5 percent for the year, driving the unemployment rate from 5.7 percent to 4.9 percent. Although the CEA predicted that $38 billion would be added to the GNP in 1965, the economy grew by $47 billion. The confidence of economic managers was almost palpable. By 1965, the CEA noted "These four years of expansion have demonstrated that the American economy is capable of sustained balanced growth in peacetime. No law of nature compels a free market economy to suffer from recessions or periodic inflations."[3]

In Johnson's 1964 State of the Union address, he announced new initiatives in civil rights and a War on Poverty. The success of these measures was intrinsically connected to the larger macroeconomic stimulus: a full employment policy would lead to higher levels of integration and create new opportunities for those in poverty if reinforced by social policy. As Johnson stated in the letter of transmittal for the *Economic Report of the President*:

> Today, as in the past, higher employment and speedier economic growth are the cornerstones of a concerted attack on poverty … . But general prosperity and growth leave untouched many of the roots of human poverty. In the decade ahead, the forgotten fifth must be given new opportunities for a better life.

This had important implications for the welfare of minorities and the success of the civil rights initiatives. In Johnson's words: "Forty-four percent of non-white families are poor. Deficiencies of education and health and continuing job discrimination depress the earnings of Negros and other nonwhites, throughout their lives."[4]

Within the next two years, Congress passed the landmark Civil Rights Act of 1964 and Voting Rights Act of 1965. With respect to the War on Poverty,

Congress passed the Economic Opportunity Act of 1964, creating a number of anti-poverty programs including Head Start and the Job Corps, and the Food Stamp Act of 1964. The next year, Congress passed the Social Security Act of 1965 creating two new entitlement programs, Medicare and Medicaid, to provide health care for the elderly and the medically indigent. These programs, combined with a liberalization of Aid for Families with Dependent Children, marked the greatest expansion of the social welfare state since the New Deal. As Sheldon Danziger and Robert D. Plotnick explain, the policy mix was premised on a faith

> that "fine tuning" could virtually guarantee prosperity and low unemployment. In retrospect, it was naively optimistic. Rising earnings that were to follow from new training and educational programs failed to materialize in a major way. Furthermore, the demographic changes and labor supply reactions to increased transfer outlays … made reductions in pretransfer poverty harder to achieve.[5]

As growing social welfare and defense spending combined with the stimulative effects of the 1964 tax cut, unemployment fell to 3.8 percent in 1966 and 1967, surpassing the full employment target of 4 percent. As inflation rates increased in 1966, the CEA began to recommend a tax surcharge and a suspension of the 1962 investment tax credits as a means of slowing the economy. Johnson was hesitant to accede to these recommendations, given the looming 1966 midterm elections and his belief that full employment was one of his chief accomplishments. By 1967, the *Economic Report* called for a 6 percent surcharge on individual and corporate taxes as a means of countering the effects of an additional $5.8 billion in defense spending.[6] Congress refused to comply unless the surcharge was combined with a reduction of domestic expenditures. Ultimately, Congress passed the Revenue and Expenditure Control Act in June of 1968, imposing a 10 percent tax surcharge and accelerating corporate tax payments. The president agreed to rescind appropriated funds and reduce appropriations for 1969. By the fall of 1968, as concerns mounted that these decisions would induce a recession, the Federal Reserve adopted an expansive monetary policy which, when combined with ongoing war spending, allowed for the resumption of inflationary forces.

As the war in Vietnam escalated, Johnson's popularity plummeted. The Democratic Party fragmented into competing factions, consisting of the old New Deal coalition, a growing antiwar contingent, and Southern Democrats alienated by the administration's civil rights efforts. Johnson decided not to pursue reelection but he was successful in getting what remained of the New Deal coalition to coalesce around the candidacy of Hubert Humphrey, his vice president, who pledged to expand upon the Great Society. In a three way race between Humphrey, the American Independent candidate George Wallace, and Republican Richard Nixon, Nixon claimed a narrow plurality of the vote.

The Nixon Administration

Richard Nixon's presidency began with incremental change and ended with the most significant economic controls of the postwar period. When he assumed the presidency in 1969, the inflation rate of over 5 percent was the highest since the Korean War and there was little chance that Vietnam War spending would end soon. Having borne the political costs of fiscal drag in his unsuccessful bid for the presidency in 1960, Nixon was hesitant to pursue price stability at the cost of higher unemployment. His initial policy of "gradualism" entailed budgetary and monetary restraint and an extension of the tax surcharge. However, by 1970, conditions had worsened as unemployment reached 6.1 percent and inflation remained largely untouched. Ultimately, Nixon would impose price controls in an attempt to restrain inflation. Before exploring these initiatives, let us turn to another of the most significant events of the postwar period: the expansion of the regulatory state.

Nixon and the New Social Regulation

Regulatory scholars commonly draw a distinction between economic regulation and the social regulation. Economic regulations control the conditions under which firms can enter and exit markets, the prices they can charge, competitive practices and the size of economic units. Progressive Era and New Deal regulations provide the classic examples. In contrast, the new social regulations force corporations to assume responsibility for the negative externalities of the production process—for example, pollution and industrial injuries and disease.[7] Although social regulations have a long pedigree in the United States, the major social regulatory initiatives were introduced in the postwar period and, more precisely, during the Nixon presidency. Ironically, as Nixon was seeking to control inflation, he was simultaneously responsible for the creation of the Environmental Protection Agency, an agency that would impose unprecedented regulatory costs on the American economy.

Environmental concern had been growing over the course of the late 1960s and Nixon clearly understood its political popularity. In his 1970 State of the Union address, he proclaimed: "Restoring nature to its natural state is a cause beyond party and beyond factions … . Clean air, clean water, open spaces—these should once again be the birthright of every American. If we act now, they can be." Nixon was refreshingly candid when speaking of the costs: "clean air is not free, and neither is clean water. The price tag on pollution control is high. Through our years of past carelessness we incurred a debt to nature, and now that debt is being called."[8] Over the course of the next year, Congress would pass the Clean Air Act Amendments of 1970 and Nixon would create the Environmental Protection Agency (EPA) via executive reorganization. Two years later, Congress would pass the Federal Water Pollution Control Act Amendments of 1972 (or the Clean Water Act)— this time over a presidential veto—with the ambitious goals of achieving zero discharges into the nation's waters. The modern environmental era was clearly underway.

In the past, regulatory statutes had provided broad grants of discretionary authority to regulatory agencies. As noted in Chapter 3, this delegation was grounded, in part, in a faith in neutral bureaucratic expertise. However, during the postwar period, there was growing concern that regulatory agencies had become overly accommodative to regulated interests or had degenerated into moribund bureaucracies.[9] Having learned the lessons of the past, the authors of new regulatory statutes delegated minimal discretionary authority to regulators. They mandated expensive pollution control technologies with little regard for cost and imposed ambitious implementation timetables backed with significant penalties. In the case of the Clean Water Act, the statutory goals could not be achieved with existing technology. Extended rule making, intervener funding, and expanded standing provided ample opportunities for advocacy groups to shape policy and sue the EPA if it failed to execute its non-discretionary duties.[10]

The new initiatives in environmental protection were combined with new regulations in occupational safety and health, most importantly, the Occupational Safety and Health Act of 1970. Nixon, simultaneously courting the support of the Teamsters and the business community, introduced a relatively weak proposal that relied on state-level enforcement and vested limited authority in the Labor Department.[11] The final act, however, was a product of the Democratically controlled Congress. It created a new agency in the Department of Labor, the Occupational Safety and Health Administration (OSHA). It directed the new agency "to assure so far as possible every working man and woman in the nation safe and healthful working conditions." It established that the employer had an affirmative obligation "to furnish to each of his employees employment and a place of employment which are free from recognized hazards that are causing or are likely to cause death or serious physical harm to his employees."[12] Like EPA, OSHA had economy-wide jurisdiction. It rapidly began to engage in rulemaking to develop detailed standards for private-sector employers and these standards often mandated costly changes to the production process or the design of industrial facilities. When Congress passed the new legislation, it did not mandate that OSHA consider costs when developing its standards and, as a result, OSHA, like the EPA, would become embroiled in seemingly endless controversies and litigation.

Nixon was also responsible for a dramatic expansion of affirmative action. In 1969, the administration resurrected the Philadelphia Plan, originally designed by Johnson. The plan mandated that contractors on federally funded construction projects establish numerical goals and timetables for the hiring of minorities, as a means of desegregating the trades and addressing poverty. The plan was expanded to include all contracts over $50,000 and it was extended to women. By 1971, a national plan was in place, proclaiming that all contractors had to have an affirmative action program designed to achieve the "prompt and full utilization of minorities and women at all levels and in all segments of the workforce." Nixon's promotion of affirmative action was more than symbolic. The budget of the Equal Employment Opportunity Commission (EEOC) increased from $13.2 million to $43 million between 1969 and 1974, and enforcement levels increased dramatically. Scholars still debate whether Nixon's policy reflected genuine support for desegregation or a strategic effort to drive a wedge between organized labor and African Americans, both key members of the Democratic coalition. Regardless, with the expansion of affirmative action, decisions over hiring and firing could no longer simply be a response to labor market dynamics.[13]

Although EPA, OSHA, and affirmative action were the most important regulatory legacies of the Nixon presidency, Nixon also promoted the reorganization and revitalization of the Federal Trade Commission and signed legislation creating two new regulatory agencies: the National Highway Safety Administration and the Consumer Product Safety Commission. Even if there was strong political support for an expansion of regulation, the nation's commitment would prove relatively unstable. As stagflation became the greatest challenge of the 1970s, critics would effectively cite regulatory sprawl and command-and-control regulation as responsible for inflation, stagnant growth, and lagging US competiveness. The decade that began with an unprecedented expansion of the regulatory state would end with deregulation and regulatory reform.

Nixon and the New Economic Policy

As Nixon was actively promoting the most expensive regulatory initiatives in the nation's history, inflation remained the most important domestic issue on the policy agenda. As noted above, Nixon's initial response of "gradualism" involved employing a mild contractionary policy to reduce inflation without simultaneously inducing increased unemployment.[14] However, in December of 1969, the nation entered a relatively mild recession that would last until the fall of the next year. In August of 1970, Congress responded by passing the Economic Stabilization Act, which gave the president the authority to impose mandatory wage, price, and rent controls. Nixon did not seek the powers, but Congress was clearly willing to assign him the responsibility—and the blame—for the state of the economy.[15] Nixon, always the political strategist, was concerned that economic performance was beginning to register in the public opinion polls and he prepared Republican leaders to expect losses in the midterm elections if unemployment remained above 5.5 percent. Moreover, as the salience of inflation grew, opinion polls revealed that 65 percent of the population supported the imposition of wage-price controls—fully 50 percent endorsed a freeze. Recent price increases by US Steel and Bethlehem Steel, combined with significance wage settlements in key industries and ongoing war spending, suggested that inflation would only worsen overtime absent intervention.[16]

Fed Chairman Arthur Burns argued that the persistence of inflation with high unemployment was a product of labor militancy and excessive wage settlements that made corporations hesitant to make investments. Nixon wanted expansionary monetary policy, but Burns countered that this policy would not have the intended impacts absent wage-price controls. The CEA forecasts suggested that economic growth would fall below projections and, as a result, there was little hope that unemployment would reach acceptable levels before the 1972 elections.[17] Following a meeting with key advisors at Camp David, Nixon unveiled his New Economic Policy on August 15, 1971. This policy had several key components. First, let us consider the international component. During the summer, the United States had weathered large balance-of-payments deficits and the dollar was under assault in international money markets. Without consulting the International Monetary Fund or any of the nation's major trading partners, Nixon unilaterally ended the convertibility of dollars into gold, thereby putting an end to Bretton Woods. He also imposed a 10 percent tariff to compel the world's central bankers to realign their currencies, thereby mitigating the impacts of an over-valued dollar.[18]

These actions could have inflationary consequences: the tariff and the depreciation of the dollar could stimulate price increases, thereby making a wage-price freeze a necessary component of the New Economic Policy. The Administration announced a 90-day price and wage freeze to be administered by a newly created Cost of Living Council. This freeze would subsequently be referred to as Phase I. In an executive order issued on October 15, Nixon announced Phase II: an extension of wage-price controls from November 14, 1971 through January 10, 1973. Responsibility was delegated to several new bodies, including a tripartite Pay Board to set wage guidelines and examine wage settlements, and a Price Commission to set standards and hear appeals. Although all firms were subject to controls, attention focused on the largest companies (i.e., with sales in excess of $50 million and over 1,000 employees) on the theory that they had a disproportionate impact on price levels. With these controls in place, it was believed, inflationary expectations could be reduced, thereby permitting more expansionary fiscal and monetary policies— an expedient combination given the elections of November 1972.[19]

This combination of policy interventions, while relatively novel in the US, was used more commonly in Western Europe. The theoretical justification for wage-price or income policy is relatively straightforward. As Fritz W. Scharpf explains: "fiscal and monetary policy measures can only be employed together to achieve one target at any one time, either inflation control, or employment stimulation, but not both at the same time." By introducing wage-price policy, one can add an additional policy instrument to the arsenal of policy tools. Scharpf continues: "If wage restraint can be relied upon to control inflation, governments will be free to fight unemployment by reflating demand. In short, the availability of an effective income policy does increase the degrees of freedom of macroeconomic policy."[20]

Nixon's landslide reelection was certainly facilitated by the economic controls and the Fed's easy money and it has been of great interest to students of the political business cycle.[21] Unemployment, which had been 6.1 percent when controls were introduced, fell to 5.3 percent. Inflation for the year was 3.3 percent, the lowest since 1967. In January 1973, Nixon responded to demands for a relaxation of controls and announced Phase III: voluntary controls that were to extend until August. However, with rising food prices and shortages of beef and gasoline, Nixon announced a new 60 day price freeze in June, to be followed by Phase IV, a sector-by-sector decontrol under the supervision of the Cost of Living Council. The efficacy of controls was undermined by political and economic events. In the spring of 1973, the revelations of Watergate rapidly eroded support for the president. Opinion polls revealed that the public attributed the recent inflation to a failure of Nixon's policies. The AFL-CIO and the National Association of Manufacturers—angered by the high costs of compliance with price controls—successfully lobbied Congress to prevent renewal of the Economic Stabilization Act.[22]

More importantly, in October of 1973, the Organization of Arab Petroleum Exporting Countries imposed an embargo on the United States in retaliation for its support for Israel during the Yom Kippur War. Within a year, oil prices increased by some 400 percent. In combination with failed world harvests that dramatically increased the price of food, these supply shocks threatened to unleash high levels of inflation. Efforts to mitigate the effects through contractionary fiscal and monetary policy resulted in a troublesome combination of inflation and unemployment that would come to define the 1970s and bedevil policymakers.

Ford, Carter, and the Political Economy of Stagflation

When Nixon initiated his policy of gradualism, inflation of 5 percent was considered high enough to justify a contractionary policy, even if it might push unemployment above 3.5 percent, as it ultimately did. By 1974, when Ford assumed office, inflation was approaching 12 percent and the unemployment rate stood at 5.5 percent. For the remainder of the decade, unemployment and inflation would prove highly resistant to policy interventions (See Figure 6.1). The rates of inflation that caused such alarm in the late-Johnson and early-Nixon administrations would be a fond memory. And the goal of full employment, realized and exceeded in the late 1960s, would prove elusive. The trade-offs central to the Phillips Curve were no longer in the opportunity set available to policymakers, raising questions about the efficacy of Keynesianism and the New Deal Regime more generally.

In an August 6, 1974 address to Congress, Gerald Ford proclaimed: "Inflation is domestic enemy number one. To restore economic confidence, the Government in Washington must provide some leadership. It does no good to blame the public for spending too much when the Government is spending

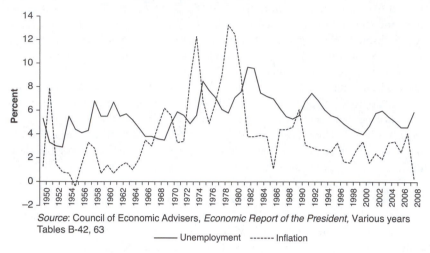

Source: Council of Economic Advisers, *Economic Report of the President,* Various years
Tables B-42, 63

——— Unemployment   ------- Inflation

Figure 6.1 Inflation and Unemployment, 1950–2008.

too much." Ford informed Congress that he had directed his administration "to make fiscal restraint their first order of business."[23] The next month, Ford presided over an Inflation Summit and presented his economic program to Congress. The contractionary policy called for a temporary tax surcharge on corporations and upper-income households combined with reduced expenditures. This policy mix had important consequences. By January 1975, the economy began a rapid descent into recession and by May, unemployment peaked at 9 percent, the highest rate thus far in the postwar era. In response, the Ford administration switched to an expansionary policy in 1975. The Tax Reduction Act of 1975 provided an $8 billion tax rebate, a $12 billion reduction in income taxes, a $1.7 billion increase in social security payments and a $1 billion earned income tax credit. Cognizant of underlying inflationary forces, Ford was hesitant to promote additional stimulation. By January of 1976, the recovery was underway but, troublingly, unemployment remained relatively high. Ford promoted additional stimulus via $28 billion in tax cuts, albeit with little effect. When voters cast their ballots in the November election, unemployment stood at 7.8 percent—largely where it had been at the beginning of the year.[24]

When Jimmy Carter campaigned in 1976, he presented the election as a referendum on fighting inflation with recession. He promised a full employment policy and provided qualified support for the proposed Humphrey-Hawkins Full Employment and Balanced Growth Act, undoubtedly as a means of courting organized labor and the Congressional Black Caucus. The proposed legislation, envisioned as a means of resurrecting the Full Employment Act of 1945, would declare explicitly the goal of full employment (with an interim goal of 3 percent unemployment). It proposed to establish an entitlement to employment, making the government the employer of last resort. The bill was premised on the belief that the problem of stagflation was primarily a problem of stagnation—a demand failure stemming from the distribution of income—and thus, full employment could be achieved without inflationary consequences.[25] Carter's tactical embrace of Humphrey-Hawkins was combined with a pledge to reduce inflation to 5.5 percent. In the end, there would be little progress toward either of the goals. Rather, the administration would move between expansionary and contractionary policies as exogenous shocks produced an unprecedented combination of inflation and unemployment.[26]

Upon assuming office, Carter pushed forward with a stimulative package comprised of tax rebates, public works and an expansion of public service employment under the Comprehensive Employment and Training Act of 1973. The administration believed that this package, combined with expansionary monetary policy, could move the economy toward recovery. Because there was excess capacity in the economy, it was believed that this could be accomplished without igniting inflation. However, when the economy appeared to be recovering at a faster pace than first believed, the administration moved toward anti-inflationary measures, including a reduction in expenditures and voluntary wage-price controls. By January 1978, the administration once again moved toward stimulation, reversing itself again when inflation began to rise in the fall of 1978.[27] The rapid cycling between expansionary and contractionary policy was emblematic of an underlying uncertainty about how to manage stagflation.

What of the goal of full employment? Given the overwhelming concern with inflation, Carter withdrew his support for the original Humphrey-Hawkins bill, and with it the guarantee of full employment, with government as the employer of last resort. In late 1977, the administration placed its support behind a scaled-back version of the bill. In a replay of the debates of 1945–46, the original goal of full employment was replaced with a target of 4 percent by 1983. The public employment provisions were eliminated; no alternative mechanism was put in its place to guarantee jobs. The final legislation included a host of additional objectives including price stability (an inflation rate of zero by 1988), growth in real incomes, productivity gains, balanced growth, balanced budgets, and additional price supports for farmers.[28] To underscore the lack of commitment to Humphrey-Hawkins, Carter announced new anti-inflationary measures three days before signing the act into law.[29] As Brad De Long notes:

> the Humphrey-Hawkins Act has had no effect on anything, save that the Federal Reserve chairman does give his periodic "Humphrey-Hawkins testimony"; as a result the workload of the Federal Reserve staff is slightly higher (and perhaps the "transparency" and accountability of Federal Reserve actions has improved).[30]

The full employment debates of the 1970s, like the debates of the 1940s, failed to elevate the goal of full employment and create the institutional framework necessary for its realization.

If the first two years of the Carter administration proved to be problematic, the last two proved economically disastrous. Productivity growth fell to new lows (from a range of 2.2–2.4 percent in 1975–77, to 0.6 in 1978 and 1.2 percent in 1979), thereby affecting how much stimulus the economy could endure without igniting inflation.[31] More important, the nation experienced a second oil crisis stemming from the Iranian revolution and a second oil embargo. Between 1978 and mid-1980, the price per barrel of oil increased from $14 to more than $35. Although the increases were smaller than experienced under Nixon, growing dependence on imported oil magnified their impact. The impact of rising energy costs took its toll, when combined with the growing costs of the new social regulations, the indexation of entitlement programs, increases in the minimum wage, new agricultural price supports, and rising costs of imports driven by a dramatic drop in the value of the dollar. The inflation rate accelerated and reached 13.3 percent for 1979.[32]

Carter attempted to stabilize the situation by appointing Paul Volcker, the president of the New York Federal Reserve Bank, as his new Fed Chairman. As a monetarist, Volcker was convinced that the Fed should pursue stability in the money supply and allow market processes to determine interest rates. In the past, it was argued, the Fed had too often failed to raise rates during upswings in the business cycle, thereby facilitating inflation. His strong anti-inflationary agenda was critical in retaining the support of the financial community. The support for Volcker would be critical in the next year, as upward revisions in the deficit—which was now projected to be fifty percent larger than originally estimated—led to chaos in the bond markets, and the prime rate increased to 21 percent. The administration met with Congress to revise the fiscal year 1981 budget that had already been submitted. Carter gave tacit support to the Fed for the introduction of credit controls.[33] Carter introduced his anti-inflation program and his plans for a 1981 balanced budget on March 14, 1980, along with a televised appeal to the public to borrow less. The combined effect was almost instantaneous and within a month, the nation was in the midst of the steepest one-quarter decline thus far in US history.[34] Unemployment increased from 6.3 percent to 7.6 percent within three months and remained at that level for the remainder of 1980. When Carter had won the election four years earlier, he had promised full employment and inflation of 5.5 percent. He stood for reelection with high unemployment and inflation of 13.5 percent.

The political consequences of stagflation were particularly severe for the Democratic Party. As noted in Chapter 4, Roosevelt's political coup had been to reinforce the New Deal coalition through public policies that distributed benefits ranging from agricultural supports to old age pensions. As the coalition began to fray in the postwar period, the limitations imposed by the 1970s had significant implications for the Democratic Party. As Robert M.

Collins explains: "stagflation imposed an unfamiliar discipline upon Democratic policymakers maneuvering uncertainty in a time of limits." The attempts to maintain the Democratic coalition were complicated by the "fact that the economic policies needed to fight inflation worked against growth and proved incompatible with the political needs of the Democratic coalition." As a result, the "Democrats found themselves immobilized as the 1970s ended ... the struggle against inflation required a regimen of restraint, sacrifice, and pain that a party coalition nurtured on economic growth and programmatic largess appeared incapable of providing."[35]

Making Sense of Stagflation

Stagflation proved to be something of a puzzle for macroeconomists. Informed by the Phillips Curve, a generation of Keynesians believed that there was an unavoidable trade-off between inflation and unemployment. Stagflation raised profound concerns about the adequacy of theory and the efficacy of macroeconomic management. As Frank E. Morris, a former Kennedy Treasury official and president of the Boston Fed, remarked in a 1978 conference entitled *After the Phillips Curve*:

> It is probably fair to say that economic policy is now being made in at least a partial vacuum of economic theory. Unlike earlier periods, no one body of theory seems to have a very broad acceptance. If Keynesianism is not bankrupt ... it is at least in disarray. Certainly, the confidence that I felt as a member of the Kennedy Treasury in our ability to use the Keynesian system to generate outcomes for the economy which were highly predictable has been shaken, and I believe a great many other people have also lost that confidence.[36]

Given the inability of Keynesian theory to provide a coherent explanation of stagflation and offer effective policy solutions, the period led to fascinating debates over how best to explain and address the vexing combination of high inflation and unemployment.

Neo-Keynesians focused primarily on the problem of inflation when considering the events of the 1970s. As Arthur M. Okun concisely stated his premises: "We live in a world dominated by cost-oriented prices and equity-oriented wages."[37] The rising wages in the immediate postwar decades created expectations of ongoing income growth governed by norms of equity. There was a "sense of fairness, that sense of wages following wages, wages following the cost of living, wages being relatively insensitive to the labour market."[38] These expectations created underlying inflationary tendencies. An exogenous shock (the oil embargo) produced price-wage spirals that were difficult to manage with traditional policy tools. Hence, neo-Keynesians concluded, there was a need for some form of incomes policy, either in the form of wage-price controls or the use of taxation to create disincentives for firms to approve wage increases that exceed productivity gains.[39] Structural unemployment could be addressed through investments in labor training and education.

Post-Keynesians departed from some of the core assumptions of the neo-Keynesians, placing a greater emphasis on the role of oligopolistic pricing. More importantly, they interpreted the business cycle as reflecting competition between organized economic groups over the distribution of GDP. This led to theoretical support for a more activist state role and the development of consensual institutions for managing industrial conflicts and wage-price fluctuations.[40] Here, attention commonly focused on the corporatist institutions employed in northern Europe. Other heterodox economists combined these insights with arguments regarding the impact of aging capital stock—contributing to the slowdown in productivity in the 1970s—and the growing competitive challenges resulting from postwar trade liberalization. These arguments led to support for a consensual incomes policy and an active labor market policy.

In addition, there was growing interest over industrial policy to promote sectors of the economy that promised opportunities for growth and high-wage employment. Manufacturing in the United States had been in long-term decline during the postwar period but this trend accelerated in the 1970s. Some 31 percent of the workforce was involved in manufacturing in 1960, declining slightly to 27.4 percent by 1970. But between 1970 and 1980, this figure would drop to 20.7 percent (with a decline to 10.5 percent a quarter century later).[41] This was of great concern given the higher wages available in manufacturing relative to service industries, particularly for workers with lower levels of skill acquisition. Analysts offered competing explanations of "de-industrialization." But common variables included an aging capital stock that undermined productivity and growing pressure from international competition. During the decade of the 1970s, the nation's share of the world's manufactured exports fell by 23 percent and, by the end of the decade, 70 percent of the domestic market for manufactured goods faced foreign competition.[42] Japan, in particular, was gaining great strength in export markets and its products, increasingly, were gaining a reputation for quality.

Faced with cost-based challenges, corporations might have invested more heavily in their productive capacity. But under the trying economic conditions of the 1970s, other options proved more attractive (e.g., migration to "right-to-work" states or outsourcing to foreign facilities). As Barry Bluestone and Bennett Harrison described the situation:

> The strategies adopted by corporate management to cope with international competition, organized labor, and the social welfare state have clearly taken their toll. More than 30 million jobs lost to plant closings and permanent physical contractions in a single decade, the virtual abandonment of older industrial cities, and the helter-skelter development of Sunbelt boomtowns are merely the most obvious manifestations of an economy that has failed to provide steady growth, secure employment, or

stable policies, and that no longer competes effectively in the global market place.

The very factors that led to impressive levels of growth in the immediate postwar period—trade liberalization and a capital stock intact at the end of the war—now created the foundations for decline. Additionally, the "hyper-mobility" of capital could be contrasted with the immobility of labor, thereby undermining "the personal security of workers, their families, and their communities."[43]

What was the solution? Analysts looked to the example of nations that had developed industrial policies to stimulate technological gains and channel capital into export-oriented sectors. Japan's Ministry of International Trade and Industry provided one potent example of how the state could transform its industries through effective policy interventions. By the late 1970s, scholars began to make the case for a new industrial policy, drawing either on the example of Japan or depression-era institutions like the Reconstruction Finance Corporation. Carter's Economic Policy Group explored the potential for industrial policy and, during the summer of 1980, Carter announced an Economic Revitalization Plan that included the creation of an Economic Revitalization Board to coordinate a targeted industrial policy and advise the president on the creation of an "industrial development authority" that would finance industrial transformation. These proposals were relatively imprecise and, in the end, Carter's 1980 defeat rendered them irrelevant.[44]

Whereas neo-Keynesians, post-Keynesians, and various heterodox political economists saw the answer to stagflation in new policy instruments (e.g., wage-price policy, industrial policy) and an expansion of the state, their counterparts on the Right were united in the belief that excessive state intervention was the primary cause of the troubles besetting the nation. Scholars drawing on various strands of monetarism, rational expectations, and supply side economics argued that if markets were to function effectively, there would need to be a rejection of active fiscal policy combined with an embrace of deregulation, welfare reforms, and tax reductions. Analysts in a growing network of policy think tanks correctly identified stagflation as creating an opportunity for significant policy change. By linking the burgeoning regulatory-welfare state to the economic problems of the decade, they could propose reforms that would have been unthinkable a few years earlier.

Milton Friedman, the chief advocate of monetarism, argued that inflation is primarily a monetary phenomenon. He argued that in the late 1960s and 1970s, the accelerated growth of the money supply was a product of increased government spending, the pursuit of full employment, and the misguided policies of the Federal Reserve. In Friedman's words:

> When a country starts on an inflationary episode, the initial effects seem good ... . But then the increased spending starts to raise prices; workers find that their wages, even if higher in dollars, will buy less; businessmen

find that their costs have risen, so that the extra sales are not as profitable as they anticipated, unless they can raise their prices even faster. The bad effects start to emerge: higher prices, less buoyant demand, inflation combined with stagnation.

Given this portrayal of the problem, the solution was clear: a reduction of government spending, the rejection of full employment goals, and a slower rate of monetary growth. Friedman argued that the Phillips Curve trade-off was based on a false dichotomy. In the long run, the only question is "whether we have higher unemployment as a result of higher inflation or as a temporary side effect of curing inflation."[45] The barriers to stability are political and inherently the product of the activist state.

The rational expectations school, best represented by Robert E. Lucas and Thomas J. Sargent, concluded that the flaws in Keynesianism were fatal. Anything systematic can be learned and adapted to by rational actors. As a result, policy interventions can be successful only if policymakers have the ability to foresee shocks that are not apparent to private actors and can incorporate this information into policy interventions that are both unanticipated and related to the economic problems in question. In short, "effectiveness ... rests on the inability of private agents to recognize systematic patterns in monetary and fiscal policy." Since these conditions rarely hold, Lucas and Sargent claimed that active monetary and fiscal policy had, at best, a disruptive impact. What are the implications for policy? Rational expectations "directs attention to the necessity of thinking of policy as the choice of stable 'rules of the game,' well understood by economic agents."[46] Much as with Friedman, these rules would include monetary stability, balanced budgets, and a reliance on market forces.

Supply-side economists reinforced the insights of the rational expectations school and argued that excessive government spending—a product of the welfare-regulatory state—forced tax rates that created disincentives to work and invest. Supply-side arguments, promoted by economists Robert Mundell and Arthur Laffer, and popularized in the editorial pages of the *Wall Street Journal*, had significant policy implications. The way out of the economic malaise would be found in rolling back the state and reducing marginal tax rates. Advocates argued that the clearest evidence for the efficacy of supply-side forces could be found in the 1964 tax cut—a supply-side triumph that had been erroneously attributed to Keynesianism.[47]

The Triumph of Conservative Political Economy

When one examines the debates surrounding stagflation, one discovers something of a paradox. While all OECD economies faced a common set of problems, the difficulties faced by US policymakers were not universal. Northern European nations, in particular, had lower rates of inflation and unemployment. As a generalization, they adopted corporatist systems of interest intermediation as a means of managing inflation. That is, governments negotiated agreements with peak labor and business associations to control wages and prices, and reinforced the commitments with more expansive social welfare policies and various supports for business (e.g., trade promotion, research and development subsidies). By creating institutions to manage the competition and conflict inherent in the business cycle, policymakers were free to use fiscal and monetary policy to promote growth. Much as post-Keynesians and heterodox theorists suggested, there were institutional means of managing economic crises and invariably, these means entailed a more expansive role for the state. Indeed, nations with successful corporatist institutions also had the largest welfare states among OECD countries.[48]

Although there have been some corporatist experiments in the United States, they were of limited duration and arose under conditions of crisis (e.g., the National Recovery Administration, wartime mobilization agencies). Durable corporatist institutions, in contrast, depend on a rather unique configuration of historical, institutional, and cultural factors that are difficult to replicate.[49] The monetarist, rational expectations, and supply-side arguments conclude that the best remedy for stagflation was the market free from the regulatory-welfare state. Even if one stipulates that corporatism cannot be easily transplanted in foreign soil, it is difficult to examine the cross-national experience with stagflation and find uniform support for the proposition that excessive state intervention was the cause of the economic problems of the 1970s.

Despite the empirical record, the policy interventions in the late 1970s and the 1980s were premised on a growing faith in the market and a rejection of the interventionist state. Although the 1970s began with unprecedented regulatory expansion, under the pressure of inflation and lagging economic growth, policymakers embraced deregulation. In financial regulation, the regulatory firewalls created by the Glass-Steagall Act of 1933 were eroded and interest rates were deregulated. In transportation, the changes were even more significant. The airline industry was deregulated and the Civil Aeronautics Board was eliminated. The railroad and trucking industries were deregulated and the Interstate Commerce Commission was phased out. Less dramatic deregulation occurred in energy and communications. In each case, deregulation was advocated through appeals to price theory and a faith that market competition could produce greater gains in consumer welfare than regulation.[50]

Although the new social regulations proved less vulnerable to the deregulatory fervor, they were increasingly burdened by regulatory review requirements centralized in the Office of Management and Budget. During the 1970s, each successive administration imposed additional review requirements, mandating the use of cost-benefit analysis to justify significant new regulations. This was particularly troublesome for EPA and OSHA regulations. They are characterized by large initial costs and often produce a stream of benefits that are negatively affected by a methodology that discounts costs and benefits to present value. These requirements would become far more onerous in the 1980s, when the Reagan administration essentially stopped the regulatory process for agencies failing to comply with the requirements and showing that their regulations yielded net present benefits.[51] Although there was growing support for additional policy changes in tax and welfare policies, they would not translate into successful reform proposals until after the 1980 election, when Republicans gained control of the presidency and the Senate.

An explanation of these changes consists of several components. First, in the wake of Vietnam, Watergate and stagflation, public opinion exhibited dramatic erosion in public support for government institutions. Between 1973 and 1980, the percentage of Americans with great confidence in the executive branch declined from 29 percent to 12 percent, with comparable declines in confidence in Congress (from 23 to 9 percent).[52] The decay in confidence reinforced an anti-statist policy agenda. The growing costs of regulation could be linked, at least rhetorically, to runaway inflation, the failure of businesses to reinvest, and the growing challenge posed by foreign-based producers. The excesses of the welfare state could be linked to high marginal tax rates. In essence, stagflation created an environment that was conducive to mounting a challenge to the policy legacy of the New Deal and the Great Society.

The challenge, however, was far from spontaneous. A second component of the explanation can be found in the corporate counter-mobilization. As David Vogel notes, the changes in regulation were of particular importance. The new social regulatory agencies had economy-wide jurisdictions, thereby affecting business as a whole and "the entire balance of power within the economic system." As a result, Vogel argues, "the fight over government regulation became the focus of class conflict for the first time in American history" and became "analogous to the struggle over the adoption of the welfare-state and the recognition of unions that defined class conflict during the 1930s."[53] Businesses and conservative foundations began to invest far more heavily in politics, via advertising, lobbying, and campaign contributions. Under the provisions of the Federal Election Campaign Act Amendments of 1974, businesses increasingly donated money to candidates through the use of political action committees. By the end of the decade, PACs representing corporations and trade or business associations constituted 61.6 percent of political action committees, responsible for 58.9 percent of total PAC giving. The same story can be told more generally. By 1980, 72 percent of the organizations with Washington representation were corporations or trade and business associations, compared with 57 percent two decades earlier.[54]

As business was mobilizing ever-greater resources into the electoral arena, core partners in the New Deal coalition were losing strength. Consider organized labor. As noted above, unionization rates fell from 27.3 to 23 percent over the decade of the 1970s. During the 1940s and 1950s, labor unions prevailed between 80 and 85 percent of the time in National Labor Relations Board representation elections. By 1980, the unions were winning 50 percent of the time, as businesses increasingly made the case that higher labor costs were forcing them to outsource production.[55] By 1980, labor constituted

5 percent of the organizations with Washington representation. Union PACs constituted 1.9 percent of all political action committees, responsible for 2.9 percent of PAC giving. The comparison with the figures on business representation and giving are striking.[56]

A final and related component came in the war of ideas. Corporations and foundations dramatically increased investment in conservative policy think tanks, the largest being the American Enterprise Institute, the Heritage Foundation, and the Cato Institute. At the same time, as Andrew Rich notes, "many of the older, more progressive foundations were disappointed by what they perceived as the failures of Great Society programs in which they had invested" and "many of the older, nonconservative foundations were operating with less. The endowments of many of the largest foundations lost hundreds of millions of dollars when the stock market declined in the 1970s."[57] Although there were clear ideological differences among the think tanks—the Heritage Foundation adopted a social conservative position, for example, whereas the Cato Institute was committed to libertarianism—there was common support for deregulation and regulatory review, welfare reform, and tax reductions. The institutes worked tirelessly to shape policy debates through publications for experts and lay audiences. They also organized testimony before Congress and administrative agencies and developed model legislation and regulations. If there was any consistent message being presented by the think tanks, it was this: the core policies and institutions created during the New Deal and Great Society had failed. Governmental expansion had been beset by myriad commitments to interest groups, many of which took the form of policies that interfered with market processes. Any competent response to stagflation would demand a withdrawal of the federal government, delegation of authority to the states, and a reliance on markets—and by implication, the very corporate decision-makers who had mobilized in opposition to the regulatory-welfare state.

Conclusion

The Great Society embodied the boldest aspirations of those who advocated full employment and social Keynesianism in the late 1930s and 1940s. The Johnson administration combined an aggressive fiscal policy with an expansion of the social welfare state. Keynesian fine-tuning proved triumphant in the achievement of a full employment economy. Social welfare, the administration argued, was a right of social citizenship. In the next several years, new civil rights and regulatory statutes transformed the role of the state in the economy. Yet, once the Great Society encountered the great stagflation, the trajectory of political-economic development changed once again. A decade after the Johnson presidency ended, the policy debates were dominated by those who called for deregulation, welfare reform, a rejection of Keynesianism, and an embrace of market forces.

Crisis plays a central role in regime change. The depression of the 1890s created the electoral foundations for the Progressive Regime. The Great Depression set the stage for the New Deal Regime. Even if the stagflation was comparatively less damaging than the earlier events, it nonetheless created a window of opportunity for rapid and substantial policy change. The confluence of declining public opinion support for public institutions, a corporate counter-mobilization, and the conservative engagement in the war of ideas set the stage for a new period of change. When the electorate, soured by a decade of poor economic performance, expressed its discontent at the polls, there were ample resources to support Republican candidates making the case for a new approach to the political economy. The consequences of this change are the subject of Chapter 7.

7 The Neoliberal Regime and the Return of the Market

In 1970, economist Arthur Okun introduced the "economic discomfort index," the sum of the unemployment and inflation rates, as one means of capturing the success or failure of economic management. In the next several years, the index assumed a new name—the misery index—and became a staple of political campaigns. In 1976, for example, presidential candidate Jimmy Carter cited a misery index of 12.8 when building a case against Gerald Ford's economic record. Carter promised full employment and price stability and, as noted in the previous chapter, both proved illusive. Indeed, the misery index peaked at 22 in 1980, as Carter was in the midst of his unsuccessful bid for reelection. Reagan secured a decisive victory, winning 44 states and 489 electoral votes. More impressively, the Republicans won control of the Senate for the first time since the Eisenhower administration and added thirty-five seats in the House, thereby giving them a working majority on key issues where they could rely on the support of conservative Southern Democrats.

Any incumbent would have encountered difficulties under these conditions. But many interpreted the election results as carrying far greater significance. Ronald Reagan framed the nation's economic and political malaise as the inevitable product of government expansion, welfare spending, overzealous regulation and confiscatory tax policies. He offered a remedy grounded in a diminution of the state via deregulation and welfare reform, a rejection of Keynesian management, and the promotion of free markets more generally. Although Republican gains in 1980 hardly constituted a realignment comparable to what occurred during the New Deal, they nonetheless provided a foundation for a period of rapid and substantial change, resulting in the emergence of a new regime. The term "neoliberalism" is commonly employed to describe the mix of policies that characterized the decades following the Reagan election (and those promoted simultaneously in other nations, most notably in the United Kingdom under the direction of Prime Minister Margaret Thatcher). Thus, we shall refer to this new regime as the Neoliberal Regime.

Before exploring the policy changes in greater detail, it is useful to present an overview of the economic conditions of the period. In 1981, the first year of the Reagan presidency, unemployment stood at 7.6 percent. By 1982, the economy fell into a prolonged and deep recession largely as a product of Paul Volcker's anti-inflationary program at the Federal Reserve. The GDP declined by 1.9 percent and unemployment peaked at 10.8 percent in late 1982, before the economy entered a period of prolonged expansion. By 1989, unemployment had fallen to 5.3 percent and inflation was under control for the first time in almost two decades. Another relatively mild recession would occur in 1990–91, raising unemployment briefly to a peak of 7.5 percent by 1992 and dashing George H.W. Bush's reelection bid. But during the next eight years, the economy entered a period of steady growth, and by 2000, the unemployment had fallen to 4 percent, the lowest in three decades. Another mild recession marked the first year of the George W. Bush presidency, raising unemployment to a high of 6 percent, before returning to a low of 4.6 percent in 2006 and 2007. Between 1981 and 2008, inflation adjusted GDP more than doubled (from $5.2 trillion to $11.7 trillion in 2000 dollars). This growth, combined with low unemployment and price stability marked an economic environment that had eluded policymakers throughout the 1970s.[1]

Yet, there were persistent problems, including the dual deficits, one budgetary, the other in trade. Despite the promise of balanced budgets, the Reagan administration ran persistent deficits (See Figure 7.1). In 1981, the deficit was 2.6 percent of GDP. By 1983, following a drop in revenues generated by recession and tax cuts, it reached 6 percent of GDP, the highest level since 1946. Although the budget would move briefly into surplus during Clinton's second term, the budget deficit and debt would be persistent problems. Within a quarter century, the public debt would double relative to the economy, rising from 32.6 percent of GDP (1981) to a peak of 67.5

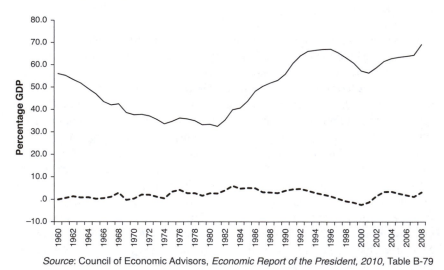

Source: Council of Economic Advisors, *Economic Report of the President, 2010*, Table B-79

- - - - Deficit   ——— Debt

Figure 7.1 Deficits and Debt, 1960–2008.

percent of GDP in 2008. At the same time, the national savings rate fell from 8.5 percent in 1981, to 2.8 percent by 1993, improved to an average of 6.1 percent (1997–2000) as the nation moved to a balanced budget and surpluses. But after 2001, as the pattern of high deficits returned, the net national savings rate fell to an average of 2.1 percent, actually turning negative in the final year of the Bush presidency.[2]

The trade deficit also became a source of growing concern. During the period in question, the nation became far more integrated into the global economy. Consider the growth of imports and exports, the total value of which increased from $634.4 billion in 1980 to $3.46 trillion in 2008 (2000 dollars). While the economy grew by some 225 percent during the period, the total value of exports and imports grew by some 545 percent. The United States began to generate troubling trade deficits in the late 1960s and 1970s. In 1981, the nation ran a slight trade surplus ($8.3 billion, in 2000 dollars). But from that point forward, the trade deficit began to grow dramatically, reaching a peak of $616.6 billion in 2005 (2000 dollars).[3] The mounting trade deficit was a product of a debt-inflated dollar that made imports ever cheaper and the remarkable growth in newly industrialized countries that were competing in export markets.

There was also a continuation of two trends that had marked much of the postwar period: the decline of manufacturing and the fall in unionization. In 1960, 64.7 percent of the non-agricultural workforce was employed in services. By 1980, this figure had increased to 73.2 percent and would increase again to 84.1 percent by 2008. Between 1977 and 2007, manufacturing value-added as a percentage of GDP fell from 21.6 percent to 11.7 percent.[4] The category of "services" includes occupations ranging from food services to professional, scientific, and technical occupations. Although there was an expansion of high wage service sector occupations, the dominant story was one of a shift of employment out of manufacturing into low-paying service positions. At the same time, there was a continued decline in unionization, from 19.5 percent of the nonagricultural workforce in 1980 to 12.5 percent a quarter century later. Given the size of the union premium (estimated to range from 17 to 24 percent), the decline of unionization had implications for wages, which largely stagnated.[5]

Another point of concern could be found in the persistence of poverty and growing inequality. In 1968, the last year of the War on Poverty, 12.8 percent of the population fell below the poverty line. Over the next four decades, the percent of the population below the poverty line would never fall below 11 percent and, under conditions of recession (1982–83, 1993), the poverty rate would rise to 15 percent.[6] The Gini coefficient, a standard measure of statistical dispersion used to measure degrees of income equality (0 represents pure equality, 1 represents pure inequality), reached a postwar low (i.e., greatest level of equality) of .348 in 1968. By 1980, the Gini coefficient had increased to .365. From that point forward, levels of income inequality reached the highest levels in the postwar period, peaking at .444 in

2006.[7] As a result, the United States had higher levels of inequality than any other wealthy democracy.

Reaganomics

In his first inaugural address, Reagan articulated themes that suggested monumental changes in the role of the state. He famously noted:

> government is not the solution to our problem; government is the problem. From time to time we've been tempted to believe that society has become too complex to be managed by self-rule ... Well, if no one among us is capable of governing himself, then who among us has the capacity to govern someone else?[8]

Reagan indicted government spending that mortgaged the future and a tax burden that penalized achievement and destroyed incentives. These themes would find an expression in the Economic Recovery Program of 1981, the key components of which included significant tax reductions, domestic spending cuts, and regulatory reform. They would be combined with increases in defense spending. The Federal Reserve would also play an important role in shaping the economic policy of the 1980s, as Chairman Volcker used monetary policy to squeeze inflationary expectations out of the system. Let us examine the core components of Reagan's economic policy in greater detail.

Taxation and the Laffer Curve

The central component of Reagan's economic policy came in the form of the Economic Recovery Tax Act (ERTA) of 1981, co-sponsored by Representative Jack Kemp (R-NY) and Senator William Roth (R-DE). The proposal found its intellectual justification in the Laffer Curve, developed by Arthur Laffer and popularized by Jude Wanniski in the pages of the *Wall Street Journal*. According to the Laffer Curve, if the marginal tax rate is 100 percent, revenues will be zero; rational actors will not work for free. If the marginal rate is zero percent, revenues will also be zero. By reducing marginal tax rates, one can increase the incentives for economic activity, thereby claiming a smaller share of a much larger economic pie. Fiscal conservatives found these arguments dubious and argued that austerity should precede tax cuts, otherwise the effects could be inflationary. Those on the supply side believed the order should be reversed, since tax cuts would stimulate growth and new revenues. In the end, the supply-side argument prevailed, one suspects, because of its political utility.[9]

ERTA had two key components. The first was the Kemp-Roth reduction in personal income taxes—a 23 percent reduction in individual tax rates, to be phased in over three years, with the top marginal rate falling from 70 percent to 50 percent. It also raised the exemption for married couples and phased in an increase in estate tax exemptions. Importantly, ERTA indexed income brackets for inflation, thereby eliminating "bracket creep" (i.e., nominal increases in income forcing tax payers into higher income brackets). The second component was an accelerated cost recovery system promoted by a powerful business coalition. It replaced the complicated asset depreciation schedule with a simplified schedule that accelerated depreciation and provided a host of additional benefits. When the provisions were combined, ERTA constituted the largest tax cut in the nation's history.[10]

Even if one accepts the logic of the Laffer Curve, there is no evidence that ERTA provided empirical validation. According to the Treasury, in the four years after the passage of ERTA, revenues fell by an annual average of 13.3 percent. Indeed, within months of the passage of ERTA, continued inflationary forces and new deficit projections led the administration to revisit the tax cuts. The administration negotiated the elimination of the scheduled increases in accelerated depreciation, a 10 percent withholding on interests and dividends, and additional tax increases for business. The Tax Equity and Fiscal Responsibility Act of 1982 increased revenues by 5.7 percent, the largest increase since Johnson's 1968 Revenue and Expenditure Control Act.[11]

Although there were several additional changes in tax policy during the 1980s, the second most important piece of tax legislation took the form of the Tax Reform Act (TRA) of 1986. One of the great critiques of ERTA was that it provided most of its benefits to the wealthy and further complicated the tax code. The TRA reduced top marginal rates once again—the top rate falling from 50 percent to 28 percent—while raising the lowest rate from 11 to 15 percent, thereby reducing dramatically the progressivity of the tax system. The impact was partially offset by the increase of the individual exemption that removed 4.3 million low-income families from the tax rolls. Moreover, the earned income tax credit, first introduced in 1975 as a work bonus for low wage workers, was increased to its original inflation-adjusted level and indexed for future inflation. The top corporate tax rate was also reduced from 46 to 34 percent. The new legislation was designed to be revenue neutral; the personal income and corporate tax reductions were to be offset by the repeal of the investment tax credit, accelerated depreciation, and a variety of tax loopholes. In the four years after its enactment, revenues grew by an annual average of $100 million.[12]

The Budget: Guns, Butter, and Deficits

The impact of falling revenues could have been offset by comparable budget cuts. In 1981, with control of the Senate and House Democrats demoralized by the electoral outcome, the administration moved forward rapidly with revisions in the budget initially submitted by Carter. Using the reconciliation process to achieve his goals, Reagan's budget reduced 1981 spending by some $36 billion, with impacts on over 250 programs and long-term spending reductions of some $130 billion. As part of Reagan's new federalism, the

Omnibus Budget Reconciliation Act (OBRA) of 1981 consolidated 57 categorical grant programs into nine block grants, dramatically reducing funding levels but giving states greater discretion. The accelerated process left little time for advocacy groups to evaluate the proposed cuts and mobilize opposition. Although the administration's success in achieving domestic spending cuts was stunning, the success experienced in 1981 would be elusive in subsequent years.[13]

Domestic budget cuts were combined with dramatic increases in defense spending. At the height of Vietnam, defense spending peaked at 9.5 percent of GDP (1968). The Carter administration had allowed defense spending to decline to between 4.7 and 4.9 percent of GDP.[14] For Reagan, and the growing number of neoconservatives gravitating to the GOP, these decisions facilitated the Soviet invasion of Afghanistan, Sandinista victories in Nicaragua, and the Iranian Hostage crisis. Reagan promoted the largest peacetime expansion of the military in US history. His support for a 600-ship Navy and the B-1 bomber, and the promotion of a new B-2 Stealth bomber and the Strategic Defense Initiative had significant budgetary implications. In 1981 alone, inflation adjusted defense spending increased by 17 percent and by 1985, it had increased by 53 percent.[15] Even though Congress became less supportive of Reagan's defense spending over the course of his presidency, defense peaked at 6.1 percent of GDP, claiming 28.1 percent of government outlays—the largest level since Vietnam.[16]

When candidate Reagan denounced Democratic economics, he routinely cited the large deficits generated by the Carter administration as evidence of fiscal irresponsibility and promised balanced budgets. ERTA failed to generate the increase in revenues and Congress and the administration refused to exercise spending restraint. As the nation fell into the deepest recession of the postwar period, the budget deficits and debt ballooned. The 1981 deficit more than doubled to 6 percent of GDP by 1983, the highest level since World War II demobilization. For the remainder of the Reagan presidency, the deficit would exceed the peak deficits of the previous administration.[17] Ironically, an economic program premised on supply side assumptions was rapidly transformed into a program that relied on high levels of fiscal stimulation that was difficult to distinguish from what might have been pursued by an administration committed to Keynesianism. With the heavy reliance on defense spending, it could be more accurately described as military Keynesianism.

Monetary Policy

The story of the 1980s cannot be told without emphasizing the role of monetary policy. Arguably, the most important component of inflation is expectational. If consumers and businesses project high levels of future inflation, they will incorporate these expectations into wage demands, purchase decisions, and contracts, making them a self-fulfilling prophecy. Federal Reserve Chairman Volcker, freed from the constraints of the Carter administration, moved aggressively to tighten the money supply to squeeze inflationary expectations out of the economy. The Fed raised the Federal funds rate to 20 percent and the economy entered a deep recession that lasted from July 1981 until November 1982. With a peak unemployment rate of 10.8 percent, it was the deepest recession since the Great Depression.

Supply side economists objected that Volcker's restrictive policies could forestall recovery. When the White House and Congress agreed to the Tax Equity and Fiscal Responsibility Act in 1982, Volcker modified his approach to monetary management and the economy began to expand.[18] When recovery came, the high inflation rates of the past did not re-emerge—the inflation rate in 1983 was 3.2 percent, a number unimaginable during the 1970s. The elimination of inflation was a major accomplishment of the monetary policies of the 1980s. But critics raised two questions. First, to what extent was the recession deeper than necessary? Second, in a representative democracy, should decisions affecting the lives of so many citizens be delegated to the least democratic part of the American state? Given that the Reagan administration had rejected active fiscal policy, the central role in economic management was left, by default, to the Federal Reserve. This would become part of a long-term trend. As policymakers were constrained by the budget deficit, the Fed would become the central actor in the definition of economic policy.

Welfare Reform

During the 1970s, conservative policy think tanks had emphasized the failure of welfare state policies, focusing on the persistence of poverty and growing intergenerational dependency. In the 1980s, much of this research found its expression in Charles Murray's *Losing Ground,* routinely cited as one of the blueprints of the Reagan revolution. Murray's proposal was dramatic. He proposed "scrapping the entire federal welfare and income-support structure for working-aged persons ... . It would leave the working-aged person with no recourse whatsoever except the job market, family members, friends, and public or private locally funded services."[19] While Murray's solution was never adopted in full, the Reagan administration marked the beginning of a long process of reform. OBRA did more than reduce spending. It made the most significant changes in AFDC since the Johnson Administration. But where Johnson had sought to expand participation through liberalized requirements, the Reagan administration had the opposite intentions.

The administration aspired to make AFDC "a safety net rather than a guaranteed income."[20] In the past, states had been able to disregard some portion of income and allow for the deductibility of job-related expenses when determining eligibility. Now, OBRA set strict limits on incomes, deductions, and the assets that could be in the possession of recipients. Given that access to AFDC was often a gateway to other benefits (Food Stamps, Medicaid), the termination of participation was devastating for the working poor. Moreover, new restrictions were placed on payments to pregnant women to create disincentives for procreation while on assistance. Eighteen year olds could no longer receive benefits unless they were attending high school.[21] "By 1983," David Stoesz notes, "the consequences of the 1981 OBRA were clear. Some 408,000 families had been terminated from welfare; another 299,000 had their benefits reduced."[22] The most important changes in welfare were yet to come. In 1981, the administration began to grant states AFDC waivers to promote "welfare to work" experiments.[23] In 1986, Reagan drew on these state experiences and called for a significant reform; Congress complied with the passage of the Family Support Act of 1988. The Act mandated that states extend AFDC to two-parent families under the condition that at least one parent be looking for employment or participate in a workfare program. Single parents (with children above the age of three) were required to participate in education or job training through a newly created Job Opportunities and Basic Skills Training program. The workfare requirements were introduced gradually and accompanied with federal funding, but within a decade, the reform process would lead to the elimination of AFDC.[24]

Another target of reform was Social Security. During the 1970s, there were clear concerns about the long-term viability of Social Security in light of demographic trends. Analysts in conservative think tanks were arguing for privatization and incentives for retirement savings.[25] The 1980 Social Security trustee's report projected that the Old-Age and Survivors Insurance Trust Fund would be depleted by late 1981 or 1982. One step toward reform came with ERTA, which allowed individuals to save pre-tax dollars in Individual Retirement Accounts. Although Reagan's OMB Director David Stockman proposed immediate benefit reductions for early retirees, the Senate repudiated the plan and it was withdrawn. Reagan created a bipartisan National Commission on Social Security Reform, chaired by Alan Greenspan. When the Commission issued its report in 1983, it did not recommend any significant restructuring of the system (Republican losses in the 1982 midterm elections had been attributed to the proposed benefit cuts). Ultimately, the Social Security Act Amendments of 1983 brought a new infusion of revenues through accelerated increases in the FICA tax, increases in the self-employment tax, and taxation of benefits for high-income recipients. It reduced expenditures through a delay of cost of living adjustments and a gradual extension of the retirement age. Social Security received an extended lease on life and significant reform was deferred for another day.[26]

Regulatory Reform

Although macroeconomic issues captured the attention of the public, the administration also addressed the regulatory expansion of the previous decade. Reagan could not claim credit for the deregulation of railroads, trucking, finance and commercial aviation, all of which were initiated in the 1970s. But regulatory growth was primarily the product of the new social regulation. Reagan's approach had four components. First, Reagan's agency appointments were skeptical if not openly hostile to regulation. Second, there were significant budget cuts. The EPA, for example, lost one-third of its budget and one-fifth of its staff. Third, there was an unwillingness to support significant new regulatory statutes. Finally, Reagan imposed new executive review processes grounded in cost-benefit analysis.[27] This last component constitutes the largest regulatory legacy of the Reagan administration and is one worth exploring in greater detail.

During the 1970s, presidents sought to impose various schemes of regulatory review concentrated in the Office of Management and Budget, albeit with limited impact. Upon assuming office, Reagan issued executive order 12291 requiring that all significant new regulations be accompanied by cost-benefit analyses showing that they generated net positive benefits. Reagan gave the OMB's Office of Information and Regulatory Affairs the authority to prevent agencies from publishing notice of rulemaking in the *Federal Register* if they failed to conduct an acceptable analysis, essentially ending the regulatory process. As noted in Chapter 6, during the 1970s, Congress had written highly detailed regulatory statutes thereby expanding legislative control over the bureaucracy. The imposition of new review requirements vested greater power in the presidency.[28] The provisions of executive order 12291 fell particular hard on social regulatory agencies. Under the budgetary constraints imposed by Reagan, the costs of complying with executive order 12291 were often prohibitive. As a result, the number of new regulations fell significantly. The expansion of the social regulatory state, if not terminated, had been constrained.

Free Trade

During the latter half of the 1970s, concerns over deindustrialization and growing interest in industrial policy led to a host of proposals, many of which involved some combination of export subsidies and trade barriers to protect industries from imports. Candidate Reagan had embraced free trade as part of the larger economic program and, in 1981, the *Economic Report of the President* declared: "the open trading system that contributed so importantly to rising prosperity in past decades must be strengthened in the face of increasing pressures to adopt protective measures and the temptation to indulge in 'beggar-thy-neighbor' policies." Reagan's CEA argued that protectionist measures "intensify inflation directly by reducing competitive pressures, and they increase economic rigidities by sheltering excessive wages, profits, and other incomes in particular sectors from the discipline of the market."[29] Over the course of the next several years, the administration would promote an expansion of free trade, albeit with some inconsistency.

During the 1980 campaign, Reagan had proposed a free trade agreement between the United States and Mexico. Although this would not come to pass for more than a decade, there was nonetheless progress toward this end. In 1982, the administration proposed the Caribbean Basin Initiative "to promote economic revitalization and facilitate expansion of economic opportunity" and in 1983, Congress passed the Caribbean Basin Economic Recovery Act, which authorized preferential treatment for most goods imported from Caribbean countries. Thereafter, the administration obtained a waiver under GATT Article I, which requires all members to provide most-favored nation status to all other members. Moreover, in 1986, the administration began negotiating the US-Canada Free Trade Agreement, removing tariff barriers in trade between the two nations. The agreement, finalized in 1988, set the stage for subsequent negotiations with Mexico that culminated in the 1993 North American Free Trade Agreement.[30] Similarly, the Reagan administration supported the Uruguay Round of GATT, which began in 1986 and would ultimately set the groundwork for a new World Trade Organization.

Free trade was combined with selective protectionism. In a 1980 campaign speech at a Chrysler plant, Reagan proclaimed the government had a legitimate role "to convince the Japanese one way or another, and in their own best interest, the deluge of cars into the United States must be slowed while our industry gets back on its feet." Once elected, Reagan pressured Japan for voluntary export restraints, arguing that they would be superior to the mandatory quotas favored by congressional Democrats.[31] In 1982, Harley-Davidson petitioned the International Trade Commission for tariff relief from imported heavy motorcycles. Under Section 201 of the Trade Act of 1974, firms can seek remedies if imports are threatening or injuring domestic industry. In 1983, when the commission found in the company's favor, Reagan imposed new tariffs. Similarly, growing steel imports led the administration in 1984 to negotiate voluntary restraints with major exporters, once again backed by the implicit threat of mandatory restraints. As I.M. Destler concludes: "What all this amounted to was systematic circumvention of the rules for enforcing fair trade, for creating a level playing field, to which the administration, and Congress, claimed to give highest priority!"[32]

Whether this was "systematic circumvention" or what a former Reagan CEA chair would refer to as a "strategic retreat," it is clear that the administration did not exhibit fidelity to free trade.[33] Nonetheless, the growth of imports during the Reagan presidency was simply stunning. Between 1981 and 1988, the value of imports grew from $319.1 billion to $561.4 billion (in 2000 dollars), an increase of some 76 percent; US exports increased by a far more modest 39 percent during the same period.[34] Moreover, the support for expanded free trade in the Americas and the strengthening of GATT would bear fruit in the next decade as the North American Free Trade Agreement was signed into law and the World Trade Organization replaced GATT.

Reaganomics as Prologue

Reagan initiated a significant shift in governing philosophies, but rhetoric exceeded results. For example, Reagan vowed to reduce the size of the state, only to expand federal outlays well above the average for the Carter presidency (and the peak of Johnson's Great Society). Nonetheless, many of the changes initiated by Reagan were continued, albeit with some refinements or marginal adjustments. While this should not be surprising with respect to the presidency of George H.W. Bush, Reagan's vice president and immediate successor, continuity was also exhibited in the Clinton presidency. Clinton won the 1992 election with 43 percent of the vote in a three-way race that included Bush and independent Ross Perot, whose embrace of balanced budgets and opposition to the North American Free Trade Agreement (NAFTA) attracted 19 percent of the vote. Although President Clinton began with a concerted effort at health care reform and expanded public investment, the defeat of these proposals and the 1994 election of Republican majorities in both chambers of Congress forced change in the administration's policy orientations. It quickly shifted to a mix of policies that gave substance to some of Reagan's aspirations. Another surprise: if there were a single significant departure from the Reagan agenda, it would occur not under Clinton but under the two-term presidency of George W. Bush. We will reserve a discussion of the Bush presidency for the final pages of this chapter.

Fiscal and Monetary Policy

First, consider taxation. By the end of the Reagan presidency, the top rate had fallen to 28 percent (although a 5 percent surcharge created a *de facto* 33 percent rate for some wealthy tax payers). George H.W. Bush pledged not to raise taxes. But the pressure of persistent deficits led him to accept modest increases in the top marginal rate to 31 percent. With the Clinton election and unified Democratic control of Congress, the top marginal rate was increased to 39.6 percent, well above the Reagan record but lower than in any year between World War II and 1981. With the election of George W. Bush and unified Republican control of the Congress, the top marginal rate fell to 35 percent, one half of the 1970s level.[35] During the 1960s and 1970s, when top marginal rates ranged from a high of 91 percent to a low of 70 percent, government receipts were, on average, 17.97 percent of GDP. In the period 1981–2008, with top marginal rates at roughly one half of the earlier era, receipts averaged 18.32 percent of GDP.[36] Lower rates did not reduce revenues, they simply changed the distribution of the tax burden.

Second, the decline of Keynesianism would mark a broader disengagement from active fiscal policy. Reagan consistently argued that a primary reliance must be placed on markets, a position echoed by George H.W. Bush. Yet, when Clinton entered office, there was once again great continuity. As the former head of the centrist Democratic Leadership Council, Clinton had a healthy respect for market mechanisms. Consider the basic statement of economic philosophy presented in the 1996 *Economic Report of the President*. "Private enterprise lies at the very heart of our modern economy. Individuals and corporations provide the initiative and innovation ... and the underlying dynamism of markets is fundamental to the continued improvements in living standards." The *Report* conceded "unfettered markets occasionally fail" and made an argument grounded in the positive theory of market failure. However,

> not every market "problem" calls for government action. In order to raise living standards, government actions therefore must meet two criteria: they must address some serious imperfection in the private marketplace, and they must be designed so that their benefits outweigh their costs.[37]

By the 1990s, many openly questioned whether the business cycle had finally been defeated. Much of the praise for the economic climate was given to Alan Greenspan, first appointed to the chairmanship of the Federal Reserve by Ronald Reagan in 1987. Greenspan, a monetarist and former disciple of Ayn Rand, was a staunch advocate of free markets. There is no greater testament to the continuity in economic policy than Greenspan's tenure at the Federal Reserve, which extended for two decades and four presidencies. Under Greenspan's direction, and in the absence of active fiscal policy, the Federal Reserve became the single most influential actor in economic policymaking.

The Quest for Balanced Budgets

Bourgeoning deficits significantly altered budgetary politics. When Reagan had proposed cutting the deficit through a freeze on key Democratic social programs, Congress responded with a more structured process. Under the Gramm-Rudman-Hollings Balanced Budget and Emergency Deficit Control Act of 1985, Congress created a series of fixed deficit targets, with the goal of a balanced budget by 1991. The Act mandated automatic across-the-board spending reductions if these targets were exceeded. The triggering mechanism—forced sequestration at the order of the Comptroller General—was declared unconstitutional in 1986 insofar as it delegated executive powers to an agent of the legislature, thereby forcing some alterations in the Act.[38] The Budget Enforcement Act of 1990 sought to achieve the same goals, but without the deficit targets. The Act established caps on annual spending and, more importantly, a "pay-as-you-go" process. Spending increases in each sub-committee would have to be offset by equal reductions or increased revenues. Failure to achieve these goals would result in sequestration of spending in non-mandatory programs. The Balanced Budget Act of 1997 extended the new system, created in 1990.

Critics on the right argued that the various procedures for budgetary control would not be sufficient absent a constitutional amendment mandating balanced budgets. Critics on the left interpreted the various schemes to reduce deficits as emblematic of a larger strategy to kill the welfare state. Under the various approaches, there could be no real expansion of discretionary welfare spending unless there were cuts in other related programs or politically unpopular tax increases. Some argued that the ultimate goal was to cut the largest entitlement programs. This strategy—often referred to as "starving the beast"—assumed that large deficits and debts could not be eliminated without structural reforms in Medicaid, Medicare, and Social Security. The concern over deficits and debts was viewed as a strategic ploy to force systematic welfare state retrenchment, essentially using seemingly neutral procedures to accomplish changes that would be politically unpopular.[39]

In the end, Gramm-Rudman-Hollings was responsible for modest reductions in the projected deficit.[40] The greatest progress came during the Clinton presidency following the 1994 midterm elections, when Republicans assumed control of both chambers of Congress for the first time since the Eisenhower presidency. Restraint in budgetary growth, both a product of ideology and the shrinking post-Cold War defense budget, combined with significant revenue growth to generate the first surplus in decades. Ultimately, the respite from looming deficits and debts was temporary. When the Balanced Budget Act of 1997 expired in 2002, the Republican-led Congress refused to reauthorize it. Subsequently, large tax cuts, the largest single expansion of the welfare state in almost four decades, and two wars produced deficits and debts that were greater than those generated by Reagan.

Regulation: Reinvention and Withdrawal

At the end of the Reagan-Bush era, critics hoped that subsequent administrations would reject the reliance on cost-benefit analysis. Although Clinton revoked Reagan's executive order 12291, he imposed a new system of regulatory review that, once again, vested authority in the OMB and continued to rely heavily on cost-benefit analysis. This should not be a surprise given the role of market failure in the above-quoted passage from the *Economic Report* that used the language of cost-benefit analysis to frame the case for limited government intervention. The consensus on the role of cost-benefit analysis was so strong that when George W. Bush assumed the presidency in 2001, he retained the Clinton regulatory review process.

Rather than seeking a statutory expansion of regulatory authority, Clinton pursued a strategy of "regulatory reinvention." Reminiscent of Hoover's associationalism, new public-private partnerships were created by regulatory agencies in the hope that cooperation could achieve results beyond what could be gained under regulation. As the administration noted in a 1995 report on environmental protection:

> Pollution is often a sign of economic inefficiency and business can improve profits by preventing it. We have learned that better decisions result from a collaborative process with people working together rather than from an adversarial one that pits them against each other.[41]

While the regulatory reinvention activities produced improvements that would not have been otherwise forthcoming, there were ongoing concerns that corporate voluntarism would preempt new statutory authority and business cooperation would be fragile, contingent on their profitability.[42]

During the post-Reagan years, there was little in the way of new regulatory statutes. The most notable exception, the Clean Air Act Amendments of 1990, extended regulation to the problem of acid rain but, tellingly, employed market mechanisms to achieve its ends. Although the Clinton administration gave some support for regulatory expansion by signing the Kyoto Protocol on Global Climate Change, it never submitted it for Senate ratification, thereby guaranteeing that it would not go into force. Where changes in regulation occurred, they were overwhelmingly deregulatory in nature. The deregulation of finance was the most important case in point. Despite the tragic collapse of the saving and loan industry at a taxpayer cost of some $160 billion during the George H. W. Bush presidency, deregulation continued. With the support of the Clinton administration, Congress passed the Gramm-Leach-Bliley Financial Services Modernization Act of 1999, eliminating the vestiges of the Glass-Steagall Act of 1933. A detailed discussion of the consequences of financial deregulation will be reserved for Chapter 10.

Welfare Reform: The Death of an Entitlement

By the end of the Reagan presidency, welfare reform seemed to reach an impasse. In 1987, Frances Fox Piven and Richard A. Cloward suggested "popular support constitutes a major obstacle to the success of the attack on the welfare state, as we predicted it would at the outset of the Reagan era. Despite some administrative restructuring and budget cuts, the income-maintenance programs remain basically intact." They explained that "the enlarging role of government in the economy has undermined the legitimacy of traditional *laissez-faire* ideas and given rise to a greatly strengthened popular belief that the state is responsible for economic well-being."[43] Within a decade of writing these words, AFDC, the largest means-tested income support entitlement, would be terminated at the hands of a Democratic president.

In his 1993 State of the Union address, Clinton announced his intentions to "end welfare as we know it." He elaborated:

> I want to offer the people on welfare the education, the training, the child care, the health care they need to get back on their feet, but say after 2 years they must get back to work, too, in private business if possible, in public service if necessary.

In part, Clinton hoped to sharply expand the earned income tax credit (EITC): "we will make history; we will reward the work of millions of working poor Americans by realizing the principle that if you work 40 hours a week and you've got a child in the house, you will no longer be in poverty."[44] Clinton embedded this goal in a more ambitious program that included a $30 billion investment program focusing on infrastructure, new community investment banks, an active labor market policy, and comprehensive health care reform. Concerns over the deficit limited congressional willingness to concede to most of the president's wishes. Congressional Democrats supported the expansion of the EITC, thereby transforming it from a "work bonus" to what would ultimately become the largest means-tested anti-poverty program.[45] Comprehensive health care reforms, unveiled in 1993, died in Congress. Following the midterm elections, the new Republican majority, united behind the Contract with America, proposed legislation that would have placed mandatory work requirements on AFDC recipients after two years and imposed a 5 year lifetime limit on participation, along with additional provisions to discourage teen pregnancy and reproduction while on public assistance.

Although the initial legislation met with a presidential veto, Congress ultimately passed the Personal Responsibility and Work Opportunity Reconciliation Act of 1996, achieving most of what had been promised in the Contract. It formally terminated AFDC and replaced it with Temporary Assistance for Needy Families (TANF), a block grant given to states. Under TANF, participation was limited to five years (although states could set shorter limits) and work requirements. The process of reform that began with state "welfare to work" demonstration projects in the 1980s, the Family Support Act of 1988 with its modest work requirements, and a host of state-level reform efforts in the early 1990s, found a final expression in TANF.

The Extension of Free Trade

The Reagan administration negotiated a free trade agreement with Canada that went into effect in 1988, beginning a process that would end with NAFTA. Negotiations over NAFTA spanned the presidency of George H.W. Bush and the agreement was signed in December of 1992. The task of steering the agreement through Congress fell to the Clinton administration. NAFTA was of some concern to environmentalists, and thus the administration negotiated the North American Agreement on Environmental Cooperation to monitor environmental impacts. Similarly, organized labor feared that NAFTA would place downward pressure on US wages, and thus the administration negotiated an additional side deal, the North American Agreement on Labor Cooperation. NAFTA went into effect on January 1, 1994.

Critics argued that NAFTA would exacerbate wage stagnation and growing inequality. Some advocates, in contrast, argued that NAFTA would be an engine of economic growth. Preliminary analyses of the impacts of NAFTA suggest that its effects were, in fact, minimal. Trade with Canada was already liberalized and the Congressional Budget Office concluded that 85 percent of the increased exports to Mexico and 91 percent of the increased imports from Mexico would have occurred even if NAFTA had not been implemented.[46] A comprehensive analysis of NAFTA by Gary Clyde Hufbauer and Jeffrey J. Schott concluded:

While NAFTA succeeded in its core goal—eradicating trade and investment barriers—trade pacts only create opportunities. ... NAFTA never
had the potential for luring droves of US firms or sucking millions of
US jobs into Mexico. Nor could NAFTA create "jobs, jobs, jobs" or
significantly raise wages ... . Those gains essentially depend on good
macroeconomic policies, a flexible labor force, better worker skills, and
effective use of information technologies.[47]

The other major event in the post-Reagan era came in 1995, when the
Uruguay round led to the creation of a new World Trade Organization to
replace GATT, which had never been designed to serve as a permanent institution. In addition to providing a permanent structure for overseeing trade, the
new WTO had a stronger dispute resolution procedure—an important factor
given the growing complexity of trade disputes (e.g., intellectual property
rights and trade in services are far more complicated than multilateral tariff
reductions). The WTO was based in consensual decision-making, and one of
the great concerns was that processes were so protracted that parties would
circumvent it and work within bilateral or multilateral trade agreements that
had the potential to divert globalization into regionalization (e.g., NAFTA, or
the European Union). Like NAFTA, the WTO would become the target of
many groups concerned with the impacts of globalization on labor, the
environment, and the preservation of indigenous cultures.[48]

These concerns became most pronounced in the 1990s because of the
literally unprecedented expansion of world trade. During the 1990s, the volume of trade grew 2.5 times faster than world GDP—a sharp departure from
the postwar period when trade grew at 1.5 times the rate of overall economic
growth. And these changes were the most striking in developing countries.
As the World Bank's Roberto Zagha and Gobind T. Nankani note: "Between
1990 and 2000, developing countries' export revenues doubled as a share
of GDP, rising from 12.5 percent to almost 25 percent." Moreover, "the
composition of developing countries' exports shifted dramatically from agricultural and resource exports into manufactures, which now constitute nearly
80 percent of exports from all developing countries."[49] The growing presence
of international trade was clearly evident in the United States. During the
1990s, the total value of exports and imports doubled, from $1.16 trillion to
$2.31 trillion; by 2008, it had tripled, reaching $3.46 trillion (all values in
2000 dollars). Trade deficits became most troublesome, growing from $54.7
billion in 1990 to a record of $616.6 billion by 2005 (in 2000 dollars).[50]

The Bush Administration as a Departure

The key components of the Neoliberal Regime—a rejection of active fiscal
policy, balanced budgets, low taxes, welfare reform, regulatory reform, and
free trade—were articulated by Reagan and found a concrete expression
during the Clinton presidency. By 2000, the nation was enjoying budgetary

surpluses with low marginal tax rates, full employment with stable prices. The largest means-tested income maintenance program had been eliminated. Regulatory review was institutionalized, deregulation continued, and the government was increasingly relying on public-private partnerships. Levels of global economic integration had never been greater and, with the end of the Cold War, the ties that connected nations were largely commercial.

In this context, the George W. Bush presidency (2001–9) was both a period of continuity and radical departure, and where these departures were the most distinctive, they marked a sharp movement away from the policy commitments of the past two decades. First, let us examine the continuity. The Federal Reserve, still under the control of Greenspan, remained the central actor in economic policymaking. In the areas of regulation and welfare reform, there was little more than stasis. New public-private partnerships were created in agencies like the EPA and OSHA. The welfare reforms of 1996 continued with no significant modifications, and with the exception of an unsuccessful effort to provide a modest "carve out" in Social Security old age pensions, there was little in the way of additional reform efforts. The major domestic policy departures came in two areas: the budget and the welfare state.

When Bush was inaugurated in 2001, the budget was in surplus. There was a strong case for devoting future surpluses, initially, to buying down the national debt. Although the national debt had fallen from a peak of 67.3 percent of GDP (1996) to 57.4 percent of GDP (2001), it remained well above historical levels.[51] But as Greenspan recalled:

> Now the projected surpluses were so large that debt repayment would be completed within a very few years … any surpluses thereafter would have to be held in some form of nonfederal assets. In 2006 the surpluses would break $500 billion. Thereafter, more than a half trillion extra dollars would flow into Uncle Sam's coffers each year.[52]

Greenspan believed that persistent surpluses of this magnitude would only lead to the creation of new government obligations. Thus, attention turned to using surpluses to bolster the Social Security and Medicare trust funds, both of which were headed toward insolvency. Alternatively, one might fund a transition to a privatized system of pensions, thereby realizing one of the decades-old goals of conservative critics of the welfare state.[53]

The Bush administration embraced a different option: tax cuts. In June of 2001, the Congress passed the Economic Growth and Tax Relief Reconciliation Act. Under the Act, the highest marginal tax rate was scheduled to fall from 39.5 percent to 35 percent, with 3 percent reductions in lower brackets (except the 15 percent bracket, which was converted to a new 10 percent bracket). The reductions were to be phased in through 2006. It also phased in an increase in the estate tax exemption, leading to its full repeal by 2010. Additional provisions (e.g., increases in IRA contribution limits) were designed to promote additional savings and investment. All of the changes in the tax code were designed to sunset on January 1, 2011, as a means of circumventing a Senate rule (the Byrd Rule) that facilitates blocking new legislation that will significantly increase the deficit for more than ten years.

In March of 2000, the tech-heavy NASDQ rose to historical levels before the so-called "dot com" bubble burst. By March of 2001, the nation had entered a brief recession that was extended by the domestic terrorist attacks of September 11, 2001. The Fed responded by flooding the financial system with liquidity and the administration secured additional tax cuts. The Job Creation and Worker Assistance Act of 2002 provided a few additional benefits for businesses (e.g., in their expensing of capital asset purchases and their treatment of operating losses). Its impact was quite limited, however, when compared with the Jobs and Growth Tax Relief Reconciliation Act of 2003, which accelerated the schedule for phasing in the 2001 reductions and provided additional cuts for dividends and capital gains. These changes were subsequently extended through 2010.[54]

The Bush tax cuts raised two sources of significant concern. First, the effects were particularly regressive given the reduced taxation of dividend income and capital gains, both of which are far more important sources of income for the wealthy. As William G. Gale and Peter Orszag explain:

> The top 1 percent of the population earns about one-tenth of the total wage and salary income but almost half of all the capital income. Shifting away from a tax on all income and toward a tax on just wages thus moves the tax burden on to lower-earning workers.

How were these changes politically possible? The capital gains and dividend components were packaged with some reductions in marginal rates for the middle class and a host of additional benefits (e.g., increased deductions for child care expenses, reduction of the "marriage penalty," increased deductions for IRA contributions). But as Gale and Orszag suggest, the middle-class components "were just a remarkably successful marketing ploy" that disguised "the much more regressive and expensive components."[55]

The second concern involved the budgetary implications. Between 1993 and 2000, federal revenues grew from 17.6 percent of GDP to 20 percent of GDP while expenditures fell from 21.4 percent of GDP to 18.4 percent of GDP, the lowest level since 1966. Combined, these trends provided the largest surplus since the Truman presidency. With the passage of significant tax cuts in 2001–3, revenues fell to a low of 16.4 percent of GDP in 2004, before recovering slightly. At the same time, high levels of domestic spending and the wars in Iraq and Afghanistan drove levels of federal spending back above 20 percent of GDP. By 2004, the federal government ran a deficit of 3.5 percent of GDP, the highest since the Reagan administration, and the debt ultimately increased by $1.4 trillion, to 67.5 percent of GDP.[56]

Some economists make the argument that deficits simply do not matter. Rational actors understand that the deficit constitutes a decision as to whether to tax now, or tax in the future, and thus they adjust their savings accordingly.[57] But the consensus position is that deficits are important because they reduce national savings and, through the effects on interest rates, domestic investment. In a global economy, these effects may be mitigated by inflows of foreign capital, but this nonetheless creates long-term obligations of debt repayment. With this in mind, one of the great concerns was the long-term implication for growth. According to one analysis, the ramifications could be profound, reducing national income by between 1 and 2 percent by 2015.[58] Supply side doctrines were grounded in a belief that lower taxation combined with reduced government spending would free capital and create new incentives for investment and growth. Clearly, the budgetary decisions of the Bush presidency could have the opposite result.

The late 1990s revealed that budget deficits can be eliminated and debt can be retired if policymakers exercise fiscal discipline. Yet, these measures will have minimal impact on the long-term growth of entitlement programs (see Chapter 8). With respect to welfare, the most significant change came with the passage of an administration-backed proposal in 2003 that dramatically expanded the costs of Medicare. Previous reform efforts met politically insurmountable obstacles given that Medicare, like Social Security, is backed by a strong coalition of groups representing the elderly. In the 2000 campaign, Bush had promised a new benefit for prescription drugs. As the 2004 reelection campaign approached, the Bush administration sought to make good on this promise while introducing new cost-containment provisions. However, as the bill moved through Congress, cost-containment was abandoned and the benefit was added for all Medicare participants. In the 2003 State of the Union address, Bush predicted that the costs of Medicare reform would be $400 billion over the next decade. Two years after passage, the estimated ten-year cost (2006–15) had risen to $724 billion, and by 2008, the Medicare Trustees Report placed the cost estimates (2008–17) at $966.9 billion.[59] The new drug benefit put additional stress on Medicare, one that will be the major source of unfunded liabilities in the next generation. In the judgment of Comptroller General David Walker, the drug bill was "probably the most fiscally irresponsible piece of legislation since the 1960s."[60]

Conclusion

The two decades following the Reagan election witnessed important changes in the role of the state in the American political economy and the rise of a new regime. By the end of the Clinton presidency, the nation experienced a prolonged record of growth, a reduction of government relative to the economy, growing budget surpluses, growing levels of global economic integration, and daily records being set in the stock markets. And yet, this impressive record had a dark side. While many Americans lived in a full-employment economy, African Americans remained subject to double-digit unemployment and, by 2006, levels of income inequality had reached the highest levels of the post-war period.[61] Long-term structural changes in the US economy provided very limited economic opportunities for those with lower levels of skill acquisition. Should they fall into poverty, the largest means-tested income maintenance program, AFDC, was no longer available. As policy analysts note, there is often a trade-off between efficiency and equity. Under the Neoliberal Regime, it was clear which of these two values had been privileged.

Even if there appeared to be a bipartisan celebration of the market, this consensus would be severely tested in the last years of the Bush presidency. Beginning in the mid-1990s, the nation experienced a booming real estate market, an asset bubble driven by changes in tax policy and underwriting standards, and low interest rates, the product of the Federal Reserve's easy money policies and the influx of dollars from abroad. When the real estate bubble burst, the effects quickly moved through the housing market and the financial system. By the end of 2007, the nation entered a prolonged recession that would soon rival the deep recession of 1982. Rather than relying on the market, policymakers of both parties turned to the state. In the fall of 2008, Congress and the Bush administration secured some $700 billion to shore up the financial system. As an indictment of past policy decisions, Democratic presidential candidate Barack Obama resoundingly defeated centrist Republican John McCain and, once inaugurated, successfully secured a large stimulus package and directed his administration to take an unprecedented role in failing businesses. A period that began with the claim that "government is the problem, not the solution" ended with corporate and financial bailouts, *de facto* nationalization of the automobile industry, and concerted efforts to reverse financial deregulation.

Attention also turned to a host of major new policy initiatives that stand in stark contrast to the old neoliberal paradigm. The administration initiated efforts to provide universal health care—an accomplishment that eluded the past Democratic presidents. In addition to designing a new regulatory architecture for finance, the administration advocated new carbon regulation to address the problem of global climate change. This, combined with a new "green" industrial policy, was framed as a means of providing the new, high-wage, manufacturing jobs of the future. These proposals constitute significant departures from the policy orientations that predominated since the era of stagflation. There remain unanswered questions. The combined costs of the financial crisis and the stimulus package forced the largest issuance of debt since World War II. The nation's balance sheet, already woefully out of control, was made far worse. Will this mandate the return to higher levels of taxation? Will this opportunity be used to address growing problems of income inequality? And what of entitlements? The date when the unfunded portions of Medicare and Social Security old age pensions will begin to claim a growing share of the budget is quickly approaching. Will this reality forestall the provision of universal health care or will the new health care policies be used to restructure existing entitlements? We turn to some of these questions in the chapters that constitute Part III of this book.

Part III

Neoliberalism and Its Discontents

8   The Two Welfare States and the Coming Entitlement Crisis

In the 1988 State of the Union address, Ronald Reagan wryly proclaimed: "My friends, some years ago, the Federal Government declared war on poverty, and poverty won." After reviewing the spending record, he asked:

> What has all this money done? Well, too often it has only made poverty harder to escape. Federal welfare programs have created a massive social problem. With the best of intentions, government created a poverty trap that wreaks havoc on the very support system the poor need most to lift themselves out of poverty: the family.

With these words, Reagan accelerated a program of welfare reform that would lead, in less than a decade, to the elimination of Aid for Families with Dependent Children (AFDC).[1] Despite Reagan's claims, there was progress in reducing the poverty. Following Johnson's 1964 declaration the poverty rate fell from 19 percent to a record low of 11.1 percent (1973). But in the next 35 years, the poverty rate would never fall below this level, and would usually be much higher, particularly during recessions. Things were markedly worse for minorities. Consider the year 2000, when the economy had been in the longest postwar period of uninterrupted growth. The poverty rate among the white non-Hispanic population was 9.5 percent, compared with 21.5 percent for Hispanics, 22.5 percent for African Americans, and 38.6 percent for female-headed African American families.[2] The persistence of poverty despite robust growth is an expression of a simple fact: the United States has the highest level of inequality among wealthy democracies.[3]

A host of factors have been introduced to explain growing inequality, including demographic trends (e.g., the growing prevalence of female-headed households), high levels of immigration, and the long-term decline in manufacturing relative to service industries. Yet, there is a strong policy component as well. During the 1960s and early 1970s, wage inequality was partially muted by expanded welfare state spending. Moreover, other policies like the minimum wage set a floor on income. Although there have been nominal increases in the minimum wage, its inflation adjusted purchasing power peaked in 1968 and has fallen steadily in the interim such that even after the 2009 increase to $7.25 an hour, a fulltime worker would still be close to the federal poverty line.[4]

Changes in taxation are also part of the story. Since 1981, there have been significant reductions in top individual and corporate tax rates, dramatically reducing the level of progressivity in the tax code. As Sandra Polaski noted in 2007, the tax code

> has been inverted from a progressive to a regressive system. Corporate income taxes have declined from 53 percent of government income tax receipts in 1960 to 34 percent today, while the top marginal tax rate for the wealthiest households has been reduced from 91 to 35 percent over the same period.[5]

Of course, one can exaggerate extent of progressivity even during what advocates of redistribution would consider to be the halcyon days of old. As Benjamin I. Page and James Roy Simmons remind us, "from the beginning—and increasingly over time—a series of exclusions, deductions, and tax shelters undermined progressivity by allowing much or most of wealthy people's income to escape taxation."[6] Tax policy is made in Congress, a highly fragmented and permeable institution that provides many access points for interests seeking to shape policy. We will return to the issue of taxation in greater detail below.

Welfare state policies can do much to mitigate poverty and income inequality. In this context, it is vitally important to consider with some care the broad changes that have occurred as a result of the Neoliberal Regime. An analysis of these changes reveals two things. First, the efforts to reduce the size and scope of the welfare state have been highly inconsistent. Policies designed to mitigate poverty among children and provide means-tested income support for the non-elderly population have received great scrutiny, while the middle-class welfare state and large entitlement programs explicitly designed to benefit the elderly population have flourished. One result has been significant reductions in poverty among the elderly that can be contrasted with increases in poverty among children. Second, the interplay of these large entitlement programs and demographic trends has created an unsustainable situation. There is a looming unfunded liability crisis with profound implications for the role of the state in the economy. Let us explore these issues in order, by examining the two welfare states.

The Shrinking Welfare State for the Poor

The most significant change in income support for the non-elderly came in 1996, with the passage of the Personal Responsibility and Work Opportunity Act. As of July 1, 1997, AFDC was terminated and replaced with Temporary Assistance for Needy Families (TANF), which provided block grants to states, imposed a maximum 60-month lifetime limit on participation, and enforced work requirements on a growing proportion of the caseload. In 1996, AFDC supported a total of 12,320,970 people. By 2000, the number supported by TANF had fallen to 5,778,034 and by 2008, it had plummeted to 2,847,520—approximately 23 percent of the 1996 number.[7] Was welfare reform a success? As a generalization, research reveals that poverty remains a persistent problem post-TANF. As one evaluation concluded: "Many families who leave and stay off welfare long term … are still poor after they leave, and many lack access to important benefits for which they are probably still eligible, such as Food Stamps and health insurance." Many remain without employment "because of a range of potential barriers to work, such as low education and little prior work experience, and not because they left welfare for marriage. These leavers need services to help them find and keep jobs."[8]

The 1996 Act had implications for other programs. For example, in order to achieve larger savings in welfare expenditures, it made notable changes in the food stamp program. When determining eligibility, recipients are permitted to take a standard deduction off of their incomes to reflect basic costs of living. This standard deduction was indexed to inflation until 1996, when the deduction was frozen, thereby making it more difficult to qualify. Since 1977, the support level had been set at 103 percent of the USDA's "Thrifty Food Plan," to compensate for the fact that the food budget was based on the costs from the previous year. In 1996, Congress changed this to 100 percent. These changes, combined with restrictions on access to food stamps for legal immigrants and unemployed childless adults generated savings of some $28 billion over the next six years. By 2008, these policy changes reduced levels of support for a family of three by $37 per month, allowing approximately $1 per person per meal in support.[9]

The period also witnessed changes in public housing. Traditionally, the Department of Housing and Urban Development (HUD) provided public housing agencies with capital and operating funds. Most of the public housing stock was in place by the 1970s and, due to deterioration, much of it had been demolished. In 1992, the federal government created the HOPE IV fund to provide grants to rehabilitate or demolish and rebuild public housing, on the expectation that state and local agencies would use these funds to leverage private capital.[10] Yet, construction of new units lagged behind demand. Most eligible families can harbor no expectation of support. As a recent Urban Institute report noted:

> Only 5.5 million (31 percent) of the total 18.0 million eligible households with housing needs actually receive assistance. That number represents just 23 percent of the 23.6 million that are eligible, regardless of whether they have housing problems. Even among extremely low income renters, only 34 percent of those that are eligible receive housing assistance.[11]

As support for public housing lagged, in the 1990s the federal government encouraged lending institutions to liberalize underwriting standards to facilitate the access of lower-income families to real estate markets. Although this policy generated significant increases in homeownership rates, much of these gains were vanquished by the subsequent collapse of the real estate and credit markets (see Chapter 10).

The only means-tested policy that has continued to expand overtime is Medicaid, which provides medical assistance for low-income citizens. The federal government and the states jointly fund Medicaid, with the federal government providing 56.2 percent of the funding.[12] Spending levels have been a great concern since the 1970s, given the rapid growth in cost. In 1981, the Reagan administration proposed setting a cap on Medicaid, indexed for inflation, while providing states with far greater discretion in the use of funds. Congress rejected this proposal, but imposed across-the-board reductions and established spending target rates to account for medical inflation. The next year, the administration unsuccessfully proposed that the federal government assume full responsibility for Medicaid in exchange for states accepting the full burden of other welfare programs.[13] Nonetheless, over the course of the 1980s and 1990s, states were granted far greater discretion in restricting services provided to patients and in reimbursing healthcare providers (as long as payments were "reasonable and adequate"). Required to accept the Medicaid reimbursement as payment-in-full, many physicians refused to serve Medicaid patients.[14]

The 1990s brought an expansion and a contraction of medical support for the poor. Prior to the 1996 reforms, AFDC recipients were eligible for Medicaid. The new law decoupled the two, thereby allowing individuals to receive Medicaid after exiting TANF, a fact that many potential recipients did not understand. The 1996 reforms also barred immigrants who entered the nation after August 1996 from Medicaid for all but emergency care for their first five years of residence.[15] A year after passing welfare reform, Congress created the State Children's Health Insurance Program (SCHIP) as part of the Balanced Budget Act of 1997. The new program was designed to provide insurance coverage for children of the working poor who make too much to qualify for Medicaid but too little to afford healthcare. Like Medicaid, the federal government and the states jointly fund SCHIP. Following the precedent set in 1996, legal immigrants were banned from the program for the first five years of residence. On two occasions in 2007, Congress passed legislation to expand SCHIPS, but met with a presidential veto. In 2009, the newly inaugurated President Obama signed legislation providing additional funding and extending coverage to an additional 4 million children, including legal immigrants, and mandating that states provide dental and mental health coverage.[16]

Growth in means-tested spending has been driven primarily by Medicaid. In 2008, inflation adjusted federal spending for Medicaid ($201.4 billion) was 5.99 times greater than it was in 1980. In contrast, other forms of federal family assistance increased by 41.7 percent during the same period, for a total of $25.1 billion. Adjusted for inflation—but not for the population—the nation spent more on family assistance in 1972 than it did in any year during the post-1980 period. As for public housing, inflation adjusted spending in 2008 was precisely what it was in 1980, $350 million. To place these figures in context, since 1980 inflation-adjusted GDP more than doubled.[17] With the exception of Medicaid, the growth in national wealth has not found an expression in the growth of the means-tested welfare state.

The Burgeoning Middle-Class Welfare State

Although the Social Security Act of 1935 created the foundation for universal and means-tested policies, subsequent debates over welfare increasingly narrowed the concept of "welfare" so that it became synonymous with policies providing income support for the non-elderly poor. But if we accept a broader conception of welfare to include policies that provide income support, medical care, and housing regardless of income, then it is clear that the welfare state as a whole has expanded dramatically in the past several decades and its benefits have been directed away from the poor. This should be no surprise. In a system permeable to mobilized interests, we should expect interests with higher incomes to be more successful in achieving transfers. As E. E. Schattschneider remarked in the *Semisovereign People*: "The flaw in the pluralist heaven is that the heavenly chorus sings with a strong upper-class accent."[18]

The Hidden Welfare State

Much of the middle class welfare state is what Christopher Howard has described as the "hidden welfare state," a product of the complex network of tax expenditures in the nation's tax code. These tax expenditures may be invisible to critics of welfare, but they serve important social welfare functions with benefits that accrue primarily to upper income citizens. As Howard explains:

> Heavy subsidies for employer benefits are one reason that more affluent citizens are the main beneficiaries of the hidden welfare state. As a general rule, these benefits are most likely to be available to workers in larger companies, unionized industries, and better-paying occupations. In addition, some tax expenditures reward behaviors that less affluent taxpayers cannot afford to engage in (e.g., owning a home) .... Essentially, the more progressive the tax rates, the more upper-income taxpayers benefit from tax expenditures. As the tax bite increases, so does the value of avoiding taxation. Without some deliberate effort to cap benefits, a progressive tax system will always contain regressive tax expenditures.[19]

Howard's best estimate is that only 10 percent of the value of the tax expenditures supports low-income citizens, an estimate that predated the tax cuts of the George W. Bush administration.

The OMB reports the size of tax expenditures annually in its *Analytical*

Perspectives. A few examples should suffice to give a sense of the magnitude of these expenditures. For 2008, the exclusion of employer contributions for medical insurance premiums and healthcare cost $151.8 billion. The exclusion of pension contributions and earnings cost an additional $105.4 billion. The deductibility of mortgage interest and state and local real estate taxes for owner-occupied housing cost $111.2 billion.[20] As one might expect, the major tax expenditures deliver their greatest benefits to those in the top income groups. In 2007, the top fifth of households had incomes of more than $100,000 and according to the Joint Committee on Taxation, households earning more than this sum assume some 84.8 percent of the tax liability. But they also claim 73 percent of the benefits from the mortgage interest deduction, another 69.7 percent of the benefits from the real estate tax deduction, and 84.4 percent of the state and local income, sales, and personal property tax deduction.[21]

Many tax expenditures directly subsidize consumption of goods and services by the middle- and upper-income population. However, others provide benefits directly to corporations. Corporate welfare—the provision of various subsidies to business—can take myriad forms, including direct subsidies, loans and loan guarantees, tax expenditures, trade barriers, and regulations that protect companies (and their market shares) at a cost to consumers. Estimates of the annual costs of corporate welfare are necessarily imprecise, ranging from $90 billion (as claimed by the libertarian Cato Institute) to $125 billion (as claimed by Public Citizen).[22] As noted in Chapter 7, the corporate tax rate fell significantly in the post-1980 period. Nonetheless, the United States has a high statutory corporate tax rate relative to other OECD countries. Yet, corporate tax revenues in the United States are 1.8 percent of GDP, well below the weighted average for OECD countries (2.5 percent of GDP).[23] The explanation for this discrepancy is simple: the United States combines high statutory marginal tax rates with a host of tax expenditures that effectively reduce their impact.[24]

Social Security Old Age Pensions

Old age pensions were created, in Roosevelt's words, to be "one leg on a three-legged stool" (the other two legs were to be pensions and private savings). Benefits were added for survivors in 1939, and for disabled workers in 1954. During the postwar period, the costs of social security escalated as a product of two factors: the growing size of benefits and the growing number of beneficiaries. Originally, Congress passed legislation raising benefit levels and, at times, the increases were steep. Between 1950 and 1973, Congress authorized ten across-the-board benefit increases ranging from a low of 7 percent to a high of 77 percent.[25] Since 1975, annual adjustments have been based on the Consumer Price Index for Urban Wage Earners and Clerical Workers (CPI-W).

As benefits increased, the Social Security system also expanded in terms of participants. Regularly employed farm and domestic workers, initially excluded from the program, were incorporated in the 1950s. However, the greatest source of growth was demographic. In 1940, there were 9 million Americans over the age of 65. On average, males lived 12.7 years and females 14.7 years after reaching retirement age. By 2000, this number had increased to 34.9 million, with males living an average of 15.3 years after retirement, and women an average of 19.6 years. Reflecting these trends, between 1980 and 2008, inflation-adjusted spending on Social Security increased by 217 percent. By 2008 there were approximately 51 million Americans receiving benefits from the system at a cost of some $509 billion, approximately 4.4 percent of GDP.[26]

With an aging population and benefit levels growing faster than inflation, increased levels of taxation were unavoidable. Between 1937 and 1949, employers and employees paid a combined 2 percent tax. Over the course of the next half-century, the tax rate increased steadily, reaching a combined 12.4 percent after 1990. By design, Social Security has a contribution and benefit base, essentially an income cap beyond which taxation would cease. In the early years, the base was $3,000 and it increased on an annual basis after 1971, reaching $106,800 by 2009.[27] Since all working individuals pay the same percentage of tax on income below this threshold, the tax has a regressive effect, even with the 1983 reforms that included taxing benefits of higher income recipients. The increased levels of taxation have allowed the Old-Age and Survivors Insurance Trust Fund to remain solvent to date. However, the combination of demographic trends creates a source of significant concern, that has been heightened by the recession that began in 2008. Initially, the Social Security Trustees predicted that the revenues into the fund would be less than the payments flowing out by 2014, forcing a reliance on general revenues. Yet, under conditions of recession, this critical date arrived four years early.[28] We will turn to the long-term implications below.

Medicare

The other significant entitlement program is Medicare, created in 1965 to provide medical services to the elderly. Medicare, like Social Security, is funded through a payroll tax (currently a combined 2.9 percent split equally between employer and employee). Although the Medicare tax was initially subject to a contribution limit comparable to Social Security, this cap was eliminated in 1994 to enhance the solvency of the system. Medicare Part A provides hospital insurance, covering 100 percent of the costs for the first twenty days and additional coverage for the following 80 days with a copayment. Medicare Part B is voluntary and provides a supplemental outpatient medical insurance. As a cost containment measure, Congress created a new Medicare Part C in 1997 that allowed beneficiaries to participate in Medicare Advantage plans, private insurance offered by networks of providers that receive a monthly fee, often with a copayment. Finally, as noted in Chapter 7, a new drug benefit (Medicare Part D) was added in 2003.

Medicare spending, driven both by the demographic trends that ail Social Security and the medical inflation rate, has been a long-standing source of concern. Between 1980 and 2008, the number of beneficiaries increased by 59 percent while federal spending on Medicare grew by 522 percent. In 2008, Medicare covered 45.2 million Americans and paid out $462 billion in benefits. The number of beneficiaries is projected to double to 91.4 million by 2050. Although Medicare spending is currently much less than Social Security, it is projected to become the single largest entitlement program by the 2020s.[29] Indeed, the 2009 Trustees Report projected expenditures

> to increase in future years at a faster pace than either workers' earnings or the economy overall. As a percentage of GDP, expenditures are projected to increase from 3.2 percent in 2008 to 11.4 percent by 2083 ... Growth of this magnitude, if realized, would substantially increase the strain on the nation's workers, Medicare beneficiaries, and the Federal Budget.

To date, revenues into the system have covered the impact of growing expenses. But the trustees project that the Hospital Insurance trust fund will be depleted by 2017 and by 2030, a majority of Medicare funding (52.6 percent) will have to be drawn from general revenues.[30]

Although advocates for the means-tested welfare state have been incapable of tempering the fervor over welfare reform, policies affecting the elderly are politically untouchable due to high levels of mobilization. Cross-nationally, there has been a common pattern. "The differences among the protections for the elderly in various countries demonstrate the potency of political organization in determining who gets help in many countries, including the United States."[31] Yet, this trend has been far more pronounced in the United States. Federal spending for children grew from 1.9 percent of GDP to 2.6 percent of GDP between 1960 and 2006, whereas spending on the elderly more than tripled from 2 percent of GDP to 7.6 percent of GDP. For every dollar that the United States transfers per child, it transfers $8.12 per elderly citizen.[32] The relative success of various groups in securing welfare state benefits has had one clear expression: different experiences with poverty. In 1959, 35.2 percent of the elderly fell below the poverty line. This number fell steadily over the course of the next several decades, reaching a record low of 9.4 percent by 2006—compared with an overall poverty rate of 17.4 percent. In contrast, the poverty rate among children fell from 26.9 percent in 1959 to a low of 13.8 percent in 1969, before increasing again to an average of 15.5 percent in the 1970s, 19.9 percent in the 1980s, and 20 percent in the 1990s, before declining to an average of 16.7 percent for the period 2000–2007.[33] The United States not only developed the most unequal wealth distribution among industrialized nations, it also had the highest child poverty rate after government transfers among the same comparison group.[34]

The Looming Entitlement Crisis

David M. Walker, Comptroller General from 1998 to 2008, devoted much of his time to publicizing the problem of unfunded liabilities. As of 2006, the long-term liability exposure of the US government was some $50 trillion. To illustrate the magnitude of the problem, Walker stated: "if we wanted to put aside today enough to cover these promises, it would take $170,000 for each and every American or approximately $440,000 per American household."[35] That is, if these amounts were placed in an interest bearing account now, it would generate a flow of revenues sufficient to cover the unfunded portion of the long-term liabilities. Another illustration: if revenues remain at existing levels relative to GDP, by 2015, taxes will be insufficient to cover interest on the debt, Social Security, Medicare and Medicaid—not to mention all the other things that government might want to do (e.g., national defense, education, infrastructure). By 2020, revenues will be totally absorbed by interest on the debt and a portion of Social Security, leaving nothing at all for Medicare, Medicaid, or discretionary spending. As Walker noted:

> without policy changes on the spending and/or revenue sides of the budget, the growth in spending on federal retirement and health entitlements will encumber an escalating share of the government's resources. A government that in our children's lifetimes does nothing more than pay interest on its debt and mail checks to retirees and some of their health providers is unimaginable.[36]

The problem of long-term structural deficits is a product of program design and demographic trends. Restraining discretionary spending or raising taxes, while necessary, will not prevent the day of reckoning, nor can the solution be found in economic growth. In Walker's words:

> substantive reform of Social Security and our major health programs remains critical to recapturing our future fiscal flexibility … given demographic and healthcare cost trends, the size of the spending cuts necessary to hold revenues at today's share of GDP seems inadequate and implausible.

According to the Government Accountability Office (GAO),

> if no action is taken, balancing the budget in 2040 could require actions as large as cutting total federal spending by 60 percent or raising federal taxes to 2 times today's level. There are no "easy answers" and everything must be on the table.[37]

Walker's testimony on this subject over the course of his career as the head of the GAO had little discernible impact and thus, in 2008, he resigned and became the head of the Peter G. Peterson Foundation, a think tank devoted to making the case for fiscal responsibility.

The Congressional Budget Office has arrived at very similar long-term projections. In its 2009 *Long-Term Budget Outlook*, the CBO reported: "The number of people age 65 or older will grow by 90 percent by 2035, compared with growth of just 12 percent for those aged 20 to 64 ... . About 92 million people will be collecting Social Security benefits in 2035, CBO projects, compared with about 52 million today." As a result, "unless changes are made to Social Security, spending for the program will rise from 4.3 percent of GDP in fiscal year 2008 to 6.0 percent by 2035." The projections for medical entitlements are even direr. The CBO projects that total Medicare spending will increase to 8 percent of GDP by 2035 and to 15 percent by 2080. The CBO considers competing scenarios for drawing out the long-term implications. It calculates the "fiscal gap" representing the difference between the present value of the future stream of revenues and the present value of the future stream of outlays. This value represents the amount by which the federal government would need to "immediately and permanently raise tax revenues, cut spending, or use some mix of both." Under competing scenarios, the seventy-five-year fiscal gap is between 3.2 percent and a staggering 8.1 percent of GDP.[38]

The CBO draws some painful scenarios for members of Congress. Under current projections, the resulting deficits "would reduce national saving, leading to more borrowing from abroad and less domestic investment, which in turn would depress income growth in the United States ... and seriously harm the economy." To avoid these deficits, the government could raise taxes, but this would require "tax rates ... to reach levels never seen in the United States."[39] Unprecedented levels of taxation would also depress rates of growth and, as a result, both scenarios end in the same place. The focus must turn to significant changes in the design of the large entitlement programs. This, in turn, is a difficult task given, once again, the popularity of programs for the elderly and the incentive structure in Congress. The fifty year and seventy-five year projections may be far less salient to legislators than the projections for upcoming elections.

At first glance, it is difficult to understand why the situation is so troublesome. For both programs, the difference between revenues and the outlays is stored in trust funds and these trust funds have accumulated large surpluses. Presumably, when outlays exceed revenues, the Social Security Administration (SSA) will simply draw on these resources. However, as the OMB explains:

> These funds ... do not consist of real economic assets that can be drawn down in the future to fund benefits. Instead, they are claims on the Treasury, that, when redeemed, will have to be financed by raising taxes, borrowing from the public, or reducing benefits or other expenditures.[40]

Indeed, as the OMB noted in 2003:

the Treasury will have to turn to the public capital markets to raise the funds to redeem the bonds and finance the benefits, just as if the trust funds had never existed. From the standpoint of overall government finances, the trust funds do not reduce the future burden of financing Social Security of Medicare benefits.[41]

The long-term difficulties with Social Security and Medicare have a common demographic driver. Yet, given that the problems associated with the two programs are somewhat different, it is useful to examine them separately and consider the options open to policymakers. In each case the avenues for reform are limited and pose some significant challenges. Moreover, the most viable options seem to stand in clear opposition to the basic precepts of neoliberalism.

Reforming Social Security

The greatest problem associated with Social Security Old Age Pensions is simply a product of demographic trends and their impact on the support ratio, (i.e., the ratio of beneficiaries to workers). As the support ratio falls, the costs of supporting the system must be borne by relatively fewer taxpayers. As the Urban Institute's C. Eugene Steuerle explains:

> Close to one-third of the adult population is scheduled to be on Social Security within about 25 years. Including adults on other transfer programs, we are approaching the day when the majority of the adult population will depend upon transfers from others for a significant share of its support.[42]

According to the SSA, the ratio of workers per beneficiary was approximately 8:1 in 1960, stabilized at 3.3:1 in the 1970s, but is projected to fall to 2:1 by 2040.[43] Short of dramatic increases in immigration or fertility, little can be done to manipulate the support ratio. Taking demographics off the table, there are limited leverage points for reform: taxation, benefits, and the rate of return on the investments. Each carries with it a host of inherent difficulties. Let us consider them in turn.

The level of taxation has increased significantly, as noted above, from a combined 2 percent to the current level of 12.4 percent. The tax applies to all income below an earnings cap (in 2009, for example, taxes were paid on the first $106,800 of income). Since the tax rate is the same for all taxpayers, its effects are highly regressive. The two serious proposals on the revenue side would be to increase the statutory tax rate (e.g., raise it from a combined 12.4 percent to 14 percent) and/or eliminate or increase significantly the earnings cap. The latter approach would increase the effective marginal tax rate for high-income earners, thereby adding greater progressivity to the system. But by the SSA's own calculations, this alone would be insufficient—it would only delay the inevitable.[44]

Opponents to tax increases argue that Social Security is already a poor investment, characterized by low rates of return relative to private retirement funds. To increase taxes would be to further worsen the rate of return. However, Social Security was designed as insurance. It provided early participants with benefits that greatly exceeded their contributions. One can think of these costs as a "legacy debt" that has been passed on to future generations. Peter A. Diamond and Peter R. Orszag have suggested that some 3 to 4 percentage points of the current tax constitute the "legacy debt." On equity grounds, they suggest, some portion of this cost should be borne by those who are not formally in the system by mandating participation for newly hired state and local government employees who would otherwise be covered by public pension systems. Additionally, some portion should be borne by higher-income workers (e.g., a 3 percent legacy tax on earnings above the earnings limit) with phased-in increases in a universal legacy charge from 2023 forward.[45] These changes, seemingly modest, would cover part of the long-term financial difficulties while partially increasing progressivity.

Benefits constitute a second leverage point. They can be reduced in various ways, including raising the retirement age or reducing the size of payments. In 1983, following the work of the Greenspan Commission, Congress gradually increased the age at which retirees could receive full benefits from 65 to age 67 by 2027. With growing life expectancies, increasing the retirement age once again would seem to be a reasonable reform. However, this would have negative ramifications for minority citizens, given the differences in life expectancy. As the GAO reports:

> Because blacks, on average, already can expect to spend fewer years in retirement than whites as a result of their shorter life expectancy, they would experience a greater relative reduction in benefits, compared with whites, from an increase in the Social Security retirement age.[46]

By removing many minority citizens from the pool of beneficiaries, these changes would potentially reinforce the racial disparities in income and wealth distributions.

In this context, three alternative ways of reducing benefits seem to make great sense: increasing the taxation of benefits, reducing benefits for higher-income workers, and changing the formula for future increases. Let us consider them in turn. In 1983, Congress made 50 percent of the benefits of higher income recipients taxable; a decade later, Congress increased the tax to cover 85 percent of benefits, with the additional revenues earmarked for Medicare's Hospital Insurance Trust Fund. One proposal to reduce benefits (and raise revenues) would be to extend taxation to 100 percent of benefits above an income threshold, thereby subjecting Social Security to the same treatment as other forms of income. By the SSA's own analysis, this would have a positive but limited impact on the solvency of the trust fund.[47]

Additionally, one might consider reducing benefits for higher-income workers. Diamond and Orszag, for example, suggest reducing the highest tier of the benefit formula in recognition of the fact that "people with higher earnings and more education are increasingly tending to live longer ... . This hurts Social Security finances and reduces progressiveness on a lifetime basis, since the highest earners receive payments over an increasingly longer period compared to everyone else."[48] Indirect means testing may be attractive for normative reasons, yet there may be concerns over its political impact. Geoffrey Kollmann of the Congressional Research Service observes that opponents

> dislike the concept of indirect means testing because it makes Social Security appear more like welfare, where need determines the level of benefits ... . They assert that, as the country's only national social insurance system, which provides a bedrock level of protection to nearly all workers and their families from loss of income due to the death, retirement, or disability of the worker, Social Security is special and should be so treated.[49]

The key question is a political one: would the transition from a universal insurance to a means-tested program subject Social Security to the kinds of pressures exhibited with respect to other means-tested forms of income support?

Another means of reducing the flow of benefits would be to change the formula employed in making cost of living adjustments. As noted above, since the mid-1970s, benefit levels have been increased automatically, indexed for growth in wages using the CPI-W. Historically, wages have grown faster than prices and as a result, indexing based on the CPI-W has provided each successive generation of retirees with benefits that have greater purchasing power while providing workers with a comparable replacement rate (i.e., benefits replace 39 percent of the wages for a career-long, average-wage worker). One means of limiting the magnitude of the future unfunded liability would be to index benefits based on the CPI rather than the CPI-W.

According to the SSA, this would be more than sufficient to address the long-term solvency of the trust fund but it would dramatically reduce the extent to which benefits would replace earnings. For example, the average-wage worker who can currently expect a 39 percent replacement rate, could only expect to receive a 16 percent replacement rate by 2080 under full price-indexing. Alternatively, one might promote progressive indexing, retaining the CPI-W for low-wage workers but introduce CPI indexing for high-wage workers, with a blend of the two for average-wage workers. If such a system were employed, by 2030, high-wage earners would receive 51.5 percent less than under current law, average-wage earners would receive 35.7 percent less, whereas low-wage workers would be unaffected. The SSA calculates that this would eliminate 74 percent of the seventy-five-year deficit.[50] Progressive indexing would maintain current levels of benefits for those least likely to have private savings or pensions. Moreover, the changes would be gradual, allowing future recipients time to acquire alternative sources of income. However, this method would turn Social Security into a means-tested program and could, overtime, undermine its broad popular support.

A third leverage point is the rate of return. Social Security provides a defined-benefit pension. That is, participants receive a benefit based on earnings and years of employment. This can be contrasted to a defined-contribution pension (e.g., an individual retirement account) in which income is a function of the total contributions, investment decisions, and rates of return. Critics of Social Security have, incorrectly, treated it as a defined-contribution pension with an abysmal rate-of-return. While the first generation of recipients enjoyed inflation-adjusted rates-of-return of some 25 percent, the real rate-of-return for the "baby boom" generation is in the order of 2 percent.[51] Moreover, unlike Social Security, investors have property rights in their portfolios and can thus leave their retirement savings to their heirs, thereby allowing for intergenerational wealth transfers.

These observations fueled proposals for changes in the Social Security trust fund, or full or partial privatization. In the first instance, the trust fund could make investments in the market, thereby becoming a genuine store of wealth. Opposition to this proposal has focused on the implications of the government having a large equity stake in corporations and the politicization of investment decisions. With respect to privatization, the approach would be quite the opposite. Social Security would be terminated for citizens below a certain age, to be replaced with a system of mandatory retirement contributions. The argument for full privatization rests on comparisons between the rate-of-return offered to current participants and what could be achieved through private investments. A worker making $30,000 a year would pay $120,000 in taxes to the Social Security system, generating benefits of $185,000 (a 2 percent rate of return). The same funds, if invested at 4.6 percent (the historical rate-rate-of return for a balanced portfolio, minus administrative costs) would produce $344,000. The difference between these two figures is the opportunity cost of participating in Social Security, as borne by the worker.[52] A less dramatic alternative to full privatization would be to mandate a "carve out" allowing participants to place a portion of their Social Security tax in an individual account earning market rates-of-return or an "add on," introducing mandatory private savings in addition to Social Security.

The last concerted attempt to reform Social Security came during the George W. Bush presidency. In 2001, Bush created the President's Commission to Strengthen Social Security that offered several alternatives, combining the creation of private funds and changes in the indexing. Following the 2004 presidential election Bush announced his intent to use his "political capital" to transform the program. In the 2005 State of the Union address, he unveiled guidelines for reform, which included a "carve out" of up to 4 percent of covered earnings (a maximum of $1,000 per year) to be placed in a personal account managed by the government. Participation would be voluntary, limited to those born after 1950. Subsequently, he added, progressive indexing of benefits that would continue to index the benefits for low-wage workers on the basis of the CPI-W while changing the formula for average and upper-income workers as described above.[53] Congressional Democrats, organized labor, and the AARP mobilized in opposition to what was portrayed as a risky privatization plan. Although many Republicans and the conservative Club for Growth supported the Bush proposal, it was too timid to attract privatization advocates. Analysts noted that the majority of the savings would come through the changes in indexing and private accounts would be insufficient to compensate for the larger reductions in benefits.[54] Some opponents clearly understood the potential long-term political consequences. As Dean Baker and David Rosnick explained: "As the traditional Social Security benefit becomes less important for middle-income workers, Social Security will increasingly become a poor people's program. This may be a clever strategy if the purpose is to undermine political support."[55]

Between the November reelection and June of 2005, public support for the president fell from 51 percent to 42 percent, with even steeper declines for the Republican-led Congress. As for Social Security reform, only 25 percent supported the proposed changes. The nation was evenly divided on the merits of individual accounts and, paradoxically, given the progressive indexing, a majority believed the changes would benefit the wealthy. Following the disastrous response to Hurricane Katrina, which devastated coastal Mississippi and New Orleans, the president's political capital was all but expended. Democrats reclaimed control of both chambers of Congress in the 2006 midterm elections, effectively sealing the fate of Bush's reform proposals.[56] Support for some form of privatization was seriously diminished as the stock market and housing bubbles burst in 2007–8, reminding citizens that the extraordinary market returns of the previous decade were not guaranteed.

Reforming Medicare

The long-term problems associated with Social Security pale in comparison to those of Medicare. The impact of demographic pressures is magnified by the medical inflation rate. Although there have been ongoing proposals to reform the program and contain costs by eliminating "waste, fraud, and abuse," given the magnitude of current and future expenditures, it is impossible to separate the debates over Medicare reform from the large question of healthcare provision. Thus, it will be addressed in this context. First, it is useful to examine briefly two recent efforts by Congress to make significant changes to Medicare.

In 1986, President Reagan called on the Department of Health and Human Services (HHS) Secretary to develop a proposal to cover seniors from catastrophic illnesses. These efforts ultimately resulted in the passage of the Medicare Catastrophic Coverage Act of 1988. The Act provided full coverage for hospital stays of any length, with a $560 deductible for hospital costs and a $1,370 deductible for doctor bills. Additionally, it covered 80 percent of the cost of prescription drugs with a $600 deductible, along with a host of additional benefits. According to the CBO, "Medicare benefit payments would exceed Medicare premiums payable by 23 percent or more."[57] Given that the Act expanded benefits and was endorsed by the AARP, it seemed a perfect means to win the support of the elderly in the upcoming election. After passage, however, it became clear that the President and Congress had made a strategic miscalculation. The elderly were enraged by the premiums and deductibles, particularly those who had comprehensive coverage from a former employer.[58] One of the most memorable images of 1988 was that of House Ways and Means Chairman Dan Rostenkowski (D-IL) being chased down the street by senior citizens protesting the Act. As David Hyman remarks: "Although Mr. Rostenkowski was reelected, the debacle reinforced the risks of 'messing with Medicare' for even the dullest member of Congress."[59] Congress had learned an important lesson regarding the potential political costs of reform and passed the Medicare Catastrophic Repeal Act of 1989.

In the 2000 presidential campaign, both major candidates promised to provide additional drug benefits but, based on the experiences of 1988–89, it was clear that participation would have to be voluntary. After the election, the Bush administration began considering means of providing a new drug benefit before the 2004 campaign season began. The administration, also concerned about escalating costs, sought to link the new benefit to cost controls. In 1997, Congress authorized the delivery of Medicare benefits through participation in new Medicare Part C plans that were organized like Health Maintenance Organizations. They often provided additional benefits but did so for a monthly capitation fee, thereby creating a mechanism for cost controls. The Bush administration hoped to increase levels of participation by creating a new drug benefit linked to Part C plans as an incentive to move out of more expensive fee-for-service coverage. Congressional Democrats attacked the proposal as an underhanded effort to privatize Medicare; fiscal conservatives were concerned about costs. As the legislation evolved, the links between the new drug benefit and cost containment were severed, and when the Medicare Prescription Drug, Improvement, and Modernization Act of 2003 was finally passed, the benefit was made universal in a new Medicare Part D. During the debates, the administration, the CBO, and the HHS Centers for Medicare and Medicaid dissembled about the costs of the program in an effort to inveigle fiscal conservatives. The final cost of the plan would prove to be a multiple of the figure announced in 2003, exacerbating Medicare's long-term fiscal problems.

What are the lessons of Medicare reform efforts to date? First, beneficiaries constitute a large and growing constituency capable of effectively mobilizing to preserve and expand benefits. Second, while there may be universal recognition of long-term solvency problems, the short-term political benefits associated with preventing reforms may be too attractive for most members of Congress to ignore. Congressional debates about Medicare, like Social Security, make good politics but rarely result in good policy. Yet, as the size of the pool of beneficiaries continues to grow and the costs of Medicare claim a larger share of GDP and general revenues, the need to make significant changes will be unavoidable.

As suggested above, it is difficult to discuss Medicare reform without simultaneously addressing the larger issue of healthcare delivery. In the United States, healthcare expenditures as a percentage of GDP increased from 5.9 percent in 1965 to 16.2 percent in 2007, and are projected to exceed 20 percent of GDP by 2018. Given that healthcare programs constitute some 34 percent of total spending, the budgetary implications are enormous.[60] Healthcare expenses have outpaced GDP growth in all OECD countries, reflecting the aging of the populations and growth in benefit levels regardless of age. But the United States has both the fastest rate of growth and spends the largest percentage of GDP. In 2007, the United States spent an average of $7,290 per capita, compared with an OECD average of $3,075. And yet, on the basis of basic indicators like the child mortality rate and life expectancy, the United States actually performs worse than other OECD countries. Moreover, the United States, unlike other wealthy democracies, has a large and growing population of uninsured, constituting over 15 percent of the population.[61] These facts have combined to place comprehensive healthcare reform on the policy agenda.

The present system of healthcare delivery creates significant barriers to managing the growth in healthcare costs. As a comparative analysis of ten OECD countries suggests, "The fiscal fallout [from the future growth of healthcare expenditures] is likely to be particularly severe for the United States." Unlike other OECD countries, the United States

> appears to lack both the institutional mechanism and political will to control its healthcare spending. America's elderly are politically very well organized, and each cohort of retirees has, since the 1950s, used its political power to extract ever greater transfers from contemporaneous workers.

They conclude:

> There is, of course, a limit to how much a government can extract from the young to accommodate the old. When that limit is reached, governments go broke. Of the ten countries considered here, the U.S. appears the most likely to hit this limit.[62]

As shown above, there is little evidence that Congress has been capable of achieving meaningful Medicare reforms. The electoral costs of reform and the electoral benefits of derailing reforms are simply too great. In contrast, by folding Medicare into a comprehensive healthcare package, it could be possible to shift costs to younger generations that are outside of the risk pool. At the same time, the comparative experience of other nations with comparable demographic trends and levels of wealth reveals that nations can effectively spend a far smaller percentage of GDP on healthcare without sacrificing outcomes. In this context, the problems inherent in Medicare may be best addressed through an expansion of the role of the state.

The model for comprehensive healthcare reform has been hotly contested since the 1980s. Conservatives, hoping to preserve the private sector, have made the argument for measures to force greater competition and a larger role for market incentives. A core argument is that escalating healthcare costs are, in part, a product of excess demand which has resulted from a simple economic fact: when goods are discounted, people consume more. Overuse is a product of the incentive structure created by insurance. Advocates frequently cite the RAND Corporation's Health Insurance Experiment that ran from 1971–82. Some 7,700 individuals were randomly assigned to one of five groups, one offering free care, three requiring different levels of cost sharing (25 percent, 50 percent, or 95 percent), and one offering access to an HMO-style health service. The study found that higher levels of cost sharing resulted in lower levels of healthcare consumption—fewer doctor visits, fewer hospitalizations, fewer prescription drugs, dental visits, and mental healthcare. What was somewhat surprising, however, was that "in general, the reduction in services induced by cost sharing had no adverse effect on participants' health."[63] Based on this study, advocates argue, the best response to escalating healthcare costs is to change the incentive structure. Medical savings accounts combined with a high-deductible insurance policy would drive down the costs of healthcare while minimizing government intervention in healthcare markets. This could be combined with other measures, including tort reform and the deregulation of health insurance, which is regulated on a state-by-state basis. During the 1990s, Republicans promoted medical savings accounts as the cornerstone of reform, and accounts were authorized on a pilot basis with the Health Insurance Portability and Accountability Act of 1996 and extended, as Health Savings Accounts, with the Medicare Modernization Act. To date they have been employed only as adjuncts to the system.

While these reforms might contain costs, critics note they would do little to extend coverage to the uninsured. One alternative is "pay or play," a model that mandates that all employers pay a tax to fund coverage under a public program, but provides a credit for costs incurred in insuring employees. In essence, the employer mandate creates a source of funding for many who are currently uninsured and may be extended through the provision of public funds.[64] Advocates cite the public program as being an important means of promoting cost containment. If private insurers cannot provide comparable rates, employers would pay the tax rather than continue insurance coverage. Critics argue that this, or any other system with a public option, would force a transition to a "single-payer" system in which hospitals and healthcare providers are compensated fully by the state.

In 1993, the Clinton administration unsuccessfully proposed universal healthcare reform that would have included employer mandates and the creation of regulated regional healthcare alliances as a means of addressing simultaneously the problems of coverage and cost. As Jonathan Oberlander notes:

> Perhaps the Clinton administration's greatest mistake was excessive ambition. The plan attempted simultaneously to secure universal coverage, regulate the private insurance market, change health care financing through an employer mandate, control costs to levels enforced by a national health board, and transform the delivery system through managed care ... although there is a substantive rationale for taking all of them on at once, it was a politically treacherous task. Indeed, each dimension of the Clinton plan galvanized opposition.[65]

The employer mandate mobilized the opposition of the National Federation of Independent Business. Changes in insurance regulation and the imposition of federal cost controls mobilized the Health Insurance Association of America, which unleashed a successful series of television ads with the tagline "They choose, we lose." Middle- and upper-income voters who already enjoyed insurance feared that the changes would jeopardize the status quo. Conservatives rejected the bureaucratic structure envisioned by the proposal while Democrats were dismayed by the administration's failure to engage them in the development of the proposal at a point where they could have forged the compromises necessary to build a supportive coalition. Despite unified Democratic control of the Congress and presidency, the Clinton proposal died a slow death. The 1994 Republican landslide is often cited as one of the byproducts of the administration's efforts to introduce comprehensive reforms.

Since that time, the problems of costs and coverage have continued to grow more severe, and many US corporations cite high healthcare costs as one of the factors that undermines competitiveness in the global economy. The classic example was General Motors, that estimated in 2005 it added more than $1,500 to the price of each vehicle to cover the costs of providing healthcare insurance secured through its labor contracts with the United Auto Workers.[66] On a per vehicle basis, the costs of healthcare exceeded the costs of steel, contributing, ultimately, to the bankruptcy of GM and other auto manufacturers. With unified Democratic control of the presidency and Congress following the 2008 election, the government bailout of GM and Chrysler, and projections of unsustainable growth in healthcare costs, comprehensive reform moved back on to the policy agenda.

Following a raucous yearlong debate, President Obama achieved something that had eluded his predecessors: comprehensive health care. The Patient Protection and Affordable Care Act of 2010 is a complicated piece of legislation with several provisions that will be phased in over an eight-year period. Ultimately, the Act will extend insurance to some 30 million uninsured Americans using a combination of policy instruments. The Act imposes a mandate on individuals, requiring that all purchase insurance or face a penalty. Individuals with an income of up to 133 percent of the poverty line will be covered through an extension of Medicaid, whereas those who are between this threshold and 400 percent of the poverty line will receive subsidized insurance. Insurance companies are prohibited from denying coverage to, or imposing higher premiums or lifetime spending caps on, individuals with pre-existing conditions. The costs of the new healthcare plan are to be financed through fines imposed on companies that fail to insure their employees, an excise tax on expensive insurance plans, and reductions in the growth rate of Medicare expenditures. This last provision is of particular interest given that the Act also expands coverage of pharmaceuticals under Medicare Part D.

The Obama administration and the Democratic majorities have projected that the new healthcare act will slow the growth of medical expenditures, thereby reducing the long-term growth in the deficit. Whether this occurs— and whether the Act ultimately extends insurance to 30 million Americans— remains an open question. As noted above, key provisions are to be phased in over an eight-year period. Republican members of the House and Senate— none of whom voted in support of the legislation—have announced their intention to seek repeal based on grounds ranging from concerns over the budgetary implications to the potential use of public funds to subsidize abortions. Several states have announced their plans to challenge the constitutionality of various provisions of the Act (most importantly, the individual mandate). Critics have scrutinized the stylized assumptions incorporated into the Act and question whether there are sufficient provisions for cost containment. Ultimately, if the Patient Protection and Affordable Care Act survives these challenges, it will mark the largest expansion of the American welfare state since the Great Society. Whether it has the felicitous budgetary impacts claimed by its advocates or only further worsens the entitlement crisis will only become clear once it is fully implemented.[67]

Conclusion

An accurate description of the contemporary welfare state would have to note that the welfare state has never been larger. Despite the anti-welfare state rhetoric of past decades, there has been ongoing expansion. And yet, this expansion has been asymmetrical. Means-tested income support policies have languished and the welfare state for the non-elderly poor has never lived up to its aspirations. In sharp contrast, the welfare state for middle- and upper-income Americans has grown dramatically though the labyrinth of tax expenditures and entitlements for the elderly. Given the rhetorical framing of welfare in the United States, the greatest opponents of the welfare state likely do not realize that they are, in fact, its chief beneficiaries. Nonetheless, the most popular programs, as currently designed, are unsustainable given current demographic trends. In the past, presidents and the Congress have been more than willing to defer reform. The date for trust fund insolvency seemed to be well in the distance and of little concern relative to the short-term political costs of reform. But the day of reckoning cannot be put off indefinitely.

The Neoliberal Regime was premised, in part, on a faith in markets, a reduced role for the state, tax reductions, and skepticism toward traditional welfare state policies. Can these beliefs be retained given the need for genuine reform in the large entitlement programs? Given important functions served by Social Security and Medicare and their popularity, we can assume that they will not be abandoned. Yet, the opportunity set facing policies makers is quite constrained. They may choose to introduce dramatic increases in marginal tax rates to generate the general revenues necessary to offset the imbalances in the trust funds. They may decide to reduce the trajectory of growth through explicit or implicit means testing. They may embrace larger, overarching reforms, building on the Patient Protection and Affordable Care Act of 2010. While the future of the nation's large entitlement programs is impossible to predict, it is clear that reforms will be necessary and in each case they will force a departure from the governing principles of the Neoliberal Regime. At date uncertain, a future president may be able to declare that neoliberals declared a war on the welfare state, and the welfare state won.

9 The Global Economy and the Persistence of the State

A specter is haunting the economies of the world—the specter of globalization. Reminiscent of the Communist Manifesto, many tracts on globalization identify an inevitable process that will dramatically and permanently transform the economies and polities of the world, rendering irrelevant old relations of production and, perhaps, the nation state itself. Globalization's sharpest critics are convinced that the expansion of trade and economic integration constitute a disaster characterized by the loss of manufacturing jobs in nations like the United States, growing inequality both nationally and globally, and a trade-induced regulatory race to the bottom with unparalleled environmental costs. In sharp contrast, the celebrants of globalization see a process that will bring a new world of unprecedented prosperity, endless consumer choices, and a dramatic diminution of the state. For neoliberals, this new world has been possible only because so many nations have discovered the benefits of free trade and rejected the interventionist state.

These are extreme positions, to be certain. A sober evaluation suggests that globalization is a complex process with costs and benefits; sweeping conclusions are inferior to a careful consideration of both sides of the ledger. Even if one concludes that the benefits exceed the costs, there is little to suggest that globalization marks some world-historical triumph of the market. As argued in previous chapters, public policy and institutions play a central role in constituting the economy and shaping patterns of economic interaction. This is true whether one is considering a national economy or the international economy. The key question is whether the existing configuration of policies and institutions—national and international—is adequate. When examining the process of globalization, there is much to suggest that it is not. Ironically, the success of globalization may depend not on the absence of institutions and public policies, but on their strength and robustness.

The term "globalization" has been defined in a vast variety of ways. As Douglas Kellner notes, the term "is often used as a code word that stands for a tremendous diversity of issues and problems and serves as a front for a variety of theoretical and political positions" ranging from imperialism and "the imposition of the logic of capital" to "the continuation of modernization and a force of progress, increased wealth, freedom, democracy, and happiness."[1] Here the term globalization will simply be used to describe "the cluster of technological, economic, and political innovations that have drastically reduced the barriers to economic, political, and cultural exchange."[2] This chapter explores globalization of trade and finance and the implications for labor, the autonomy of national policymakers, and the environment. Advocates of globalization argue that the expansion of the global market necessitates the diminution of the state. But if the economy—in its local, national, *and* international manifestations—is constituted by decisions about policy and institutional design, then the expansion of the global economy cannot be fruitfully viewed as some inexorable trend driven by the logic of the market. It may be the case that policies and institutions are ill-suited to manage the dynamics of the international economy, but this is a far different claim. If the instability and dislocations are a product of the disjunction between the expansion of the global economy and existing policies and institutions, there is a strong case for addressing the imbalance.

Globalization of Trade and the Organization of Production

The chief benefits of trade derive from the theory of comparative advantage. Every nation has a certain endowment of resources, labor and capital that allows it to produce certain kinds of goods and services more efficiently than other goods and services. Trade creates the opportunity for specialization. Even if a nation has no absolute advantage, it can still gain through specialization, thereby contributing to higher levels of prosperity. Even if nations do not gain equally through trade, theoretically, trade should provide all nations with higher levels of wealth than would exist under autarky. Additionally, the heightened competition induced by trade should provide consumers with lower prices, higher quality, and a greater range of consumption options.

As explained in Chapter 5, the General Agreement on Tariffs and Trade (GATT) initiated a process that resulted in dramatic reductions in trade barriers. This combined with cost-saving changes in transportation technologies (e.g., air transportation, containerization, bulk shipping) and enhanced means of coordinating exchanges (e.g., through telecommunications and the internet) facilitated an expansion of trade. There was also dramatic growth in the number of nations involved in international markets, largely as a result of changes in development strategies and the collapse of the Soviet Union. Early in the postwar period, developing countries focused on import-substitution industrialization, using a combination of tariffs and public investments to develop industries to provide goods for domestic consumers. As part of the turn to neoliberalism, the International Monetary Fund (IMF) and the World Bank began to impose the "Washington consensus," which mandated export-based development strategies, privatization, deregulation, and price stabilization as the preconditions of assistance. Between 1982 and 1999, 40 Less Developed Countries (LDCs) reduced their tariffs by an average of

60 percent, with comparable reductions in non-tariff barriers. Similarly, the percentage of LDCs with open trade increased from 15 percent in the early 1970s to 64 percent by 1999. Trade dependence (the combination of imports and exports) increased from an average of 55 percent of GDP in 1970 to an average of 85 percent three decades later.[3]

Participation in trade would become a vital component of growth. For the 24 nations that belong to the Organization for Economic Cooperation and Development (OECD), trade grew at almost twice the pace of output in the decades following 1960.[4] For the period 2000–2007, for example, world GDP and merchandise production increased by an annual average of 3 percent, whereas merchandise exports grew by 5.5 percent, and manufacturing exports by 6.5 percent.[5] A comparable story can be told for LDCs. Jeffrey Sachs and Andrew Warner, for example, found that open economies experienced a 2 percent higher level of growth in per capita income than nations that were closed to trade. Most recently, Romain Wacziarg and Karen Horn Welch found that nations that liberalized trade experienced annual growth rates that were some 1.5 percent higher than before they liberalized.[6]

The positive relationship between trade expansion and income growth needs be qualified in two senses. First, although the percentage of the world living in extreme poverty fell from 52 percent to 25 percent between 1981 and 2005, some regions of the developing world seem relatively untouched by trade liberalization and its beneficial impacts on growth.[7] Poverty in Sub-Saharan Africa, most notably, remains virtually unchanged. Second, while globalization had positive ramifications for the poor, it also exacerbated global income inequality. As Joseph A. Stiglitz warns:

> Hidden beneath the surface in these econometric studies of globalization is another subtext: because globalization has proven so good for growth and poverty reduction, critics of globalization must be wrong. But these cross-sectional studies cannot address the most fundamental criticisms of globalization as it has been practiced: that it is unfair and that its benefits have disproportionately gone to rich people.

Stiglitz cautions that

> econometric studies on globalization, growth and poverty have been a misleading distraction, shifting the debate away from where it should be— on the appropriateness of particular policies for particular countries, on how globalization can be shaped (including the rules of the game) and on international economic institutions, to better promote growth and reduce poverty in the developing world.[8]

The impact of growing trade has had mixed implications for the United States. During the post-1960 period, the United States became far more integrated into world trade, as revealed by statistics on imports and exports. In

1960, combined imports and exports constituted 7.9 percent of GDP, a figure which grew to 12.3 percent of GDP by 1980. This number would rise to 29.7 percent by 2008. Adjusted for inflation, the combination of imports and exports in 2008 was 5.5 times greater than it had been in 1980. Yet, as a result of a growing number of participants in the global economy, the growth in US import-export activity would be combined with a reduction in its international economic power. In the immediate postwar period, the United States was responsible for 28.1 percent of the world's exports, making it the world's largest exporting nation. However, this share would fall precipitously over the next six decades to 8.5 percent by 2007, placing it behind Germany (9.7 percent) and China (8.9 percent). At the same time, the United States has remained the largest importer, responsible for 14.5 percent of world imports in 2007. Thus, what became an increasingly source of concern was the mounting trade deficits. The trade deficits that began to widen in the 1980s, expanded at a far more dramatic pace during the post- 2000 period. Indeed, by 2005, the trade deficit was almost as great as the inflation-adjusted sum of imports and exports in 1980 and constituted some 5.6 percent of GDP.[9]

The growing integration of the United States in the world economy coincided with changes in the organization of production. During much of the twentieth century, US manufactures employed systems of mass production and mass consumption commonly referred to as Fordism (a reference to Henry Ford, who combined mass production of the Model T with pricing that made it available to a mass market). In contrast, post-Fordism was grounded in "a higher degree of specialization, greater flexibility and faster turnover time," which was facilitated by transportation and communication innovations. As James H. Mittelman explains, this forced a "spatial reorganization of production." That is, corporations in the United States (and other wealthy democracies) increasingly outsourced production as developing nations with lower labor costs "upgraded their manufacturing industries, initially through labour intensity, and climbed to a higher position in the global division of labour."[10] Many US firms that were once manufacturing their products domestically, could now purchase components from producers in multiple nations in hopes of gaining cost-based and differentiation-based advantages.

The impact of this reorganization of production is evident in the decline in US manufacturing. Consider the case of iron and steel production, an area that the United States once dominated. The US share of iron and steel exports has fallen steadily, and as of 2007, it constituted a mere 3.2 percent of world exports. At the same time, the United States is the world's largest importer of steel (7.7 percent). While the United States was losing market share, China's iron and steel industry was growing at a phenomenal pace. Between 2002 and 2007, China's iron and steel exports increased by an average annual rate of 73 percent, making it the world's largest exporter of iron and steel by 2007 when it claimed 10.9 percent of the world's exports. In automobile products, the United States' share of world exports fell from 11.9 to 9.2 percent of world exports between 1980 and 2007, while it remained the world's largest automobile importer (18.5 percent).[11] The bankruptcies of General Motors and Chrysler in 2008–9 were a striking testament to how much the terms of trade had changed.

One might not bemoan the decline of these old industries if they were replaced by high-tech industries that would provide an alternative source of high-income manufacturing jobs for blue-collar workers. But here the record is relatively clear. In telecommunications and electronic data processing equipment—important fields given the ubiquity of computers—the United States' share of world exports has fallen rapidly. In 1980, the United States was the world's second largest exporter after Japan, claiming 19.5 percent of world markets. This share fell steadily to 8.9 percent by 2007. Once again, the United States was the single largest importer of these goods, accounting for 16 percent of world imports. Similarly, the United States' share of the world's electronic data processing equipment exports fell from 7.4 to 4 percent between 2000 and 2007, making it a net importer. In integrated circuits and electronic components, the United States' share of world exports fell from 20.4 to 12.1 percent between 2000–2007.[12]

One of the few areas where the US exports held up is in the area of business, professional and technical services. Here, the United States is second only to the combined nations of the European Union. In 2006, the United States exported some $61 billion worth of these services. And this sector employed over 16 million people—more than employed in manufacturing—to provide some $1.4 billion in value-added and accounting for 11 percent of GDP.[13] Yet, many of these positions were occupied by what Robert Reich referred to as "symbolic analysts," workers who "solve, identify, and broker problems by manipulating symbols." They are "distinguished from the rest of the population by their global linkages, good schools, excellent health care, and abundance of security guards." It is Reich's contention that the benefits of globalization accrue to these individuals, leaving the remainder of the population "growing gradually poorer ... powerless to alter these trends."[14] Indeed, the decades that witnessed this transformation coincided with the growth in income inequality and reduced investments in that part of the welfare state designed to assist those who would have benefited from the industrial jobs that were no longer available.

One of the most salient issues in US domestic politics (and elsewhere in the OECD countries) has been the impact of trade on wages. Let us begin with the general argument before exploring the empirics. The argument regarding the impact of trade on wages usually takes one of two forms. One variant compares the high levels of capital mobility to the relative immobility of labor. As barriers to trade and investment have been reduced, many argue that corporations seeking the highest rates of return have responded by outsourcing to nations with lower labor costs and less stringent workplace regulations.[15] Nations hoping to attract investment (or prevent capital flight) have responded by being less accommodating to labor. The second variant of the argument is grounded in factor-price equalization. That is, absent trade barriers, the prices of outputs will equalize, and with it, the factors of production. In the long run, one should expect a convergence of wages among trading partners. The model assumes that nations engaged in trade employ the same technologies and are functioning under conditions of perfect competition. They will thus confront common marginal productivity relationships that will dictate a common set of wages and rents for a given price. These stylized conditions rarely hold and there is a host of policy-related and institutional factors that create a good deal of cross-national variation (for example, minimum wage laws, more generous welfare benefits, levels of unionization). Nonetheless, one should expect free trade to place downward pressure on the wages in high wage countries like the United States, and raise the wage levels in nations with lower wage structures. As the wages for low-skilled workers decline, the gap in incomes between low- and high-skilled labor within nations should grow, giving rise to higher levels of inequality.

There is little question that growing levels of global integration have been combined with declines in unionization levels in the United States and, to a lesser extent, other OECD countries. In the so-called Golden Age of the 1950s and 1960s, productivity gains were commonly passed on to labor (See Chapter 5). Yet, in recent decades, the threat and reality of outsourcing has limited union gains and reduced their appeal more generally. As George Ross notes:

> Intensified economic internationalization was bound to increase the vulnerability of Western unions because it ended the relative insulation of postwar national political economies. Spillovers from increasing trade, globalized financial markets, and corporate regime shopping reduced the effectiveness of national policies. Other national regulatory capacities declined, while the costs of national policies running counter to international market logics rose. Capital found new options to exit from national contexts and new ways of expanding the spatial scope of markets.[16]

One should not be surprised that since the 1970s, the only areas that have witnessed gains in unionization rates are low-end service industries and the public sector, both of which are largely insulated from the forces of global competition.

Given that unionization has led, historically, to higher wages, the decline in unionization has coincided with downward pressure on the wages of less-skilled workers in the United States over the course of the last several decades. This, in turn, is one of the factors that has contributed to growing levels of income inequality. In 2008, for example, the OECD reported that with the exception of Turkey and Mexico, "the United States is the country with the highest inequality level and poverty rate across the OECD." The average income of the top 10 percent of the population is the highest in the OECD, whereas the lowest 10 percent is 20 percent below the OECD average. The trend in growing inequality dates back to the 1970s, but accelerated since the mid-1980s and was greater in the United States than in other member nations, creating the highest levels of postwar inequality.[17]

Growing inequality and the stagnant incomes of unskilled and low-skilled workers is a complex phenomenon, and there is little question that it reflects a host of factors including demographic trends and changes in social policy. Opponents of free trade who attribute overwhelming importance to globalization may overstate their case. There is something of a consensus that trade with low-wage countries has been responsible for some 15 percent of the reduction in demand for unskilled and less educated labor. In nations with rigid wage structures and high levels of social spending, the result tends to be a rise in unemployment. In nations like the United States, with more flexible labor markets, the impact falls on wages. There is also evidence that the jobs created for export markets tend to pay salaries that are 12 to 17 percent higher than those they eliminate. Yet, without active labor market policies in place that facilitate the transition and provide displaced workers with the skills they need to assume the new positions, the alternatives may be unemployment or employment in low-end non-traded service positions that provide lower salaries.[18]

Globalization of Finance

Globalization is not simply a matter of production but extends to finance as well. As noted in Chapter 6, Nixon ended the dollar's convertibility into gold in August of 1971. The subsequent oil crisis and the inflation-driven disintermediation of the 1970s led to a massive influx of dollars into global capital markets, which became increasingly important in funding industry and government debt. The Eurodollar market—US denominated dollars in banks outside of the nation's borders and beyond the reach of US financial regulators—would become of ever-greater importance in subsequent decades, adding liquidity to the world economy. But there were significant problems as well. First, and most obviously, the growth of international financial markets complicated domestic economic management (e.g., the Fed's control of monetary aggregates and its ability to predict the impact of open market operations). Second, the lack of an international institution that could manage the market, exert regulatory oversight, and serve a lender of last resort function, meant that central bankers and finance ministers would increasingly have to discover means of cooperating in the face of foreign exchange crises.

While the financial system can be modeled as free floating capital moving through self-equilibrating markets, such characterizations fail to recognize the dense network of institutions and actors that comprise the system. Certainly, the IMF and World Bank remain the largest institutions, and the IMF's role has become increasingly complex in a post–Bretton Woods world of floating exchange rates. But there are also financial institutions—banks and large institutional investors—that shape the dynamics in global financial markets. As several analysts have observed, while it is true that there has been a greater diffusion of stock ownership in the past several decades, control of these investments has been concentrated in a relatively small number of large institutional investors. As Adam Harmes argues: "By centralizing investment decision making within disintermediated capital markets, institutional investors seem to have increased the ability of investors to exercise direct forms of power over corporate and sovereign borrowers." One of the effects, according to Harmes, is that the institutional investors have used their control to reproduce "neoliberal restructuring among sovereign borrowers."[19] That is, they have favored nations that embrace market-based reforms, reduced trade barriers and capital controls, and maintain limited welfare states, thereby perpetuating this model globally. More troubling, perhaps, is the observation that large institutional investors can often engage in a form of "herd mentality." In a global context, investors rarely have sufficient knowledge of events in each individual economy. As a result, they tend to respond to relatively small triggering events or the decisions of a single large investor, exiting markets *en masse*. The consequences can be disastrous, creating financial distress for nations even if there is scant evidence to support a more general loss of confidence.[20]

The difficulties of negotiating this new international financial system and the implications for the relative position of the United States became quite evident in the 1980s. The Reagan administration's large budget deficits and high interest rates attracted international capital and inflated the value of the dollar. The strengthening of the dollar significantly worsened the US trade position, increasing dramatically the cost of US exports and threatening the durability of the recovery. Initially, the Reagan Treasury announced that it would not intervene in international markets to stabilize the dollar. In the words of C. Randall Henning and I.M. Destler,

> [US] policy was unilateral at the core. Treasury remained unmoved by the strong objections of the European finance ministries and central banks … . The pervasive attitude was that if foreign governments disliked the depreciation of their currencies against the dollar, they should adjust their macroeconomic policies to better emulate those of the US.[21]

Yet, with growing imports and, more importantly, manufacturing imports, it was clear that the exchange rate effects of the Reagan fiscal and monetary policy mix were having powerful negative impacts, much to the dismay of US-based multinational businesses and a growing bloc in Congress advocating protectionism.

When James A. Baker assumed the position of Treasury Secretary in 1985, things changed dramatically. Through quiet diplomacy, Baker convinced the other members of the Group of 5 (or G-5) finance ministers to support a cooperative realignment of currencies, an agreement that found formal expression in the Plaza Accord of September 1985. The Plaza Accord was clear recognition of the need "to employ and strengthen multilateral institutions as a means of helping to solve US as well as international economic problems."[22] With the decline of the United States as an economic hegemon, the nation could no longer adopt a unilateralist position nor could it assume the responsibilities it had embraced in the early postwar decades. International cooperation became imperative. But it was by no means easy or efficacious. The Plaza Accord coincided with a loosening of US monetary policy, thereby reducing the pressure on the dollar. Combined with the interventions of the G-5 finance ministers, this led to a 25 percent reduction in the value of the dollar relative to key currencies, but it simultaneously had strong negative implications for nations that had profited from their exports to the United States. Increasingly, Europe and Japan resented the sense that their domestic political economies were being held hostage to the high deficit policies in the United States and tired of ongoing pressure to adopt more stimulative domestic policies to increase the demand for US exports. In February 1987, the finance ministers met once again and agreed to the Louvre Accord. The United States agreed to reduce its budget deficit to 2.3 percent of GNP for fiscal year 1988, and, in turn, Japan, West Germany, and France agreed to more stimulative domestic policies. Collectively, the finance ministers agreed to intervene to maintain exchange rates within target zones of 5 percent from the rates that existed at the time, creating a system of managed floats (i.e., rates could float on a day-to-day basis without active intervention, unless they exceeded certain boundaries).

The months following the Louvre Accord were marked increasingly by instability in financial markets, a continued fall in the value of the dollar, and growing divisions between the United States and the G-5. The world's stock markets collapsed on "Black Monday," October 19, 1987, with the Dow Jones Industrial Average losing 22.61 percent of its value (and even greater losses elsewhere). According to Toyoo Gyohten, Japan's former Vice Minister for Finance, a "fundamental cause [of the market crash] was the failure to achieve real results in coordinating the macroeconomic policies of the seven major economic powers." Following Black Monday, finance ministers were hesitant to call another meeting, fearing that a failure to achieve results would lead to further instability. Instead they issued a vague "Christmas Communiqué" that said little of substance other than "any further decline of the dollar would be counterproductive." In Gyohten's judgment, this "marked the end of a somewhat confused three-year process, the results of which were not very satisfactory ... because all of our efforts in aligning exchange rates and coordinating macroeconomic policy had failed to produce tangible, clear results."[23] In subsequent decades, there have been additional efforts at coordination, often with limited results. A new institutional architecture comparable to what existed under Bretton Woods has yet to emerge to bring stability to global financial markets.

Leonard Silk identified one of the key lessons of the monetary instability of the 1980s:

In a closely integrated world it is risky for any single nation, even the largest economy in the world, acting alone, to pursue a strongly stimulative policy without weakening its trade position and its financial structure—and without posing a threat to the international system.[24]

While there was a strong theoretical case for coordination, skeptics were convinced there was simply too much uncertainty, too little consensus about the way the world works, and too many domestic obstacles for effective harmonization. As Paul Volcker described the position:

> Better, in that view, for countries to concentrate on what seems most urgent and what they know most about—their own needs—permitting the exchange rate to fluctuate as it will to accommodate imbalances .... efforts to coordinate might too easily divert attention and political effort from what needed to be done at home.[25]

With the brief exception of the late 1990s, the United States has continued to generate high trade deficits and budgetary deficits. Trade deficits contributed greatly to the flow of dollars in international markets, and these dollars became an important source of funding for the growing national debt. By the end of 2008, more than $3 trillion of US government debt was held by foreigners, the largest single purchaser being the People's Republic of China.[26] Much of the money derived by the nation's persistent trade deficit was recycled into US capital markets, artificially reducing the interest rate, producing remarkable price stability, and fueling additional consumption. As long as there was a market for the debt, a politically popular pattern of high consumption, low taxes, and low savings could continue indefinitely, or so it was believed. As Niall Ferguson notes, this was a historical anomaly.

> A hundred years ago, the global hegemon—the United Kingdom—was a net exporter of capital, channeling a high proportion of its savings overseas to finance the construction of infrastructure such as railways and ports in the Americas, Asia, Australasia, and Africa. Today, its successor as an Anglophone empire plays the diametrically opposite role—as the world's debtor rather than the world's creditor, absorbing around three-quarters of the rest of the world's surplus savings.[27]

Other nations encountered far greater difficulties. Those with exchange rates fixed to the dollar had no control over US decisions that would affect the stability of their national economies. Nations that sought to manage their currencies with adjustable pegs often became subject to speculation. The vulnerability to market volatility proved the greatest in developing countries that, at the behest of the United States and the IMF, also engaged in capital market liberalization while failing to have in place the kind of social policies that would help mitigate the effects of economic dislocations.[28]

The Asian crisis of 1997 provides the best single example of the difficulties facing developing nations. Beginning in the 1980s, a number of East Asian nations began drawing more heavily on international capital markets to fuel development. Between 1990 and 1996, foreign debt as a proportion of GDP increased dramatically in key economies (e.g., from 14 to 28 percent in South Korea, from 33 to 50 percent in Thailand), with significant increases in short-term debt as a proportion of total debt. Highly leveraged firms, in turn, became more vulnerable to fluctuations in interest rates and any forces that might result in reductions in capacity utilization. Thailand, which had been expanding exports at an annual rate of 20 percent between 1990 and 1995, encountered an economic downturn in 1996. As imports continued to flow into the nation, severe balance of payments problems emerged. Because the East Asian economies were tightly coupled, the problem spread rapidly through the region. When the Thai government, no longer capable of defending its currency against speculation, announced in July 1997 its decision to float the baht, the crisis worsened dramatically. Credit rating agencies downgraded the debt rating of these nations—in some cases to junk bond status—and large hedge funds and investors rapidly adjusted their portfolios. In 1996, some $97 billion in private capital had flooded into these countries, but in 1997, there was a reversal of $109 billion, the equivalent of 10 percent of the combined GDP of the nations in question. As Aseem Prakash notes: "It is doubtful if any country can withstand an exogenous shock of this magnitude." Following the downgrading of debt, the "herd behavior" in international capital markets took over, causing "a veritable bank run" that was exacerbated by "the absence of the international lender of last resort."[29]

In the end, the IMF initiated the largest bailout in its history, providing loans in excess of $100 billion. To prevent further depreciation, it demanded adherence to austerity measures, including a tight monetary policy and a reduction of government budgets, to be achieved through cuts in social spending, infrastructure investments, and subsidies. As many critics correctly anticipated, the emphasis on austerity served to worsen the domestic economies of the nations in question. As recessions deepened, currencies continued to lose their value, and capital flight worsened, the IMF moderated some of its demands. But the damage was done.[30] The IMF's response to the crisis was ironic. It had celebrated the rapid development of Thailand, with the highest growth rate in the world between 1985 and 1995. It supported its openness to international capital flows, and even though there were high levels of indebtedness, this debt had been incurred by the private sector rather than the government. Indeed, the government had been running budget surpluses and the IMF congratulated the Thai government for what it viewed as a "consistent record of sound macroeconomic policies" and the stable environment it had created for foreign investment. As Nicola Bullard, Walden Bello, and Kamal Mallhotra surmise, the IMF simply assumed that "left to its own devices, the market would ensure that equilibrium would be achieved in the capital transactions between private international creditors and investors and private domestic banks and enterprises. So not to worry." When the IMF was asked to come to the rescue, "it was to fix a crisis that had as one of its root causes a Fund prescription (the liberalisation of the capital account) that had led to a problem that the Fund had neither foreseen nor worried about (private sector overborrowing)."[31]

There are lively debates over how to interpret the Asian crisis (e.g., was it a product of so-called "crony capitalism" in the nations in question, a result of moral hazard stemming from the belief that international institutions would socialize the risk, a standard financial panic, followed by a "disorderly work-out, or an event triggered by banks seeking to adjust their balance sheets").[32] But regardless of which explanation one adopts, there are some overarching lessons. First, economies that were highly dependent on international capital flows as part of their development strategies were simultaneously vulnerable to changes in these flows. Second, the flow of capital in international markets is affected by large private institutions—credit rating agencies, hedge funds, large institutional investors—that are unaccountable for the negative consequences of their decisions. Third, there are often few options open to domestic policymakers when their reliance on international capital flows is so great. The high levels of external debt obligations foreclosed currency devaluation as a means to promote exports, and Japan, suffering from its own recession, simply lacked the capacity to promote an export-led recovery for the region. Finally, the international institutions that existed— most notably, the IMF—failed to serve as lender of last resort function in a timely fashion, and when it responded it eschewed a counter-cyclical response that could have prevented further collapse. In the wake of the Asian crisis, East Asian nations began to invest more heavily in regional institution-building, in part, to reduce their vulnerability to the IMF and larger financial market forces.[33]

For neoliberal advocates of globalization who celebrated what they saw and the final triumph of markets and the withering away of the state, the Asian crisis had a sobering effect. As Duncan Green and Matthew Griffith observe, as a result of the Asian crisis, "liberalization as a panacea was being called into question even by free market economists [and] ... prominent practitioners ... . Neo-liberal hubris gave way to cautious self-doubt, especially over the problems of liberalized capital markets."[34] Indeed, there is a growing body of research, reinforced by events like the Asian crisis, suggesting that the success of globalization may rest ultimately on the quality of domestic institutions and public policies. In the words of Martin Wolf,

> Globalization does not make states unnecessary. On the contrary, for people to be successful in exploiting the opportunities afforded by international integration, they need states at both ends of their transactions. Failed states, disorderly states, weak states, and corrupt states are shunned as the black holes of the global economic system.[35]

Given the potential dislocations created by globalization, it is somewhat ironic that the period that witnessed the rise of this phenomenon coincided with greater skepticism regarding the role of the social safety net in the United States. At a time when markets could create a host of new problems, policy-makers were often looking to markets for solutions.

Globalization and the Environment

One of the most salient concerns about globalization involves the impact on the environment. The core argument involves a regulatory "race to the bottom." In many ways, the argument resembles the parallel argument about the effects of globalization on wages. Reduced barriers to trade and investment have enhanced capital mobility. In their competition to attract capital, nations and states lower their regulatory standards. They prevent the introduction of regulations that would impose costs on domestic producers seeking to prevail in international markets. Globalization, in short, has unleashed a dynamic leading to the universal degradation of environmental standards. The outcome is often referred to as the "Delaware Effect," a reference to the downward pressure that Delaware's liberal requirements for corporate charters had on the laws of other states.

While the logic makes great sense, as Dan Drezner notes, "the lack of support for the ... argument is striking." Critics of globalization argue that the race to the bottom is inevitable and deterministic: "once states decide to lower their barriers to exchange, a Pandora's box is unleashed that cannot be reversed." And yet, as Drezner notes in a review of the literature:

> Although globalization has increased the size of transnational economic flows, it has not forced a race to the bottom in regulatory standards. Ideational forces have played an equally significant role in determining the rate and location of policy convergence on labor and environmental standards. Where harmonization has occurred, it has been a conscious choice of states made under the aegis of an international organization.[36]

At first glance, this conclusion seems counter-intuitive, so let us examine the question with some care.

It is commonly assumed that corporate managers have a fiduciary responsibility to maximize shareholder wealth. This should lead them to seek out the investment opportunities where costs are the lowest and regulations are weak or nonexistent. Yet, there is growing recognition that the pursuit of profitability requires the negotiation of a highly complex environment shaped by economic stakeholders (e.g., customers, suppliers, insurers, and financiers), by regulators, and social interests (e.g., environmental groups and community organizations).[37] Economic success may even require a corporate embrace of regulatory goals such as reduction of pollution and workplace disease and injuries. Certainly, some businesses may do this simply to prevent regulatory fines and liabilities, but there is clear evidence that the managers also recognize the importance of enhancing their corporate reputations among key stakeholders. As one analysis of the adoption of voluntary environmental management systems by S&P 500 firms concluded:

> while the potentially high costs of compliance with existing and anticipated regulations as well as the threat of liabilities are inducing firms to be more proactive about managing their environmental impacts, the direct effects of these pressures are not as strong as those of non regulatory pressures from consumers, investors and communities.[38]

Of course, firms may engage in a wide range of activities in hopes of managing their reputations. Some may be satisfied with public relations efforts that simply create an appearance of social responsibility; others may redesign products and processes and introduce internal management systems to reduce pollution, thereby going beyond what might be demanded by the most stringent regulations. In recent decades, several national and international trade associations have developed their own standards and model management systems for members, often in response to crises that threatened their legitimacy and led to fears of additional regulatory scrutiny. For example, the chemical industry, working through national and international associations, developed Responsible Care, a stringent self-regulatory program, in the wake of the 1984 chemical releases in a Union Carbide plant in Bhopal, India, that claimed tens of thousands of lives. These associations can create an institutional context for corporations to coordinate their behavior, share information, and develop an "industrial morality."[39] Such initiatives reflect, in part, recognition that corporations in some industries have a shared stake in industry reputation. They are, in essence, "hostages of each other," since one disaster can destroy the reputation of all and result in a rapid escalation of regulatory costs.[40]

International standards have also grown in importance with the expansion of global commerce. The International Organization for Standardization (ISO) in Geneva, Switzerland, has developed a host of standards through the participation of national standard-setting organizations (e.g., the American National Standards Institute in the United States). In the 1990s, for example, ISO began developing a series of process-based standards for environmental management systems designed to promote continuous improvement in pollution reduction. Firms seeking certification under the ISO 14001 standard must meet a rigorous set of criteria, be in compliance with laws and regulations, and, most importantly, have their compliance certified by third party auditors. By the end of 1996—the year ISO 14001 was released—1,491 organizations in forty-five countries were certified. By 2007, this number had grown to 154,572 organizations in 148 countries. Firms voluntarily accept these costs because certification is an important source of information in international markets, a means of establishing a corporate reputation under conditions of information scarcity. Moreover, many top corporations that have obtained certification will only contract with other firms that have received certification, thereby making it a *de facto* requirement for successful participation in many supply chains. In the automobile industry, for example, between 1996 and 1998, Ford Motors required that all of its facilities (some 140 plants in twenty-six countries) be certified under ISO 14001. Between 1999 and 2003, it phased in a requirement that all of its suppliers follow suit. Other firms followed Ford's example, essentially creating a single set of global environmental standards that obtained regardless of where facilities were located.[41]

In *Trading Up*, David Vogel notes: "Not only are there important conflicts between trade and regulatory policies, but their number and significance is likely to increase as regional and international efforts to promote economic integration clash with the continued disparity of national consumer and environmental regulations." But he also observes that "on balance, both global and regional economic integration has *increased* while consumer and environmental standards have become *stronger*."[42] Similarly, Aseem Prakash and Mathew Potoski conclude:

> In some ways, the WTO is not an enemy of the environment; because developed countries with stringent environmental standards absorb the bulk of developing-country exports, free trade can lead to a ratcheting-up of environmental product and process standards in developing countries.[43]

Trade associations and standards like ISO 14001 have been a central part of this process. Indeed, one should not be surprised that the nation with the largest number of ISO 14001 firms is China; exporters in a nation with weak domestic regulations have a strong stake in gaining certification to prove that their practices are acceptable to contractors and consumers in nations with stronger regulatory policies. As one analysis of self-regulation in China concluded: "globalization increases institutional and customer pressures on firms to surpass local requirements, even when they may be tempted by lax regulations and enforcement in countries offering themselves as pollution havens."[44] Once firms in export markets adopt tougher environmental standards, moreover, they have a strong incentive to seek a ratcheting up of domestic standards as a means of equalizing costs.

Although the dynamic described above is not universal, as a generalization trade has induced higher levels of self-regulation among firms and the adoption of universal standards regardless of the strength or weakness of domestic regulatory policies. Why does the race to the bottom thesis continue to be so compelling? Perhaps the political utility of the argument has simply trumped the empirics.[45] But even if the general thesis has weak empirical support, it is nonetheless the case that the global economic expansion has carried serious environmental ramifications. The high rates of industrial growth in nations like China have produced environmental problems that did not exist decades ago, exacerbating problems of climate change and endangering many critical ecosystems, many of which will disappear as a result of industrialization.

Developing nations face a difficult trade-off. The same pattern of rapid growth that compromises environmental quality also provides higher incomes, which have translated into reductions in infant mortality and growing life expectancies that were unachievable through the kinds of bilateral and multilateral assistance that were offered in the postwar period. This trade-off is not dissimilar to those faced in Western nations during a comparable stage of industrial development. The response must be one of creating viable regulatory institutions on the national level and international institutions capable of coordinating environmental policies and practices, while reinforcing the growing trend in environmental governance among firms engaged in the global economy.

The Limits of Globalization

Many observers have presented globalization as the inevitable and beneficial product of trade and financial liberalization and technological change, most importantly dramatic reductions in the costs of transportation and the broad dissemination of information technology, that have allowed for the emergence of global production networks. Yet, there may be natural limits to the process of globalization. Robert Z. Lawrence has contributed to our understanding of the limits through his comparison of shallow and deep integration. He argues that trade liberalization is best characterized as shallow integration. Nations have simply lowered barriers to the importation of goods and services. A deeper integration—the kind of integration that many associate with the term globalization—would involve a reconciliation of divergent national practices, for example, the coordination of key regulatory policies affecting the environment, health and safety standards, and competition.[46] The difficulties with deeper integration are formidable. First, it may be impossible for nations at different stages of development to adopt common policies. Some nations may not have developed a sufficient regulatory capacity or they may prove unwilling to make the trade-offs inherent in imposing new controls on producers. Second, many of the policies that would need to be reconciled to bring about a deeper integration are often insulated from change by domestic political coalitions. The stalemates encountered by later rounds of GATT and by the WTO have reflected the difficulties inherent in deeper forms of integration.

Given the potentially high costs of globalization, elected officials have a stake in providing protection for domestic constituents. Some groups have had little trouble in their search for protection. As noted in Chapter 5, GATT provided exemptions for agriculture, in recognition of the fact that the key participants in the drafting of the agreement had designed domestic programs to elevate farm incomes through setting quantitative restrictions on production. Whether or not one believes that such restrictions were justified at the time, it is clear that they have continued to create significant problems for LDCs that often have a comparative advantage in agricultural production. As the UN *Development Report* observes, wealthy nations "seldom waste an opportunity to emphasize the virtues of open markets, level playing fields and free trade, especially in their prescriptions for poor countries" while they "maintain a formidable array of protectionist barriers against developing countries" and heavily subsidize agriculture. "Hypocrisy and double standards are not strong foundations for a rules-based multilateral system geared towards human development."[47]

It is important to acknowledge, furthermore, that while the concept of globalization suggests a *global* reduction of barriers and flow of goods and services, often what is being addressed is more accurately described as regionalization. During the postwar period, as there was a strengthening of multilateral rules for trade, there was also a proliferation in regional trade agreements. As of 2005, there were 230 such agreements covering some 40 percent of world trade.[48] The North American Free Trade Agreement and the European Union are the two most significant examples of regional agreements. According to one recent analysis, the growth of regional trade agreements has actually *reduced* world trade in recent years.[49] Indeed, according to the WTO, between 2000 and 2007, trade flows within regions have been greater than trade between regions, fluctuating between 55 and 58 percent of world trade. While North America and Asia have shown something of a balance between interregional and intraregional trade, deepening economic integration within the European Union has resulted in a much faster growth of intraregional trade relative to interregional trade. In 2007, 68 percent of the trade flows of European states occurred within the European Union. Much higher levels of interregional trade, in contrast, have characterized Latin America, Africa, and the Middle East.[50] As intraregional trade expands relative to interregional trade, and policies are increasingly coordinated within regional blocs, the promise of a fully integrated world economy may never be realized.

Conclusion

If the specter of globalization is haunting the world, it is, in part, a product of decisions about policy and institutional design dating back to the immediate postwar period when nations collaborated to create the foundations for a new international economy. There is little theoretical or empirical support for maintaining the market-state dichotomy. Given that there are not two separate logics—a logic of the market and a logic of the state—there is no reason to assume that globalization is an inexorable process that mandates the diminution of the state and the elimination of policies that are insufficiently market-conforming. Even if this vision of state-economy relations has prevailed in the post-1980 period, its political utility has greatly exceeded its empirical and theoretical foundations.

And yet, even the political utility of the argument appears increasingly tattered. Recent decades have revealed the critical role that institutions can play. New, geographically dispersed, forms of production are difficult to control with regulations designed to function within national boarder. Production and outsourcing decisions can have devastating consequences for workers and communities forced to endure the collapse of established manufacturing industries, particularly if there is insufficient investment in active labor market policies designed to inculcate the skills necessary for participation in emerging industries. The decisions of large hedge funds and institutional investors can have catastrophic implications for nations, particularly those that lack strong national institutions. These are all policy problems that cannot be addressed adequately under the core assumptions of the Neoliberal Regime.

10 The Financial Crisis and the Great Recession

The financial crisis of 2008 and the subsequent recession were products, in part, of what was arguably the greatest regulatory failure of the postwar period. For some, the costs were primarily material. They lost their jobs, their homes, their retirement funds and their invitation to participate in the "ownership society." For others, the costs were ideological, as the crisis forced a reevaluation of core foundational assumptions about the political economy. Efforts to diagnose the sources of the crisis and design a new regulatory architecture began in earnest in the autumn of 2008. This episode is of great interest. Most immediately, the stakes involved are enormous. The new regulatory system could prevent a future financial crisis from occurring or, at the very least, minimize the damage. Moreover, it is of inherent interest insofar as the crisis and its economic consequences were in many ways a product of the larger neoliberal agenda that found an expression for a generation in key policy decisions.

The general description of what occurred from the mid-1990s to the collapse of the financial markets is relatively straightforward, even if the details are somewhat opaque. During the period, great demand for housing led to a significant asset bubble in real estate. Home ownership between 1998 and 2006 expanded dramatically (from 64 to 69 percent). Real estate markets showed signs of stress in the second quarter of 2006, and as prices began a decline mortgage defaults increased dramatically. By 2007, the effects spread into a financial system with large investments in mortgage-backed securities. The immediate aftermath of the collapse was significant. It forced the failure or near failure of major investment houses and commercial banks, some of which were only saved via large infusions of public funds. The federal government was forced to adopt extraordinary measures to save the government sponsored enterprises (GSEs) that had securitized mortgages to add liquidity to housing markets—the Federal National Mortgage Association (Fannie Mae) and the Federal Home Loan Mortgage Corporation (Freddie Mac)—and the American Insurance Group (AIG) that had insured the mortgage-backed securities through the issuance of credit-default swaps. The Federal Reserve stepped in to rescue Bear Stearns and Citigroup. The Federal Deposit Insurance Corporation (FDIC) increased deposit insurance from $100,000 to $250,000 and extended a guarantee to all senior unsecured bank debt. As of 2009, the combined costs of the bailout and stimulus package required borrowing $1.7 trillion, the largest one-year issuance of debt in the nation's history and (as a proportion of GDP), the largest since World War II.[1] In terms of direct expenditures, it was larger than the dual wars in Iraq and Afghanistan and the Savings and Loan bailout of the late 1980s combined. The government assumed, in addition, potential commitments of more than $10 trillion.[2]

A decade that began with celebrations of the market ended with unprecedented foreclosures and bailouts, and open discussions of the merits of bank nationalization. As analysts sought to explain the sources of the crisis, the portrayals took a few forms. One explanation focused on greedy speculators seeking to acquire ever-greater wealth, wicked mortgage bankers who preyed on the weak, and indolent regulators who shirked their duties. A second narrative indicted the ideological blindness of market zealots who stripped away regulation only to discover to their horror that markets do, indeed, fail. A third, somewhat more sophisticated portrayal described the way in which market innovations outstripped the regulatory structures introduced in the New Deal and largely caught regulators by surprise. Although each of these stories contains some truth, none is particularly compelling when taken in isolation. Getting the story right is imperative given the role that the crisis could play in stimulating change in the regulatory system.

Deregulation in Context

The history of regulatory change in the United States has been part of the larger dynamic of regime change. As noted in Chapter 2, the emergence of a new regime does not involve the elimination of old regimes. New policies are layered upon earlier policies, giving rise to a complex and at times contradictory labyrinth of policies and institutions. As a result, regulatory performance reflects not simply the efficacy of the most current regime, but the policies and institutions inherited from the past and the friction between these regimes. As shown in previous chapters, the Progressive and New Deal regimes dramatically expanded the role of regulation and by the early 1970s, the nation had a rather complicated regulatory structure comprised of public policies and institutions that had been created over the course of the past century and reflected very different assumptions regarding the justification for public policy and appropriate models of administration and agency-interest group relations.

This regulatory system came under significant pressure as economic performance deteriorated in the mid-1970s, bringing about another period of regulatory change. Stagflation and flailing US competitiveness created a window of opportunity for deregulation and regulatory reforms. The deregulatory debates were framed, in part, by the economic theory of regulation, a theory that became a staple of the public choice perspective on the state.[3] The core problem was institutional. The regulatory policy process was modeled as a set of mutually beneficial exchanges between profit-maximizing firms and vote-maximizing elected officials. Corporations sought regulation as a means of restricting competition via barriers to entry and exit, controlling flow to market, and administering prices. Elected officials were more than happy to provide these policies, which extracted significant rents from consumers. Many conservative advocates of deregulation (and regulatory reform more generally) had a powerful faith in the self-regulating capacities of markets; others, drawn from the consumer movement, simply anticipated that deregulation would deliver lower prices and greater opportunities.

Deregulation has often been characterized in relatively simplistic terms as the removal of state controls and a transfer of authority from the government to the market. Yet, as argued in Chapter 2, the law constitutes the economy and regulates the kinds of governance mechanisms that firms can use to coordinate their behavior. The key actors in the economy are legally constituted entities. Even if government agencies were no longer formally coordinating economic behavior (e.g., by assigning routes, setting prices, or maintaining barriers to entry), law nonetheless creates an institutional structure within which governance regimes evolve.[4] Myriad decisions regarding macro-economic management, tax expenditures, and social policy had dramatic and unanticipated consequences for performance. In sum, one cannot draw some clear line of demarcation between the "state" and the "market" even when discussing deregulated industries. Markets are constituted by policy decisions, even under deregulation. With this in mind, let us briefly consider the financial deregulation that gained momentum in the 1970s and continued for the next several decades.

Regulating and Deregulating Finance

The regulatory system for finance that emerged in the early decades of the twentieth century was highly complex, initially consisting of the Treasury Department's Comptroller of the Currency and, after 1913, the Federal Reserve. For state chartered banks, state regulators were the primary actors, and they were sheltered from competition by the McFadden Act of 1927, which essentially banned interstate banking. The New Deal brought massive changes in financial regulation through the passage of the Glass-Steagall Act in 1933, which separated commercial and investment banking. It empowered the Fed, through Regulation Q, to set low interest rates for savings while prohibiting interest for demand deposits (i.e., checking). The FDIC insured deposits, in hopes of preventing runs on the banks. By the end of the 1930s, regulations had created distinct financial sub-industries, each defined by the products and services it offered, each with its own set of regulators. The New Deal system provided stability in finance, a clear departure from the earlier history of financial turmoil. As Thomas H. Hammond and Jack H. Knott observe, financial regulations, like other economic regulations, created "a cartel-like regime with state and federal regulatory agencies acting as the enforcers."[5] Regulations defined markets and created barriers to entry. Interest rate regulations eliminated price competition and the FDIC prevented bankruptcies.

During the 1960s and 1970s, the financial industry—and the regulations that created it—came under increasing stress, largely as a result of growing inflationary pressures. Interest rate regulations in an inflationary era made it difficult to attract deposits, while the very regulations that delineated the sub-industries limited the capacity of financial institutions to pursue new sources of profit. During the late 1960s, "regulators responded by trying to plug every new leak in the dike of regulation as it opened up, only to find a new leak elsewhere."[6] By the 1970s, this was no longer sufficient. State-level innovations created increasing pressure on federally regulated institutions. For example, in 1972 Massachusetts authorized Negotiated Order of Withdrawal (or NOW) accounts that paid interest and provided checking, thereby giving mutual savings banks in the state a competitive advantage. Other so-called "non-bank banks" began to offer higher rates of return, thereby making them preferable in a period of high inflation. The resulting disintermediation (i.e., the flow of funds outside of regulated financial intermediaries) forced policy changes designed to accommodate market innovations.

Although deregulation began incrementally, Congress passed major deregulatory statutes that removed many of the policies and institutions that had promoted financial stability since the New Deal. In 1980, Congress passed the Depository Institutions Deregulation and Monetary Control Act (DIDMCA), which had several important implications for financial regulation. Before its passage, banks that were members of the Federal Reserve System were required to place non-interest-bearing reserves at the district Federal Reserve Bank, placing them at a competitive disadvantage and creating incentives to exit the Federal Reserve System. Under DIDMCA, there was a phased reduction of reserve requirements and the Fed's controls were extended to cover uniformly the reserves of all depository institutions. More importantly, DIDMCA phased out Regulation Q, which both prevented price competition and channeled savings toward housing markets by mandating a slightly higher interest rate for savings and loans (S&Ls, or thrifts). Interest rate deregulation could place thrifts at a disadvantage, given their portfolios of long-term, fixed-rate mortgages. Thus, DIDMCA permitted them to invest up to 20 percent of their assets in commercial paper, corporate debt, and consumer loans. It also permitted them to issue credit cards; NOW accounts were authorized for all depository institutions.[7] Ironically, as institutions were given greater latitude in the investments they could make, Congress also increased the coverage of deposit insurance (from $40,000 to $100,000).

The changes initiated by DIDMCA came too late for many S&Ls. Inflation had driven up the interest rates they had to pay to attract funds, and these rates could not be supported with the returns being generated by real estate portfolios. These problems, combined with the deep recession in the early 1980s, forced a growing number of S&L bankruptcies. In 1982, Congress passed the Garn-St. Germain Depository Institutions Act. It enhanced regulators' capacity to manage financial institutions by extending the powers of the FDIC and the Federal Savings and Loan Insurance Corporation (FSLIC) to make deposits in troubled institutions, assume their liabilities, and engineer mergers between failing and healthy institutions. The Act had major positive implications for thrifts. It authorized money market deposit accounts that would pay market rates with checking services. It also allowed depository institutions to offer NOW accounts to federal, state and local governments and to provide demand deposits. The Act permitted federal S&Ls to hold a greater percentage of commercial and consumer loans in their portfolios, and allowed them to invest in state and local government revenue bonds. Moreover, institutions could now offer adjustable rate mortgages, thereby reducing their vulnerability to inflation.[8]

If S&Ls were the big winners in Garn-St. Germain, they nonetheless found themselves in increasing turmoil. A real estate boom in the early to mid-1980s created new opportunities for profitable investments in commercial and residential real estate. But when the Tax Reform Act of 1986 reduced the tax advantages of these investments, the speculative bubble popped. As the Congressional Budget Office explained:

> When many S&Ls became insolvent or close to it, the problem of moral hazard took on an especially virulent form. Having lost all of their equity, owners had nothing more to lose. Institutions gambled for resurrection by taking inordinate risks. The deposit insurance system presented managers with a situation in which the institution got to keep the rewards if the roll of the dice paid off, but the government's insurance fund was liable if the gambles failed.[9]

In the end, some 525 insured S&Ls failed, more than five times the total number since the end of World War II. The FLSIC went bankrupt, reporting the largest losses ever incurred by a public or private corporation.[10] Ultimately, the costs would exceed $160 billion. Congress responded by passing the Financial Institutions Reform, Recovery, and Enforcement Act of 1989, eliminating the FSLIC and transferring its duties to the FDIC. It also abolished the Federal Home Loan Bank Board—the chief regulator for the thrift industry—and replaced it with two new agencies, the Federal Housing Finance Board and the Office of Thrift Supervision. A newly created Resolution Trust Corporation was given the task of managing the assets of failed thrifts and disposing of them in an orderly fashion.

Despite the S&L debacle, deregulation continued over the next decade and the regulatory firewalls established by the New Deal regulations became increasingly porous. In 1997, the Clinton administration signaled its support for a continuation of deregulation. As Clinton Treasury Secretary Robert Rubin noted: "The old lines that separated insurance, securities and banking industries have increasingly blurred as new financial services and products have appeared." Rather than retaining antiquated regulatory distinctions, the administration supported deregulation that would allow for the creation of so-called wholesale financial institutions that could accept uninsured deposits and would continue to be integrated into the payments system, but would not be classified as banks under existing regulations. Rubin argued that this would create space for additional competition and innovation within the financial industry.[11]

In 1999, Congress passed the Gramm-Leach-Bliley Financial Services Modernization Act (GLBA). It permitted the consolidation of commercial banks, investment banks, securities firms and insurance companies in financial holding companies, thereby eliminating the last vestiges of Glass-Steagall. The passage of GLBA reflected several factors, including the growing evidence that the combination of commercial and investment banking had played little or no role in the Great Depression, and the cross-national and domestic experience with firms that combined multiple financial functions. While many would subsequently attach great significance to GLBA, it did not eliminate existing regulatory authority. "Functional regulation" continued to exist, even if the functions were consolidated in financial holding companies. Moreover, while GLBA essentially revoked Glass-Steagall, many of the changes had already occurred incrementally. For example, often through mergers and acquisitions, commercial banks had already made forays into investment banking and brokerage activities, creating more diversified financial service companies.[12]

Thus, during a period beginning in the 1970s, a failure to control inflation placed what had been a stable regulatory structure under significant stress. Some of the innovative responses to inflation were unanticipated by regulators and Congress, who were placed in a reactive position. Rather than seeking to design a new regulatory architecture, Congress engaged in a piecemeal deregulatory process that lagged behind the larger economic changes. The disjunction between key decisions—most pointedly introducing price competition while reducing controls on investments and expanding insurance coverage— increased the fragility of the financial system. Although one might want to view deregulation in isolation, macroeconomic policy decisions shaped the environment within which deregulated financial institutions functioned, often generating unanticipated and, in the case of the S&L crisis, catastrophic results.

While this episode would appear to be rich in implications, policymakers seemed to draw few lessons. Once again, a set of policy decisions would create the preconditions for an asset bubble and serious problems of moral hazard. Key regulatory decisions (and nondecisions) would almost assure that this bubble, once it popped, would have impacts that would cascade through financial markets, with tragic ramifications for the domestic and international economy. With this in mind, let us turn to consider the policy decisions that contributed to a financial crisis that would make the events of the late 1980s, seem tame by comparison.

What Can Be Learned from the Financial Crisis?

Crisis has played an important role in regime change, as detailed in earlier chapters. Will the financial collapse and the great recession constitute a crisis of such significance as to force the abandonment of some of the core assumptions of neoliberalism and the emergence of a new regime? In the words of Representative Barney Frank (D-MA), Chairman of the House Financial Services Committee, the financial collapse is clearly an indictment of "America's 30-year experiment with radical economic deregulation."[13] As attractive as this conclusion may seem, one suspects that the causality is somewhat more complicated. Three things seem certain. First, public policies created the asset bubble in real estate. Second, policy decisions maximized the probability that, when the asset bubble burst, the results would have maximum impact. Third, it is difficult simply to attribute the outcomes to bad actors, ideologically inspired blindness, or the unanticipated nature of the innovations in finance, although there are elements of truth in each of these explanations.

How to Create an Asset Bubble

Asset bubbles always reflect a combination of psychological and economic factors. But there is often a strong policy component, usually involving the expansion in credit and policies that facilitate the shifting of risk.[14] The real estate bubble that emerged between 1998 and 2006 was, in part, the unintended consequence of public policy. Changes in public policy created the preconditions of the real estate boom through a number of discrete policy decisions. Once the real estate markets began to expand and there were clear warnings that a bubble was emerging, policymakers were hesitant to intervene to check speculation (e.g., by raising interest rates or limiting liquidity in real estate markets). Let us explore some of the key decisions that, when combined, facilitated the emergence of the real estate bubble.

Beginning in the late 1970s, Congress passed a series of statutes (e.g., the Community Reinvestment Act, the Home Mortgage Disclosure Act) to prevent credit market discrimination. The release of data on mortgage lending—most importantly, Community Reinvestment Act or CRA scores—was intended to shape lending decisions.[15] Following a 1992 study by economists at the Federal Reserve Bank of Boston concluding that minorities were more than twice as likely to be denied a mortgage as whites,[16] the Federal Reserve began to recommend that banks relax underwriting standards as a means of enhancing access to credit. The Boston Fed, for example, advised lenders to accept higher obligation ratios, lower down payments, the lack of a credit history (or a negative credit history with credit counseling), lack of steady employment, and income from "overtime and part-time work, second jobs (including seasonal work), retirement and Social Security income, alimony, child support, Veterans Administration benefits, welfare payments, and unemployment benefits."[17] One might question whether Congress and regulators selected the best policy instrument for promoting home ownership among low-income populations, given the risk it entailed. One suspects that the kinds of cooperative partnerships and "third way" solutions that made so much sense in the 1990s increased the attractiveness of parallel initiatives in credit markets. Moreover, given the concerns over deficits, this strategy may have been attractive because the costs could be kept off the budget.

The core assumptions of neoliberalism can explain why policymakers sought to use credit markets to achieve larger policy goals. They can also explain why the regulatory supervision of mortgage instruments and mortgage brokers was so thin. Many lenders exploited informational asymmetries and developed instruments that created significant problems for low-income borrowers but were made attractive by requiring little in the way of down payments, and offering low initial payments and adjustable interest rates. With the relaxation of underwriting standards, some sub-prime mortgage instruments were given novel names like "liar loans" (since there was no need to verify data) and Ninja loans (an acronym for "No income, no job, and no assets"). Often they required little or nothing in down payments and provided adjustable interest rates that, in an environment of low inflation, dramatically reduced the costs of ownership. The relaxed underwriting standards not only allowed low-income borrowers access to credit, they simultaneously facilitated speculation. By 2005, speculative home purchases exceeded one-quarter of all home sales. With little in the way of down payments, these purchases were highly leveraged and would be quickly abandoned once the housing bubble burst.[18]

The relaxation of underwriting standards was accompanied by new tax incentives to invest in real estate. The United States has long promoted home ownership through the tax system, including the deductibility of mortgage interest and real estate taxes. Traditionally, homeowners over 55 received a one-time exemption for $125,000 of capital gains whereas homeowners under 55 could defer capital gains taxes if they bought a house that was of equal or greater value within two years. The incentives for real estate investments were enhanced dramatically with the passage of the Taxpayer Relief Act of 1997. Under this statute, the first $500,000 in gains from any home sale was exempted from capital gains taxes for married couples (the first $250,000 for single tax payers). Since this was above the price of the median house, it essentially provided an exemption on capital gains for most Americans. Moreover, the Act reduced the marginal tax rate on all long-term capital gains, including houses. The Act, passed with overwhelming bipartisan support, created new incentives to invest.[19]

The real estate bubble was fueled by an additional policy decision: the Fed's promotion of low interest rates, which increased the attractiveness of adjustable-rate mortgages, and high levels of consumption more generally. As shown in Chapter 10, the growing US trade deficit has been a persistent problem since the 1980s, and China, which emerged as a leading exporter, benefited greatly from the seemingly endless growth of US consumption. China's heavy investments in government bonds and mortgage debt during the 1990s and 2000s—some $1 trillion generated through US purchases of Chinese exports—placed further downward pressure on interest rates and there was no effort on the part of Fed chairman Greenspan to counter this stimulus. Indeed, the Fed explicitly promoted low interest rates. During the period 2003–5, short-term interest rates were kept "unusually low" and adjustable rate mortgages "rose to about one-third of total mortgages … . This made borrowing attractive and brought more people into the housing markets, further bidding up housing prices."[20]

Freddie Mac and Fannie Mae also played a major role in facilitating the housing bubble. By purchasing mortgages and issuing a majority of the mortgage-backed securities, they added a great deal of liquidity to the markets for home finance. The government-sponsored enterprises receive a host of subsidies and, with implicit government backing, historically they have been able to borrow money at a lower rate.[21] At the same time, however, they have been assigned responsibility for executing policy goals. Freddie and Fannie have "an affirmative obligation to facilitate the financing of affordable housing for low- and moderate-income families in a manner consistent with their over-all public purposes, while maintaining a strong financial condition and a reasonable economic return."[22] The Federal Housing Enterprises Financial Safety and Soundness Act of 1992 mandated that the Department of Housing and Urban Development (HUD) set quantitative targets for GSE purchases of mortgages serving a low and moderate-income clientele. Between 1993 and 2007, the target increased from 30 percent to 55 percent, creating a large secondary market for subprime mortgages.[23] Because originators were only responsible for the performance of loans for the first 60 days, there were great incentives to backload the burdens placed on borrowers and transfer the risk to GSEs and their private sector counterparts.

When investment banks pooled mortgages, they employed sophisticated computer programs to create "tranches" or slices with different levels of risk. They then constructed new securities with different risk-return profiles. Securities were given a risk rating by one of the top credit rating agencies. Private companies, most notably AIG, could provide credit-default swaps, essentially insurance contracts covering the potential default of the mortgage-backed securities. And for a fee, the GSEs would guarantee to cover the underlying mortgage loans in the case of default. Any concerns over risk were mitigated by two assumptions. First, investors assumed that mortgage-backed securities were relatively safe investments given the seemingly endless opportunities for real estate appreciation. Second, investors could assume that with the implicit backing of the US government, securities issued by Freddie and Fannie would be sound. While the first assumption was proven faulty—all asset bubbles contain the seeds of their own destruction—the second assumption, as events would prove, was far more accurate.

How to Maximize the Damage When the Asset Bubble Breaks

All asset bubbles invariably break. The question is whether this inevitable finale will have significant repercussions. Will regulations create a firewall limiting the instability in one sector of the economy from spreading through the entire economy? Regulatory, monetary policy, and tax decisions facilitated the emergence of the housing bubble. Arguably, policymakers were also culpable for the magnitude of the effects. During the period of financial market deregulation, a new, tightly coupled system emerged that allowed for the securitization of debt and the mitigation of risk through private contracts. Although regulated commercial banks were not at the heart of the system, because there were high levels of interdependence and banks often held these securities in their portfolios, the entire system was highly vulnerable to systemic risks. Regulations could have been extended to this shadow system of finance. But at each juncture, the opportunities for regulating the emerging system of finance were squandered. Let us examine a few of the most important policy decisions.

Managing Risk

There is reason to believe that the credit rating agencies (e.g., Standard and Poor's, Moody's Investors Service) systematically underestimated the risk of mortgage-backed securities and the impact of a downturn in the housing market.[24] Although one may question the quality of their risk assessment methodologies, two factors were particularly important. First, there were clear incentive problems. The issuers of debt pay for rating services and they have a powerful stake in the outcome since the rating will determine the extent of the market (e.g., which institutions and funds can purchase the securities). Predictably, rating agencies faced conflicts of interest. Second, there were problems of information asymmetry. The sheer complexity of many of the mortgage-backed securities was so great that few other parties had the information or expertise to evaluate rating agencies' decisions.[25] Even if there were ways in which investors could manage risk—e.g., through the purchase of credit-default swaps—without accurate assessments of risk in the first instance, it is clear that many institutions had far higher risk exposure than they may have thought prudent.

Why were credit rating agencies not subject to higher levels of regulatory oversight? In part, the answer is found in the regulatory model adopted by the Securities and Exchange Commission (SEC). It relies heavily on government-supervised self-regulation and the mandated disclosure of information. Yet, the SEC often seeks a more direct regulatory role. In 2006, SEC Chairman Christopher Cox, normally a critic of regulation, requested additional oversight authority. Although Congress responded by passing the Credit Rating Agency Reform Act of 2006, it added an amendment to prohibit the SEC from extending its oversight to the methods employed by credit rating agencies. It was deemed sufficient that these methods be made public.[26] Congress refused to address the conflicts of interest that arise when the issuers of securities pay the agencies that rate them.

Investors' underestimation of risk may have been shaped by information communicated by regulators. There have been ongoing debates regarding the problems of moral hazard in financial regulation. During the past decade, moral hazard problems were undoubtedly exacerbated by the position struck by the

Federal Reserve. Chairman Greenspan consistently argued that the Federal Reserve should not use its powers to prevent or manage asset bubbles—hence the Fed's fidelity to low interest rates. Greenspan argued, however, that regulators should mitigate the fallout once the bubbles burst. Investors could act under the assumption that the risks of bad investments would be partially if not wholly socialized.[27] Moreover, investors purchasing mortgage-backed securities could assume that they would be backed by the full faith and credit of the United States. Indeed, it is commonly argued that this implicit, open-ended guarantee is one of the indirect subsidies enjoyed by Freddie and Fannie insofar as it allows them to access capital markets at a discount.[28]

Assuring Contagion

Bubbles form and they invariably break. What was striking with the collapse of the housing bubble was how quickly the impact spread through the financial community and into the domestic and international economy. Hypothetically, the damage could have been contained to a few over-leveraged institutions, requiring interventions comparable to the earlier S&L collapse. Yet, a host of regulatory decisions and non-decisions almost ensured contagion, exacerbating the recession and creating instability in international markets.

When investors consider purchasing riskier investments, they may mitigate the risk through the purchase of credit-default swaps, derivative contracts that promise to protect investors from losses. In 1994, on the eve of the housing boom, the GAO issued a report identifying concerns over the lack of regulation for derivatives. In testimony before the House Subcommittee on Telecommunications and Finance, Comptroller General Charles A. Bowsher warned that the failure of any of the major derivative issues or dealers "could cause liquidity problems in the markets and could also pose risks to the others, including federally insured banks and the financial system as a whole." He continued: "The federal government would be likely to intervene to keep the financial system functioning in cases of severe financial stress" even resulting in "a financial bailout paid for or guaranteed by taxpayers."[29] Three years later, when the chair of the Commodity Futures Trading Commission Brooksley Born solicited comments on expanded regulation of derivatives, she met with the staunch opposition of Greenspan, Treasury Secretary Rubin, and Deputy Treasury Secretary Summers. At their urging, Congress passed an appropriations rider limiting the agency's authority to regulate derivatives.[30]

There were additional regulatory decisions that increased the fragility of the system. In 2004, for example, the SEC changed its regulation for large broker-dealers (the net capital rule) that effectively allowed them to reduce their capital levels. Excess capital from broker-dealer operations could now be used for other purposes, in this case, to purchase mortgage-backed securities and credit derivatives. The five broker-dealers that took advantage of the new rule included Bear Stearns, Goldman Sachs, Lehman Brothers, Merrill Lynch, and

Morgan Stanley. At the extreme, this allowed Bear Stearns to operate at a leverage ratio of 33:1. At the same time, these investment banks—which had leverages of some $4 trillion in assets—were allowed to manage their levels of risk with their own computer models.[31]

As the large financial institutions were acquiring larger positions in mortgage-backed securities, the same was occurring in the quasi-private world of the GSEs. As noted above, HUD set quantitative targets for GSE purchases of low and moderate-income mortgages, adding liquidity to the fragile sub-prime market. Yet, it did not simultaneously mandate that Freddie and Fannie increase their holdings of mortgage-backed securities. During the decade following the creation of the Office of Federal Housing Enterprise Oversight (OFHEO) in 1992, the assets of the GSEs grew by more than 820 percent, to $1.9 trillion. As the Congressional Research Service explained, the GSEs became "two of the largest private debt issuers in the world" with outstanding debt securities "equal to nearly half of all publicly held U.S. Treasury debt." Because "financial institutions around the world hold large quantities of GSE debt ... default by either GSE could have widespread, unpredictable, and potentially serious repercussions."[32]

When accounting scandals led to the collapse of Enron in 2001 and WorldCom a year later, attention turned to the misapplication of accounting standards in other large firms. In January of 2003, Freddie Mac admitted that it had engaged in creative accounting to "smooth out" its earnings growth and mask underlying volatility. The revelations resulted in the ouster of Freddie's top managers, SEC investigations, a consent agreement combined with a $125 million fine, and, subsequently, a class action suit.[33] Following these troubling disclosures, there was growing attention to the vulnerability of the GSEs. The International Monetary Fund, for example, identified a host of problems in 2003, including the "systemic risks inherent in the agencies' large mortgage portfolios and their hedging operations" and the "lack of transparency." The IMF cautioned: "regulators need to look closely at whether agencies' capital adequacy is sufficient, especially bearing in mind the questions about internal controls that have emerged in Freddie Mac." The IMF noted it was "unclear whether [the GSEs] have taken sufficient account of the risk that the markets may not be deep enough to allow them to continuously hedge their growing portfolios in times of stress." The IMF concluded the "more volatile market environment for the agencies, potential difficulties for the market in absorbing their hedging needs, and possible lower profit margins all argue for regulators to examine closely whether the agencies' capital base is large enough to absorb the risks on their growing balance sheet."[34]

In 2004, the OMB echoed these concerns and warned:

> The GSEs are highly leveraged, holding much less capital in relation to their assets than similarly sized financial institutions ... a misjudgment or unexpected economic event could quickly deplete this capital, potentially making it difficult for a GSE to meet its debt obligations. Given the very

large size of each enterprise, even a small mistake by a GSE could have consequences throughout the economy.

The OMB went on to review the findings of a 2003 study by OFHEO that cautioned:

> should a GSE experience large unexpected losses, the market for its and other GSEs' debt might become illiquid. Institutions holding this debt would see a rapid depletion in the value of their assets and a loss of liquidity, spreading the problems of the GSEs into financial sectors beyond the housing market.[35]

Congress held hearings over the course of the next several years to consider strengthening the oversight of the GSEs and limiting the size of their portfolios. Fed Chairman Greenspan—usually skeptical of the need for additional regulation—testified that the GSEs should be forced to reduce their trillion dollar portfolios to $100 or $200 billion, a position echoed by Treasury officials. Although proposals to create a new agency to replace OFHEO were introduced in both chambers, Republicans and Democrats blocked reforms—refusing to place restrictions on the size of GSE portfolios, preventing the regulator from considering systemic risk, or tying passage to the creation of an affordable housing fund to make grants to advocacy groups—when they could have had a significant impact on reducing the vulnerability of the GSEs and the impact of their collapse on the larger economy.[36]

Regardless of ideology or partisan identification, the warnings issued by a variety of actors were insufficient to force Congress to act. There is an old saying referenced most famously by John F. Kennedy in the wake of the Bay of Pigs fiasco: Victory has a hundred fathers, but defeat is an orphan. When the asset bubble burst and the shock waves extended through the financial system into the national and international economy, many of the legislators and regulators who refused to act when it would have mattered eschewed all responsibility. What was clearly a tragedy was portrayed as a melodrama staring George W. Bush, ideological zealots, and black-hearted mortgage brokers.

The Aftermath

When the housing bubble collapsed, the aggregate costs of past decisions and non-decisions became painfully clear. As losses mounted from their holdings of mortgage-backed securities, the credit ratings for Freddie Mac and Fannie Mae were downgraded. Congress passed the Housing and Economic Recovery Act of 2008 and the GSEs were placed into conservatorship by a new Federal Housing Finance Agency, the regulatory successor to OFHEO that Congress had failed to create when it would have mattered. Taxpayers assumed liability for the guarantees once made by the GSEs. As Freddie and Fannie were guaranteed an infusion of some $100 billion, the bail-out carried a significant *quid pro quo*: their combined portfolios could not exceed $850 billion by the end of 2009 and would have to be reduced thereafter at a rate of 10 percent a year until they reached $250 billion, approximately the amount recommended to Congress in 2004.

None of the large broker-dealers who had taken advantage of the changes in the net capital rule were left standing. Bear Stearns collapsed, and was purchased in March 2008 by JP Morgan Chase & Co with a $29 billion loan from the Federal Reserve, an unprecedented act given that the Fed has no jurisdiction over investment banks. In the fall of 2008, Bank of America acquired Merrill Lynch. Goldman Sachs survived, with assistance from Berkshire Hathaway and an infusion of $10 billion in government capital, albeit after deciding to become a traditional bank holding company—a decision also made by Morgan Stanley. Lehman Brothers went bankrupt and was not offered government assistance. As for AIG, a major issuer of credit-default swaps, a liquidity crisis threatened to undermine the swaps and thus bring down the institutions that had made heavy investments in CDOs. It survived only with the infusion of $152 billion in federal money.

The combination of events produced a perfect storm and many analysts feared that the recession could become a second Great Depression. In January 2008, Fed Chairman Ben Bernanke testified before Congress and raised concerns that the problems in the financial markets, increased energy prices, a drop in the stock market, and a softening of home values would likely continue to undermine consumer spending, labor markets, and business investment. He concluded that the time had come for a more aggressive fiscal policy and argued that the best fiscal policy would take effect immediately and "should be explicitly temporary, both to avoid unwanted stimulus beyond the near-term horizon and, importantly, to preclude an increase in the federal government's structural budget deficit."[37] Within a month of Bernanke's testimony, the Bush administration secured passage of the Economic Stimulus Act of 2008, providing some $152 billion via tax rebates to low- and middle-income families and special depreciation allowances for business purchases made in 2008. The modest stimulus, even when combined with an aggressive monetary policy, proved insufficient. The collapse of the financial markets took its toll on the stock markets: the Dow Jones industrial average lost 33.8 percent of its value—the worst performance since 1931—eliminating some $7 trillion of shareholder wealth. And unemployment, which stood at 4.8 percent when Congress passed the Economic Stimulus Act, ratcheted up to 7.2 percent by the end of 2008 (it would ultimately approach 10 percent).[38]

In October 2008, at the Bush administration's urging, Congress passed the Emergency Economic Stabilization Act of 2008, creating the Troubled Asset Relief Program (TARP). The Act authorized the Treasury to purchase or insure up to $700 billion of troubled assets, $350 billion of which would be made available immediately. By the end of 2008, TARP had purchased $178 billion worth of assets. The largest recipients were Citigroup, JP Morgan Chase, and Wells Fargo ($25 billion each), Bank of America ($15 billion), and

Morgan Stanley and Goldman Sachs, ($10 billion each). Citigroup and Bank of America subsequently received an additional $20 billion each through the Treasury's Targeted Investment Program. Each recipient was required to pay the Treasury a dividend of 5 percent for the first five years, and 9 percent thereafter. Moreover, the Treasury was given warrants allowing it to purchase common stock worth 15 percent of the amount invested in preferred stock. The Treasury also purchased $40 billion worth of preferred stock from AIG, $20 billion from Citigroup, and $5 billion from General Motors Acceptance Corporation. AIG received additional support through a $30 billion line of credit.[39]

In February 2009, less than a month after President Barack Obama's inauguration, Congress passed the American Recovery and Reinvestment Act of 2009, providing an additional $787 billion of stimulus. Conservatives objected to the Act, albeit on a variety of grounds. Some argued for supply-side stimulus via tax reductions. The $288 billion in tax cuts, the majority of which went to low- and middle-income families, was deemed insufficient. And much of the spending, in the minds of critics, was only remotely connected to recovery. Others used the debates over the stimulus program to revisit older debates about the efficacy of Keynesianism and the legacy of the New Deal. The libertarian Cato Institute, for example, published a letter endorsed by some 200 economists in the *New York Times* and the *Wall Street Journal*, which read:

> Notwithstanding reports that all economists are now Keynesians ... we the undersigned do not believe that more government spending is a way to improve economic performance. More government spending by Hoover and Roosevelt did not pull the United States economy out of the Great Depression in the 1930s.

The letter concluded: "To improve the economy, policymakers should focus on reforms that remove impediments to work, saving, investment and production. Lower tax rates and a reduction in the burden of government are the best ways of using fiscal policy to boost growth."[40]

The stimulus package had critics on the Left as well. In a series of *New York Times* columns, Paul Krugman made the case that the stimulus package needed to be large if the nation was to prevent a second Great Depression. He used the opportunity to revisit the causes of the depression and the argument made, most notably by Milton Friedman, that the collapse could have been managed more effectively via monetary policy. Two weeks before Obama's inauguration, Krugman argued:

> Friedman's claim that monetary policy could have prevented the Great Depression was an attempt to refute the analysis of John Maynard Keynes, who argued that monetary policy is ineffective under depression conditions and that fiscal policy—large-scale deficit spending by the government—is needed to fight mass unemployment. The failure of monetary policy in the

current crisis shows that Keynes had it right the first time. And Keynesian thinking lies behind Mr. Obama's plans to rescue the economy.

Krugman had no doubt that there would be a stimulus package, but he feared that it would be "delayed and/or downsized ... enough to slow the descent, not stop it."[41] As the details of the recovery measures took shape, Krugman concluded that the administration's stimulus package "was clearly both too small and too heavily reliant on tax cuts," a product of Obama's "postpartisan yearnings."[42] Similarly, Joseph Stiglitz argued that with one-third of the stimulus package devoted to tax cuts and almost half simply offsetting the contractionary effect of cutbacks at the state level, "it is probably not enough to restore robust growth." Stiglitz concluded that recovery would demand a much larger stimulus package and the revival of financial markets.[43]

Although TARP was initially envisioned as a means of rescuing financial firms, the Treasury agreed to lend $18.4 billion to General Motors and Chrysler, contingent on the release of the second installment of TARP money. The automakers, in turn, were required to negotiate new labor agreements and submit restructuring plans. By the end of June 2009, some $55 billion had been extended to the automakers. As GM worked through bankruptcy, the Treasury offered to extend another $30 billion in assistance, in exchange for $8.8 billion in debt obligations and preferred stock and some 60 percent of its equity. A decade which began with praises of the market ended with an interesting question: now that the federal government was the majority owner of GM—a firm that was once viewed as synonymous with American capitalism—should it become part of the federal budget?[44]

In Search of Remedies

What lessons are to be learned from this episode? One might suggest that the big lesson is simple: regulatory withdrawal carried high costs. But it is easy to overstate the extent of deregulation. Consider regulatory budgets. In 2008, the last year of the Bush presidency, the combined regulatory budget was $48 billion. To place this number in perspective, inflation-adjusted regulatory budgets grew by 310 percent since 1980, outpacing the growth of GDP. The inflation-adjusted budgets for the regulation of finance and banking grew some 316 percent during this period, 16.7 percent during the Bush presidency.[45] One might argue that this growth was insufficient, but deregulation did not lead to a massive defunding of the regulatory state. Moreover, as shown above, regulations were being actively deployed in the years leading up to the collapse, albeit in ways that were counterproductive.

Perhaps one can make a more subtle argument: Yes, the nation continued to invest in regulation, but it invested in the wrong kinds of regulation. Perhaps this is simply another case of institutional change lagging behind economic dynamics that are difficult to anticipate *ex ante*. Through the process of securitization and the issuance of credit-default swaps, a largely unregulated system emerged that was tightly coupled, vulnerable to systemic risk, and because of its integration into the regulated financial institutions, capable of doing extraordinary damage. Much of this fell outside of the regulatory structure. While few could have predicted precisely how this system would evolve, the process extended over more than a decade and policymakers had ample warning of the changes that were occurring and the potential consequences of failing to extend regulations. The GAO, the OMB, the CBO, the Congressional Research Service, and the IMF offered numerous projections of what the future might hold. Policymakers nonetheless refused to extend regulations to derivatives, hedge funds and credit rating agencies; they refused to force a reduction in the portfolios of the GSEs; they actively promoted a higher level of leveraging in the largest investment banks. Different decisions could have produced different results.

Perhaps the refusal to strengthen the regulatory state was itself the product of an ideological adherence to the free market and neoliberalism. Many regulators in the Clinton and Bush administrations were clearly enamored of the self-regulatory capacity of financial institutions. But members of both parties in the White House, Senate, and House—many of whom had been vocal critics of free market ideology—made key regulatory decisions. The fact that Congress failed to pass new regulatory legislation even when the Democrats held a majority in both chambers (and Barney Frank served as chairman of the House Financial Services Committee) leads one to discount this narrative as a complete explanation. Perhaps it must be supplemented by the insights of the economic theory of regulation (or in this case, an economic theory of deregulation). When the real estate industry is contributing some $40 million to members of the two key congressional committees during the 2004–8 election cycles and the securities and investment industry is contributing another $46.7 million, it may be difficult to introduce policies that will suppress the real estate boom and impose greater regulatory oversight.[46] Policymakers and industry actors may execute mutually beneficial exchanges regardless of ideology.

In the aftermath of the credit crisis of 2008, a number of reform proposals emerged, grounded in different understandings of the crisis. Congress, chastened by the events of the past several years, returned to some of the reforms that had been recommended before the collapse. Attention turned, once again, to the regulation of derivatives, the contracts (like credit default swaps) that are traded on "dark markets" where there is little regulatory oversight. The regulation of derivatives is complicated by questions of agency and congressional committee jurisdiction and whether regulation should extend to all derivatives or whether they should exclude more complex contracts that are thinly traded.[47] Additionally, attention turned once again to the regulation of credit rating agencies and the potential conflicts of interest that arise when they are providing rating and consulting services and derive their income from the issuers of debt.[48]

For those who understood the crisis as a product of exploitation—greedy mortgage brokers extracting profits from unsophisticated borrowers—the best response involved consumer protection regulation. Elizabeth Warren, Harvard law professor and chair of the Congressional Oversight Panel created to monitor TARP, actively promoted the creation of a Financial Product Safety Commission. Such a commission, she argued, would not only regulate the innovative mortgage instruments that created so many problems for low-income borrowers (and others who were directed into subprime mortgages), but would also oversee credit cards and other financial instruments.[49] Such an agency could prevent dangerous products from entering the marketplace. Certainly, a new regulatory agency along these lines would address one part of the problem. But as noted above, the financial crisis was not simply a product of deceptive practices or overly complex financial instruments marketed to unsophisticated consumers.

A far more ambitious response would be to rethink the very logic of financial regulation. Before the crisis, many institutions worked under the assumption that the government would come to their rescue, an assumption that proved to be correct. However, because the guarantee was implicit, it did not carry with it a level of oversight comparable to what exists in commercial banking, for example, where institutions pay for FDIC insurance and submit to regulatory oversight. In response to this situation, there have been recommended reforms that would make the implicit guarantee explicit through the creation of a new systemic risk regulator. Based on levels of systemic risk, all financial firms—regardless of submarket—would be folded into an insurance system comparable to the FDIC. Premiums could vary based on the potential risk posed by a financial institution; access to insurance would entail regulation of capital and liquidity requirements, leverage ratios, and other factors that could increase risk.

David Moss argues that such regulations would create disincentives for firms to become "too big to fail." He explains:

> it would provide financial institutions with a strong incentive to avoid becoming systemically significant. This is exactly the opposite of the existing situation, where financial institutions have a strong incentive to become "too big to fail," precisely in order to exploit a free implicit guarantee from the federal government.[50]

Under the New Deal regulatory system, when a bank fails, the FDIC assumes control and forces restructuring. Without a comparable institutional framework for other financial institutions, the response to failure is *ad hoc*. Under the proposed system, a mechanism would be in place to provide an infusion of capital before firms were on the verge of collapse and, more importantly, a process by which failing institutions would be placed in receivership and restructured, sold, or liquidated. Whether the new duties would be assigned to an agency that would replace existing regulators or executed by an inter-agency board remains an open question. But one suspects that the political opposition to new risk regulation and the imposition of insurance will be significant. The highly decentralized system of regulation and the congressional committee system provide numerous points of access for mobilized interests and, as noted above, in the recent past, this was sufficient to prevent far more modest reforms.

Conclusion

Whether the regulatory response to the collapse takes the form of incremental change or the introduction of a new regulatory architecture remains to be seen. Yet, two things are clear. First, the financial crisis has brought an end to the decades-long wave of deregulation and the boundless faith in markets. In the wake of the Great Depression, the faith in balanced budgets and the self-regulating capacity of markets was shaken to its core, leading to a new regime that shaped the evolution of the economy in the postwar period. With the collapse of the financial system, the foundations have been set for a new period of regulatory change. Second, it is clear that the deep recession has forced even broader changes that may well provide the foundations of a new regime. The supply-side and monetarist theories that gained so much support in the wake of stagflation appear to have been discredited. Keynesianism— seemingly relegated to the ash heap of history—has had a resurgence and with it, a greater level of support for state activism. Whether this resurgence marks a lasting shift will depend on numerous factors, most centrally, the success of policymakers in producing a rapid recovery.

11 Continuity and Change in the American Political Economy

This book began with a simple but important argument regarding the market-state dichotomy that has played such an influential role in shaping the way we think about political economy and public policy. The dichotomy is grounded in the belief that the market and the state exist as two fundamentally different realms of human activity. In this view, markets are self-constituting and pre-political. They arise from the innate "propensity to truck, barter, and exchange on thing for another," to use Adam Smith's phrase in *The Wealth of Nations.*[1]

Moreover, they are self-regulating. Supply and demand equilibrate, markets clear, and all self-interested utility-maximizers end the day having improved their welfare (and the welfare of society) through their voluntary transactions with other like-minded beings. The state, in sharp contrast, is that institution with a monopoly over the legitimate use of violence. While most analysts would recognize conditions under which the state is justified in intervening in the market, its warrant is not without bounds. It is commonly argued that inter-vention can be condoned only when there is clear evidence of market failure and the costs of intervention do not exceed the costs imposed by imperfectly functioning markets.

As argued in the early chapters of this book, the market-state dichotomy does nothing to advance our understanding of the political economy. Markets are institutions for the exchange of property, and property rights are defined by public policy and defended by state institutions. The right to divest oneself of property—to transfer it in the transactions that are at the heart of market exchanges—would be inconsequential, if state institutions did not provide the means of enforcing contracts and adjudicating disputes. Moreover, as we move beyond the question of property rights, it is clear that the very building blocks of the economy—corporations, trade associations, financial institutions, and labor unions—are legally constituted entities embedded in a dense network of public policies and institutions. These facts are not rarely granted any theor-etical importance by mainstream economics. As John Lie notes: "The market, it turns out, is the hollow core at the heart of economics." As portrayed by neoclassical economics, it "is shorn of social relations, institutions, or technol-ogy and is devoid of elementary sociological concerns such as power, norms, and networks."[2]

In striving to construct a more accurate conception of the economy, we must begin by recognizing that it is, in many ways, a product of public institutions and policy decisions. They not only constitute key economic actors, they define the various means by which they can pursue their objectives and the means by which they can coordinate their behavior with each other. Rather than using the term "market" as being synonymous with the economy, we must understand that "markets" constitute but one means of coordinating economic behavior. Corporations can coordinate their behavior through long-term contracting, interlocking directorates, participation in trade associations or various export and research and development alliances; they can use some of these governance mechanisms to coordinate their behavior with financial institutions and labor unions as well. Public policy and institutions also delimit the kinds of opportunities open to economic actors.

We can go beyond questions of governance to engage broader policies that seek to redistribute resources or manage the vicissitudes of the business or life cycle. They too, are constitutive of the economy. In the end, as Fred Block notes, "what we generally call 'the economy' is always the product of a combination of state action and the logic of individual or institutional economic actors."[3] Thus, one has no grounds to assume that poor economic performance is simply a product of excessive state "intervention" that undermines the "logic of markets." Rather, we must conclude that economic performance is a product of the ways in which the complex set of public policies and institutions affect the behavior of, and relationships between, economic actors. An examination of historical and cross-national experiences reveals that a variety of policies and institutions are compatible with positive economic performance.[4] At the same time, this does not give policymakers unbounded discretion in the decisions they make. To the extent that economic performance is, in part, a product of the decisions of privately owned and managed organizations, incentives matter.

Continuity and Change in the Political Economy

The interplay between the state and economy is complicated considerably when we introduce a historical dimension to the analysis. Yes, public policies and institutions shape economic performance, but not always in ways that are coherent. In part, this is a product of institutional design. In the United States, institutional fragmentation and high levels of group access have created seemingly endless opportunities for transfer seeking. It is impossible to determine with precision the aggregate impact of taxation, regulation, government contracts and subsidies. Given the design of US institutions, corporate production and investment decisions are shaped by multiple agencies, often with overlapping jurisdictions and very different policy mandates. And the story only becomes more complicated when we recognize the path-dependent layering process that is inherent in political economic development. New policies and institutions are created, but more often than not they are not reconciled with the policies and institutions inherited from the past.

Institutions are inherently conservative. They provide a means of coordinating behavior and stabilizing patterns of interaction. Within the state, they are reinforced overtime by bureaucratic development and patterns of interest group relations. Within the larger political economy, they are reinforced by corporate investment and production decisions, and broader governance regimes that coordinate the behavior of economic actors and the state. One should not be surprised that change often occurs in a path dependent fashion at what may appear to be a glacial pace. The structurally induced equilibria that form around key public policies can successfully limit the rapidity and magnitude of change. But they can also break down—sometimes with tragic consequences—when confronted by crisis. The ramifications for subsequent development may take forms that few actors or analysts could have predicted.

Who might have predicted, on the eve of the 1929 crash, that the next decade would witness the reorganization and regulation of finance, governmental recognition of the right of workers to organize, and the creation of social entitlements covering a majority of the population? Who could have foreseen, at the height of the Great Society, when macroeconomic fine tuning had allowed for the realization of a full employment economy, that in little more than a decade Keynesianism would lay in ruins and policymakers would be eliminating previously stable regulatory subsystems and introducing a process of welfare reform that would result, ultimately, in the elimination of Aid for Families with Dependent Children, the nation's largest means-tested income maintenance entitlement? As detailed in previous chapters, the history of the American political economy is one of stability, but this stability is punctuated by periods of rapid and substantial change forced by economic crises. And while the New Deal Regime did not eliminate the key initiatives of the Progressive Regime, and much of these two regimes survived the rise of the Neoliberal Regime, it is nonetheless the case that each of these periods changed significantly the trajectory of political economic development.

Of course, crises are not self-interpreting. There was nothing inherent in the depression of the 1890s, the Great Depression of the 1930s, or the stagflation of the 1970s that dictated a particular policy response. Thus, we must consider the role of ideas, interests, and institutions. As argued in previous chapters, reform doctrines and economic theories are difficult to divorce from interests. The debates between the New Nationalist and New Freedom strands of Progressivism had important implications for institutional design and the state's relationship with the corporate economy. In the case of the Federal Reserve, commercial banks were directly integrated into a state institution, thereby increasing their power over monetary policy. In stark contrast, the period also witnessed the creation of a new institution, the Federal Trade Commission, with a mandate to write and enforce detailed rules to prevent the concentration and exercise of corporate power. During the New Deal, the competing theoretical explanations of the Great Depression justified different kinds of policy responses, each of which could prove instrumental in securing the support of various economic interests ranging from organized labor and farmers to pensioners. To the extent that different explanations were embodied in new policies and institutions, the resulting changes may have worked at cross-purposes, thereby adding to the incoherence of the state. During the 1970s, the rapid deployment of market-based doctrines shaped the reform debates to focus on the elimination of regulatory and welfare state policies inherited from the Progressive Era and the New Deal and significant changes in the tax code that would have important implications for income distributions. The market-based arguments had positive ramifications for the state's relationship with corporations, much as one should expect given the heavy corporate investment in conservative policy advocacy.

In each case, pre-existing institutions and policies limit the extent and direction of change. These limitations can take at least three forms. First, there may be difficulties reconciling new initiatives with the powers exercised by existing institutions. Progressive and New Deal initiatives, for example, routinely ran afoul of courts that limited the growth and reach of the administrative state through reference to the interstate commerce clause and the nondelegation doctrine. Following the passage of the Employment Act of 1946, presidential control over fiscal policy remained contingent on Congress, which closely guarded its powers over taxation and budgetary decisions. Second, the success of specific initiatives is dependent on prior patterns of institutional development. The success of the National Recovery Administration, for example, was compromised by the failure of the Commerce Department to develop the analytical and administrative capacities to regulate corporations and associations during the 1920s, when the agency was influenced by Hoover's associationalism and the experience of the War Industries Board. Third, the success of new policy and institutional change may be compromised by the commitments established in the past. The commitment to free trade established under the General Agreement on Tariffs and Trade conflicted with subsequent efforts in the 1970s to achieve full employment. The large entitlement programs created under the New Deal Regime, when combined with postwar demographic trends, have proven increasingly irreconcilable with the principles underlying the Neoliberal Regime. Each new regime introduced significant changes, but the changes unfolded in ways that were often unanticipated.

Conclusion

The stage may be set for another period of significant change. As in earlier periods, crisis has emanated from, and revealed the limitations of, existing institutions and policies. Who could have imagined that a decade that began with a bipartisan celebration of the market and the "ownership society" and projected annual budget surpluses of $500 billion, would end with the collapse of the financial system, the *de facto* nationalization of parts of the automobile and banking industries, and deficits that were unprecedented in the postwar era? Who could have imagined that a decade that was initially interpreted as the culmination of a conservative revolution complete with the first unified

Republican control of the presidency and Congress in half-a-century would end with unified Democratic control and the election of the nation's first African American president? From the perspective of future analysts, the first decade of the twenty-first century may well mark another transformative period that gave rise to a distinctive regime. It is clear that the looming entitlement crisis will demand higher levels of taxation and, potentially, dramatic changes in the public provision of health care. It is also evident that the changes wrought by the growing globalization of the economy will create pressure for new policies, a "corrective counter-movement," to use the term of Karl Polyani. The collapse of the financial system and the efforts to prevent the recession from becoming a depression have forced a reconsideration of the prudence of deregulation, even among some of its staunchest advocates, and a resurrection of Keynesianism.

As of this writing, it is impossible to predict how (or whether) these problems, when combined, will result in a dramatic redefinition of the political economy. What appears to constitute a landmark shift in electoral allegiances can be short-lived (e.g., the unified Republican control after the 1952 elections). As the distance between the collapse of 2007–8 and the initiation of financial reform grows, the sense of crisis may dissipate, allowing for incremental changes in the existing regulatory structure and continued adherence to the broad support for deregulation. Certainly, the collapse of the savings and loan industry and the Federal Savings and Loan Insurance Corporation only had a temporary impact on deregulation. Similarly, the threat of trust fund insolvency may be muted by incremental changes. The same threat of insolvency existed in the early days of the Reagan presidency, and modifications to the Social Security tax, the retirement age, and the taxation of benefits were sufficient to delay the day of reckoning. Ultimately, change is inevitable. And if history is any guide to the future, its ultimate impacts will be shaped and constrained by the legacy of the past in ways that few will fully anticipate.

Notes

1 Beyond the Market-State Dichotomy

1 Robert Skidelsky, *Keynes: The Return of the Master* (New York: Public Affairs, 2009), 168.
2 John Maynard Keynes, *The General Theory of Employment, Interest and Money* (London: MacMillan and Co., 1936), 383.
3 John Stuart Mill, *Principles of Political Economy with Some Applications to Social Philosophy* (London: Longman's and Green, 1911), 1.
4 Martin Staniland, *What is Political Economy? A Study of Social Theory and Underdevelopment* (New Haven, CT: Yale University Press, 1985), 4.
5 See F.A. Hayek, "The Use of Knowledge in Society," *American Economic Review* 35, no. 4 (1945): 519–30, and Adam Smith, *An Inquiry into the Nature and the Causes of the Wealth of Nations* (Indianapolis, IN: Liberty Fund, 1981), 1:11–24.
6 Charles E. Lindblom, "The Market as Prison," *Journal of Politics* 44, no. 2 (1982): 332, 333.
7 David L. Weimer and Aidan R. Vining, *Policy Analysis: Concepts and Practices*, 3rd ed (Upper Saddle River, NJ: Prentice-Hall, 1999), 41.
8 Charles Wolf, *Markets or Governments: Choosing between Imperfect Alternatives* (Cambridge: MIT Press, 1993), 17.
9 Smith, 1:25.
10 Bruce Yandle, "Grasping for the Heavens: 3-D Property Rights and the Global Commons," *Duke Environmental Law and Policy Forum* 10, no. 1 (1999): 13–44.
11 Terry L. Anderson and Fred S. McChesney, "Introduction: The Economic Approach to Property Rights," in Terry L. Anderson and Fred S. McChesney, eds., *Property Rights: Cooperation, Conflict, and the Law* (Princeton: Princeton University Press, 2003), 6–7. On the role of property rights in economic development, see Hernando de Soto, *The Mystery of Capital: Why Capitalism Triumphs in the West and Fails Everywhere Else* (New York: Basic Books, 2003).
12 See John L. Campbell and Leon N. Lindberg, "Property Rights and the Organization of Economic Activity by the State," *American Sociological Review* 55, No. 5. (1990): 634–47.
13 Department of Commerce, Bureau of Economic Analysis, National Income and Product Account Tables 7.1 (2009), and Current and Real GDP (2009).
14 Office of Management and Budget, *Budget of the United States Government, Fiscal Year 2009, Historical Tables* (Washington D.C.: Government Printing Office, 2008), Table 15.3.
15 Figures on government as a percentage of GDP from Office of Management

and Budget, *Budget of the United States, FY 2010, Historical Tables*, Tables 3.1 and 15.3. Calculations by author.

16 Office of Management and Budget, *Historical Tables*, Tables 8.6 and 8.8, calculations by author.

17 Veronique de Rugy and Melinda Warren, *Regulatory Agency Spending Reaches New Height: An Analysis of the U.S. Budget for Fiscal Years 2008 and 2009* (Fairfax, VA: Mercatus Center at George Mason University, 2008), Table 5-A, calculations by author.

2 Making Sense of Institutions and Institutional Change

1 Douglass North, "Institutions, Transaction Costs, and Productivity in the Long Run" (St. Louis: Washington University, 1995).

2 Max Weber, "Politics as a Vocation," in *From Max Weber: Essays in Sociology*, trans. and ed. by H.H. Gerth and C. Wright Mills (New York: Oxford University Press, 1946), 77–128.

3 Marc Allen Eisner, *The State in the American Political Economy: Public Policy and the Evolution of State-Economy Relations* (Englewood Cliffs, NJ: Prentice Hall, 1995), 16–18.

4 James M. Buchanan, "Politics without Romance: A Sketch of Positive Public Choice Theory and Its Normative Implications," in *The Collected Works of James M. Buchanan*, Vol. 1 (Indianapolis: Liberty Fund, 1999), 48.

5 James M. Buchanan, "Rational Choice in the Social Sciences," in *The Collected Works of James M. Buchanan*, Vol. 17 (Indianapolis: Liberty Fund, 2001), 56.

6 James M. Buchanan and Gordon Tullock, *The Calculus of Consent: The Logical Foundations of Constitutional Democracy* (Ann Arbor: University of Michigan Press, 1962), 13.

7 Mancur Olson, *The Logic of Collective Action: Public Goods and the Theory of Groups* (New Haven: Yale University Press, 1965).

8 See Robert D. Tollison, "Rent Seeking," in *Perspectives on Public Choice*, 506–525.

9 See Mancur Olson, *The Rise and Decline of Nations: Economic Growth, Stagflation, and Social Rigidities* (New Haven: Yale University Press, 1982).

10 James O'Connor, *The Fiscal Crisis of the State* (New Brunswick, NJ: Transaction Publishers, 2001), 6. See also Claus Offe and Volker Ronge, "Theses on the Theory of the State," *New German Critique*, 6, Fall (1975):139–40.

11 Ibid., 9.

12 See Nicos Poulantzas, *State, Power, Socialism* (London: New Left Books, 1978), 133.

13 Jill Quadagno, "Theories of the Welfare State," *Annual Review of Sociology* 13 (1987): 116.

14 Fred Block, "Beyond Relative Autonomy: State Managers as Historical Subjects," in *The Socialist Register*, ed. Ralph Miliband and John Saville (London: Merlin, 1980), 233.

15 Richard Swedberg, *Principles of Economic Sociology* (Princeton: Princeton University Press, 2003), 1.

16 James G. March and Johan P. Olsen, *Rediscovering Institutions: The Organizational Basis of Politics* (New York: The Free Press, 1989), 160.

17 Elisabeth S. Clemens and James M. Cook, "Politics and Institutionalism: Explaining Durability and Change," *Annual Review of Sociology* 25 (1999): 442.

18 Paul Pierson, "Increasing Returns, Path Dependence, and the Study of Politics." *The American Political Science Review* 94, no. 2 (2000): 251–67.

19 Karl Polyani, *The Great Transformation: The Political and Economic Origins of Our Times* (Boston: Beacon Press, 1944), 79.

20 Fred Block, "Political Choice and the Multiple 'Logics' of Capital," *Theory and Society* 15, no. 1/2 (1986): 180.

21 See Lauren B. Edelman and Mark C. Suchman, "The Legal Environments of Organizations," *Annual Review of Sociology* 23 (1997): 479–515.

22 Ibid., 483.

23 Richard Swedberg, "The Case for an Economic Sociology of Law," *Theory and Society* 32, 1 (February 2003): 4.

24 Ronald H. Coase, "The Nature of the Firm," *Economica* 4 (1937): 386–405

25 John Micklethwait and Adrian Wooldridge, *The Company: A Short History of a Revolutionary Idea* (New York: Modern Library, 2003), xv.

26 See Alfred D. Chandler, Jr., "United States: Seedbed of Managerial Capitalism," in *Managerial Hierarchies: Comparative Perspectives on the Rise of the Modern Industrial Enterprise*, ed. Alfred D. Chandler, Jr., and Herman Daems (Cambridge: Harvard University Press, 1980).

27 See Ralph L Nelson, *Merger Movements in American Industry, 1895–1956* (Princeton: Princeton University Press, 1959).

28 Adolf A. Berle, Jr., and Gardiner C. Means, *The Modern Corporation and Private Property* (New York: Commerce Clearing House, 1932), 121. Also see Edward S. Herman, *Corporate Control, Corporate Power* (Cambridge: Cambridge University Press, 1981).

29 See Robert B. Reich, *The Next American Frontier* (New York: Times Books, 1983).

30 See John Zysman, *Governments, Markets, and Growth: Financial Systems and the Politics of Industrial Change* (Ithaca: Cornell University Press, 1983).

31 Claus Offe, "Two Logics of Collective Action," in *Disorganized Capitalism*, ed. John Keane (Cambridge: MIT Press, 1985), 176.

32 David Brian Robertson, *Capital, Labor, and State: The Battle for American Labor Markets from the Civil War to the New Deal* (Lanham, MD: Rowman and Littlefield, 2000), 257.

33 *Historical Statistics*, series D 951.

34 U.S. Department of Labor, Bureau of Labor Statistics, "Union Membership in 2008," USDL 09–0095 (January 28, 2009), 1–2.

35 See, for example, John L. Campbell, J. Rogers Hollingsworth, and Leon N. Lindberg, eds., *Governance of the American Economy* (Cambridge: Cambridge University Press, 1991), J. Rogers Hollingsworth, Phillipe C. Schmitter, and Wolfgang Streeck, *Governing Capitalist Economies: Performance and Control of Economic Sectors* (New York: Oxford University Press, 1994), J. Rogers Hollingsworth and Robert Boyer, *Contemporary Capitalism: The Embeddedness of Institutions* (Cambridge: Cambridge University Press, 1997), and Neil Fligstein, *The Architecture of Markets: An Economic Sociology of Twenty-First Century Capitalist Societies* (Princeton: Princeton University Press, 2001).

36 Neil Fligstein, "Markets as Politics: A Political-Cultural Approach to Market Institutions," *American Sociological Review* 61, no. 4 (1996): 658.

37 Ibid., 660.

38 See Oliver E. Williamson, "The Economics of Organization: The Transaction Cost Approach," *The American Journal of Sociology* 87, no. 3 (1981): 558, and more generally, Oliver E. Williamson, *The Economic Institutions of Capitalism* (New York: Free Press, 1985).

39 Greta R. Krippner, "The Elusive Market: Embeddedness and the Paradigm of Economic Sociology," *Theory and Society* 30, no. 6 (December 2001): 786.

40 Mark Granovetter, "Economic Action and Social Structure: The Problem of Embeddedness," *The American Journal of Sociology* 91, no. 3 (1985): 488.

41 Campbell, Hollingsworth, and Lindberg, 9–10.
42 This discussion draws on John L. Campbell and Leon N. Lindberg, "Property Rights and the Organization of Economic Activity by the State," *American Sociological Review* 55, no. 5. (1990): 634–47.
43 See George Bittlingmayer, "Antitrust and Business Activity: The First Quarter Century," *The Business History Review* 70, 3 (1996): 363–401.
44 See Marc Allen Eisner, "Markets in the Shadow of the State: An Appraisal of Deregulation and Implications for Future Research," in *Government and Markets: Toward a New Theory of Regulation*, ed. Edward Balleisen and David Moss (Cambridge: Cambridge University Press), 512–37.
45 Peter S. Rose, *Banking Across State Lines: Public and Private Consequences* (Westport, CT: Quorum Books, 1997), 37.
46 See Stephen D. Krasner, "Approaches to the State: Alternative Conceptions and Historical Dynamics," *Comparative Politics* 16, no. 2 (1984): 223–46
47 For a detailed discussion of path dependence, see Paul Pierson, *Politics in Time: History, Institutions, and Social Analysis* (Princeton, NJ: Princeton University Press, 2004), 17–53, and Andrew Bennett and Colin Elman, "Complex Causal Relations and Case Study Methods: The Example of Path Dependence," *Political Analysis* 14 (2006): 250–67.
48 Frank R. Baumgartner and Bryan D. Jones, "Positive and Negative Feedback in Politics," in *Policy Dynamics*, ed. Frank. R. Baumgartner and Bryan. D. Jones (Chicago: University of Chicago Press, 2002), 29–46.
49 B. Guy Peters, Jon Pierre, Desmond S. King, "The Politics of Path Dependency: Political Conflict in Historical Institutionalism," *The Journal of Politics* 67, no. 4 (2005): 1278.
50 Stephen Skowronek, *Building a New American State: The Expansion of National Administrative Capacities* (New York: Cambridge University Press, 1982).
51 Ibid., 286, 285.
52 See Frank R. Baumgartner and Bryan D. Jones, *Agendas and Instability in American Politics* (Chicago: University of Chicago Press, 1993).
53 See Robert Higgs, *Crisis and Leviathan: Critical Episodes in the Growth of American Government* (New York: Oxford University Press, 1987), 57–74.
54 See Theodore J. Lowi, *The Personal President: Power Invested, Promise Unfulfilled* (Ithaca, NY: Cornell University Press, 1985).
55 Marc Allen Eisner, *Regulatory Politics in Transition*, 2nd ed (Baltimore: Johns Hopkins University Press, 2000), 1.
56 Walter Dean Burnham, *Critical Elections and the Mainsprings of American Politics* (New York: W.W. Norton & Co., 1970), 10.
57 Mark Blyth, *Great Transformations: Economic Ideas and Institutional Change in the Twentieth Century* (Cambridge: Cambridge University Press, 2002), 32.
58 See the discussion in Blyth, ch. 3.
59 See Ibid., 49–51.
60 See David Vogel, *Fluctuating Fortunes: The Political Power of Business in America* (New York: Basic Books, 1989).
61 See Theda Skocpol and Kenneth Finegold, "State Capacity and Economic Intervention in the Early New Deal," *Political Science Quarterly* 97, no. 2 (1982): 255–78.
62 See Leon N. Lindberg, "Models of the Inflation-Disinflation Process," in *The Politics of Inflation and Economic Stagnation*, ed. Leon N. Lindberg and Charles S. Maier (Washington, D.C.: the Brookings Institution, 1985), 25–50.
63 Eric Schickler, *Disjointed Pluralism: Institutional Innovation and the Development of the U.S. Congress* (Princeton: Princeton University Press, 2001), 16. See Karen Orren and Stephen Skowronek, "Beyond the Iconography of Order:

Notes for a 'New' Institutionalism," in *The Dynamics of American Politics: Approaches and Interpretations*, ed. Larry Dodd and Calvin Jillson (Boulder: Westview, 1994), 311–30.

3 The Progressive Regime and the Regulatory State

1 United States Bureau of the Census, *Statistical History of the United States from Colonial Times to the Present* (New York: Basic Books, 1976), Series Q 321.
2 Richard Franklin Bensel, *The Political Economy of American Industrialization, 1877–1900* (Cambridge: Cambridge University Press, 2000), 291.
3 See Alfred D. Chandler, Jr., *Strategy and Structure: Chapters in the History of the Industrial Enterprise* (Cambridge: The M.I.T. Press, 1962) and Alfred D. Chandler, Jr., *The Railroads: The Nation's First Big Business* (New York: Harcourt, Brace & World, 1965).
4 See Alfred D. Chandler, Jr., *The Visible Hand: The Managerial Revolution in American Business* (Cambridge: Harvard University Press, 1977).
5 John F. Stover, *American Railroads* (Chicago: University of Chicago Press, 1961), 30–31, Lloyd J. Mercer, *Railroads and Land Grant Policy: A Study in Government Intervention* (New York: Academic Press, 1982), 7, and Morton Keller, *Affairs of State: Public Life in Nineteenth Century America* (Cambridge: Harvard University Press, 1977), 165–67.
6 Robert Sobel, *Inside Wall Street: Continuity and Change in the Financial District* (New York: W.W. Norton & Co., 1982), 334.
7 See *United States v. Trans-Missouri Freight Association*, 166 U.S. 290 (1897) and *United States v. Joint Traffic Association*, 171 U.S. 505 (1898).
8 Marc Allen Eisner, *Antitrust and the Triumph of Economics: Institutions, Expertise, and Policy Change* (Chapel Hill: University of North Carolina Press, 1991), 52–55, and George Bittlingmayer, "Did Antitrust Policy Cause the Great Merger Wave?" *Journal of Law and Economics* 28, no. 1 (April 1985): 77–118.
9 Bittlingmayer, 99.
10 Bureau of the Census, Series D 942, 943, and 945.
11 Author's calculations based on Bureau of the Census, Series D 977 and 982.
12 Author's calculation based on Bureau of the Census, Series C 89, 131, and 133.
13 Douglas W. Steeples and David O. Whitten, *Democracy in Desperation: the Depression of 1893* (Westport, CT: Greenwood Press, 1998), 53.
14 For an excellent review of the period and a critique of the realignment thesis, see Jeffrey M. Stonecash and Everita Silina, "The 1896 Realignment: A Reassessment," *American Politics Research* 33, no. 3 (2005): 3–32.
15 Dorothy Ross, *The Origins of American Social Science* (Cambridge: Cambridge University Press, 1991), 156.
16 Ronald J. Pestritto, *Woodrow Wilson and the Roots of Modern Liberalism* (Lanham, MD: Rowman & Littlefield, 2005), 6–7. Much of the discussion in this paragraph draws on this volume.
17 Herbert Croly, *The Promise of American Life* (New York: The Macmillan Company, 1911), 400.
18 See Leon Epstein, *Political Parties in the American Mold* (Madison: University of Wisconsin Press, 1986).
19 Martin Shefter, *Political Parties and the State: The American Historical Experience* (Princeton: Princeton University Press, 1994), 76.
20 James A. Morone, *The Democratic Wish: Popular Participation and the Limits of American Government* (New York: Basic Books, 1990), 98.

21 Woodrow Wilson, *The New Freedom* (New York: Doubleday, Page & Company, 1913), 46–48.

22 Francis L. Broderick, *Progressivism at Risk: Electing a President in 1912* (New York: Greenwood Press, 1989), 35.

23 William Howard Taft, "Message on Interstate Commerce and Anti-Trust Laws and Federal Incorporation, January 7, 1910," in *Presidential Addresses and State Papers of William Howard Taft*, Vol. 1 (New York: Doubleday, Page & Co., 1919), 534.

24 Theodore Roosevelt, "National Life and Character," *The Sewanee Review* 2, no. 3 (1894): 368, 369.

25 Theodore Roosevelt, "Kidds' Social Evolution," *The North American Review* 161, no. 464 (1895): 97–98.

26 Theodore Roosevelt, "The New Nationalism," in *The Works of Theodore Roosevelt* (New York: Charles Scribner's Sons, 1926), 17: 12.

27 Theodore Roosevelt, "A Confession of Faith," in *The Works of Theodore Roosevelt*, 17: 280–81.

28 William Howard Taft, *Our Chief Magistrate and His Powers* (New York: Columbia University Press, 1916), 144–45.

29 "Review," *The North American Review* 194, no. 671 (1911): 633.

30 Woodrow Wilson, "The Lawyer and the Community," *The North American Review* 192, no. 660 (1910): 610–11, 617.

31 Woodrow Wilson, "The Law and the Facts: Presidential Address, Seventh Annual Meeting of the American Political Science Association," *The American Political Science Review* 5, no. 1 (1911): 9.

32 Woodrow Wilson, "An Address to the Workingmen in Fall River, Massachusetts, September 26, 1912," in *The Papers of Woodrow Wilson* (Princeton, N.J.: Princeton University Press, 1978), 25: 261–62.

33 Woodrow Wilson, *The New Freedom: A Call for the Emancipation of the Generous Energies of a People* (New York: Doubleday, Page & Co., 1913), 201–2.

34 Ibid., 172, 173.

35 Nathan B. Williams, "The Federal Trade Commission Law," *Annals of the American Academy of Political and Social Science* 63 (1916): 2.

36 Allen Ripley Foote, "Unregulated Competition Is Destructive of National Welfare," *Annals of the American Academy of Political and Social Science* 42 (1912): 113, 112, 114.

37 See the discussion in Marc Allen Eisner, *Regulatory Politics in Transition*, 2nd ed (Baltimore: Johns Hopkins University Press, 2000), 49–58.

38 Stephen Skowronek, *Building a New American State: The Expansion of National Administrative Capacities, 1877–1920* (Cambridge: Cambridge University Press, 1982), 138–39.

39 *Interstate Commerce Commission v. Cincinnati, New Orleans, and Texas Pacific Railway Co.* 167 U.S. 479, 494–95.

40 Quoted in Interstate Commerce Commission, *Eleventh Annual Report of the Interstate Commerce Commission, December 6, 1897* (Washington, D.C.: Government Printing Office, 1897), 50–51.

41 Joshua Bernhardt, *The Interstate Commerce Commission: Its History, Activities, and Organization* (Baltimore: Johns Hopkins University Press, 1923), 21–28, Robert E. Cushman, *The Independent Regulatory Commissions* (New York: Oxford University Press, 1941), 103.

42 Woodrow Wilson, "Address to a Joint Session of Congress on Trusts and Monopolies, January 20, 1914." Available at http://www.presidency.ucsb.edu/ws/?pid=65374

43 Quoted in Benjamin J. Klebaner, "Potential Competition and the American

Antitrust Legislation of 1914," *The Business History Review* 38, no. 2 (1964): 180.

44 *Standard Oil of New Jersey v. United States,* 221 U.S. 1 (1911).

45 Senate debates, 63rd Congress, 2nd sess., June 25–August 4, 1914, in *The Economic Regulation of Business and Industry: A Legislative History of U.S. Regulatory Agencies,* ed. Bernard Schwartz (New York: Chelsea House Publishers, 1973), 3: 1765.

46 Samuel Untermyer, "Completing the Anti-Trust Programme," *The North American Review* 199, no. 701 (1914): 536, 537.

47 See Eisner, *Regulatory Politics,* 58–65.

48 Robert L. Owen, "The Origin, Plan, and Purpose of the Currency Bill," *The North American Review* 198, no. 695 (1913): 556, 560.

49 This account draws on John T. Woolley, *Monetary Politics: The Federal Reserve and the Politics of Monetary Policy* (Cambridge: Cambridge University Press, 1986), ch. 2.

50 E. M. Patterson, "The Organization and Work of the Federal Reserve Board," *Annals of the American Academy of Political and Social Science* 63 (1916): 89.

51 O. M. W. Sprague, "The Federal Reserve Act of 1913," *The Quarterly Journal of Economics* 28, no. 2 (1914): 218.

52 Frank A. Vanderlip, "How to Amend the Currency Bill," *The North American Review* 198, no. 696 (1913): 701–2.

53 Woolley, 40.

54 Quoted in J. Laurence Laughlin, "The Banking and Currency Act of 1913: I," *The Journal of Political Economy* 22, no. 4 (1914): 305.

55 Ibid., 304.

56 Owen, 567.

57 Laughlin, 314, 315.

58 Vanderlip, 703.

59 See Marc Allen Eisner, *From Warfare State to Welfare State: World War I, Compensatory State Building, and the Limits of the Modern Order* (University Park: The Pennsylvania State University Press, 2000).

60 Theodore Roosevelt, *America and the World War* (New York: Charles Scribner's Sons, 1915), 184–85, 244.

61 Grosvenor B. Clarkson, *Industrial America in the World War: The Strategy Behind the Lines, 1917–1918* (Boston: Houghton Mifflin Co., 1923), 111.

62 Frederic L. Paxson, "The American War Government, 1917–18," *The American Historical Review* 26, no. 1 (1920): 76.

63 Robert D. Cuff, "Woodrow Wilson and Business-Government Relations During World War I," *The Review of Politics* 31, no. 3 (1969): 404–5.

64 Robert D. Cuff, *The War Industries Board: Business-Government Relations During World War I* (Baltimore: Johns Hopkins University Press, 1973), 158, 174.

65 Paul Koistinen, "The 'Industrial-Military Complex' in Historical Perspective: World War I," *Business History Review* 41, no. 4 (1967): 394.

66 Jordan A. Schwarz, *The Speculator: Bernard M. Baruch in Washington, 1917–1965* (Chapel Hill: University of North Carolina Press, 1981), 74–75.

67 Bureau of the Census, series F 3. Calculations by author.

68 John Maurice Clark, *The Costs of the World War to the American People* (New Haven: Yale University Press, 1931), 44.

69 Bureau of the Census, series F 3. Calculations by author.

70 Ellis W. Hawley, *The Great War and the Search for a Modern Order: A History of the American People and Their Institutions, 1917–1933* (New York: St. Martin's Press, 1979), 18–19.

71 Eric F. Goldman, *Rendezvous with Destiny: A History of Modern American Reform* (New York: Alfred A. Knopf, 1958), 307.

72 See National Industrial Conference Board, *Trade Associations: Their Economic Significance and Legal Status* (New York: National Industrial Conference Board, 1925), app. B.

4 The Rise of the New Deal Regime

1 The period examined in this chapter is explored in detail in Marc Allen Eisner, *From Warfare State to Welfare State: World War I, Compensatory State Building, and the Limits of the Modern Order* (University Park: The Pennsylvania State University Press, 2000).

2 Edward N. Hurley, *Awakening of Business* (New York: Doubleday, Page & Co., 1916), 42, 207–8.

3 Herbert Hoover, *American Individualism* (Garden City, NY: Doubleday, Page & Co., 1922), 32–33, 17.

4 James Stuart Olson, *Herbert Hoover and the Reconstruction Finance Corporation, 1931–1933* (Ames: Iowa State University Press, 1977), 20.

5 Herbert Hoover, *The Challenge to Liberty* (New York: Charles Scribner's Sons, 1934), 41.

6 Department of Commerce, *Report of the President's Conference on Unemployment* (Washington, D.C.: Government Printing Office, 1921), 103, 159, 165.

7 Ibid., 34.

8 See Evan B. Metcalf, "Secretary Hoover and the Emergence of Macroeconomic Management," *Business History Review* 49, 1 (1975): 60–80, and William J. Barber, *From New Era to New Deal: Herbert Hoover, the Economists, and American Economic Policy, 1921–1933* (Cambridge: Cambridge University Press, 1985).

9 E. Pendleton Herring, *Public Administration in the Public Interest* (New York: McGraw-Hill, 1936), 130–31.

10 Federal Trade Commission, *Annual Report, 1927* (Washington, D.C.: Government Printing Office, 1927), 1.

11 John Kenneth Galbraith, *The Great Crash: 1929* (Boston: Houghton Mifflin, 1988), 135–45, and William J. Shultz, and M.R. Caine, *Financial Development of the United States* (New York: Prentice-Hall, 1937), 628–66.

12 Milton Friedman and Anna Jacobson Schwartz, *A Monetary History of the United States, 1867–1960* (Princeton: Princeton University Press, 1963), 418.

13 See Peter Temin, *Lessons from the Great Depression* (Cambridge: The MIT Press, 1989), 46, and Alfred E. Eckes, Jr., *Opening America's Market: US Foreign Trade Policy Since 1776* (Chapel Hill: University of North Carolina Press, 1995), 100–139.

14 Merle Thorpe, "Partners for Prosperity," *Nation's Business* 18, no. 1 (1930): 9.

15 Herbert Hoover, "Press Statement of February 3, 1931," reprinted in Ray Lyman Wilbur and Arthur Mastick Hyde, *The Hoover Policies* (New York: Charles Scribner's Sons, 1937), 375.

16 Elliot A. Rosen, *Hoover, Roosevelt, and the Brains Trust: From Depression to New Deal* (New York: Columbia University Press, 1977), 63.

17 See Paul Blanshard, "Socialist and Capitalist Planning," *Annals of the American Academy of Political and Social Science* 162 (1932): 6–11, and "A Panorama of Economic Planning," *Nation's Business* 20, no. 2 (1932): 29–32.

18 Glenn Frank, "Notes on the Renewal of America," *Annals of the American Academy of Political and Social Science* 162 (1932): 156, 159.

19 Herbert Hoover, "Message to Congress, December 8, 1931," reprinted in

Myers and Newton, 149. See James Stuart Olson, *Herbert Hoover and the Reconstruction Finance Corporation, 1931–1933* (Ames: Iowa State University Press, 1977), 33–39.

20 Olson, 65–67.

21 Jordan A. Schwarz, *The Interregnum of Despair: Hoover, Congress, and the Depression* (Urbana: University of Illinois Press, 1970), 253.

22 Bureau of the Census, series D 86.

23 Franklin Delano Roosevelt "Commonwealth Club Address, delivered 23 Sept 1932, San Francisco, CA." Available at http://www.americanrhetoric.com/speeches/fdrcommonwealth.htm

24 Franklin D. Roosevelt, "First Inaugural Address, March 4, 1933." Available at http://www.presidency.ucsb.edu/ws/?pid=14473

25 Rexford G. Tugwell, *In Search of Roosevelt* (Cambridge: Harvard University Press, 1972), 116–17, 281–82.

26 The conflict between these two positions is explored in depth in Ellis W. Hawley, *The New Deal and the Problem of Monopoly: A Study in Economic Ambivalence* (Princeton: Princeton University Press, 1980).

27 For an overview of these debates, see William J. Barber, *Designs within Disorder: Franklin D. Roosevelt, The Economists, and the Shaping of American Economic Policy, 1933–1945* (New York: Cambridge University Press, 1996) and Mark Blyth, *Great Transformations: Economic Ideas and Institutional Change in the Twentieth Century* (Cambridge: Cambridge University Press, 2002), 49–51.

28 Quoted in Gerard Swope, "Planning and Economic Organization." *Proceedings of the Academy of Political Science* 15, no. 4 (1934): 87.

29 Sidney Hillman, "The NRA, Labor, and Recovery," *Annals of the American Academy of Political and Social Science* 172 (1934): 73–74.

30 Dudley Cates, "A Current Appraisal of the National Recovery Administration," *Annals of the American Academy of Political and Social Science* 172 (1934): 135, 130.

31 Walter C. Teagle, "The Recovery Program in Operation," *Proceedings of the Academy of Political Science* 15, no. 4 (1934): 46.

32 Quoted in Michael Alan Bernstein, *The Great Depression: Delayed Recovery and Economic Change in America, 1929–1939* (Cambridge: Cambridge University Press, 1989), 196.

33 Peter H. Irons, *The New Deal Lawyers* (Princeton: Princeton University Press, 1993), 27.

34 295 U.S. 495 (1935).

35 Richard S. Kirkendall, "The New Deal and Agriculture," *in The New Deal: The National Level*, ed. John Braeman, Robert H. Bremmer, and David Brody (Columbus: Ohio State University Press, 1975), 1: 85.

36 For a detailed discussion of the AAA see J. Henry Richardson, "The 'New Deal' in the United States," *Economic Journal* 44, no. 176 (1934): 567–615.

37 Ibid., 586–87, and Richard Polenberg, *The Era of Franklin D. Roosevelt, 1933–1945: A Brief History with Documents* (New York: Macmillan, 2000), 12.

38 Joseph S. Davis, "AAA as a Force in Recovery," *Journal of Farm Economics* 17, no. 1 (1935), 8–9.

39 Harold Hoffsommer, "The AAA and the Cropper," *Social Forces* 13, no. 4 (1935): 499, 498.

40 Jonathan M. Wiener, "Class Structure and Economic Development in the American South, 1865–1955," *The American Historical Review* 84, no. 4 (1979): 989, 990.

41 297 U.S. 1 (1936).

42 Theda Skocpol and Kenneth Finegold, "State Capacity and Economic

Intervention in the Early New Deal," *Political Science Quarterly* 97, no. 2 (1982), 271, 277.

43 Susan Previant Lee and Peter Passell, *A New Economic View of American History* (New York: W.W. Norton & Co., 1979), 369.

44 W. L. Crum and J. B. Hubbard, "Review of the First Quarter of 1933," *The Review of Economics and Statistics* 15, no. 2 (1933): 69.

45 Friedman and Schwartz, 440. Figures on bank failures calculated from data, 438–39.

46 Ibid., 445–49.

47 Marc Allen Eisner, *Regulatory Politics in Transition*, 2nd ed (Baltimore: Johns Hopkins University Press, 2000), 106–11.

48 Thomas K. McCraw, "With the Consent of the Governed: SEC's Formative Years," *Journal of Policy Analysis and Management* 1, no. 3 (1982): 359.

49 John L. Lewis, "Labor and the National Recovery Administration," *Annals of the American Academy of Political and Social Science* 172 (1934): 58.

50 Fremont Rider, "Is There Any Solution for the Labor Problem?" *The North American Review* 238, no. 3 (Sep., 1934): 247.

51 Bureau of the Census, series D 970, 971.

52 David J. Saposs, "The American Labor Movement Since the War," *The Quarterly Journal of Economics* 49, no. 2 (1935): 251.

53 Bureau of the Census, series D 950, 951, 936, 937.

54 See Eisner, *Regulatory Politics*, 97–103.

55 James T. Patterson, *America's Struggle Against Poverty, 1900–1985* (Cambridge: Harvard University Press, 1986), 57.

56 Quoted in Ibid., 59.

57 Paul H. Landis, "On the Evolution of Dependency Mores in the Primary Group under Federal Relief Agencies," *Social Forces* 13, no. 4 (May, 1935): 556, 559.

58 Franklin D. Roosevelt, "Annual Message to Congress, January 4, 1935." Available at http://www.presidency.ucsb.edu/ws/?pid=14890

59 Mary Poole, *The Segregated Origins of Social Security: African Americans and the Welfare State* (Chapel Hill: University of North Carolina Press, 2006), 181.

60 Larry DeWitt, "Historical Background and Development of Social Security." Available at http://www.ssa.gov/history/briefhistory3.html

61 Bureau of the Census, series D 85.

62 W. L. Crum, R. A. Gordon, Dorothy Wescott, "Review of the Year 1937," *The Review of Economics and Statistics* 20, no. 1 (1938): 43.

63 Kenneth D. Roose, "The Recession of 1937–38," *The Journal of Political Economy* 56, no. 3 (1948): 241.

64 Friedman and Schwartz, 529.

65 Roosevelt, "Annual Message, 1935."

66 Quoted in Ronald Edsforth, *The New Deal: America's Response to the Great Depression* (New York: Wiley-Blackwell, 2000), 238.

67 W. Elliot Brownlee, *Federal Taxation in America: A Short History* (Cambridge: Cambridge University Press, 2004), 95.

68 See Patrick Renshaw, "Was There a Keynesian Economy in the USA between 1933 and 1945?" *Journal of Contemporary History* 34, no. 3 (1999): 337–64.

69 Robert M. Collins, "Positive Business Responses to the New Deal: The Roots of the Committee for Economic Development, 1933–42," *The Business History Review* 52, no. 3 (1978): 375.

70 Ibid., 378.

71 Herbert Stein, *The Fiscal Revolution in America* (Washington, D.C.: The AEI Press, 1990), 111. The summary of the Ruml memo is drawn from Stein's discussion.

72 Franklin D. Roosevelt, "On Economic Conditions." Radio Address of the President, Broadcast from the White House, April 14, 1938. Available at http://www.fdrlibrary.marist.edu/041438.html

73 Stein, 114.

74 Thurman W. Arnold, "Antitrust Enforcement: Past and Future," *Law and Contemporary Problems* 7, no. 1 (1940): 9.

75 Department of Justice, *Annual Report of the Attorney General of the United States* (Washington, D.C.: Government Printing Office, 1939), 38.

76 See Marc Allen Eisner, *Antitrust and the Triumph of Economics: Institutions, Expertise, and Policy Change* (Chapel Hill: University of North Carolina Press, 1990), 77–83.

77 Franklin D. Roosevelt, "Message from the President of the United States Transmitting Recommendations Relative to the Strengthening and Enforcement of Anti-trust Laws," *The American Economic Review* 32, no. 2, Part 2, Supplement, Papers Relating to the Temporary National Economic Committee (1942): 122, 128.

78 Robert A. Brady, "Reports and Conclusions of the Temporary National Economic Committee (U.S.A.)," *The Economic Journal* 53, no. 212 (1943): 414, 415.

79 Council of Economic Advisers, *Economic Report of the President, 2009* (Washington, D.C.: Government Printing Office, 2009), Table B-79.

80 Bureau of the Census, series D 85.

81 Tom Kemp, *The Climax of Capitalism: The U.S. Economy in the Twentieth Century* (London: Longman, 1990), 99.

82 Foster Rhea Dulles and Melvyn Dubofsky, *Labor In America: A History*, 4th ed (Arlington Heights, Ill.: Harlan-Davidson, 1984), 322–23.

83 Bureau of the Census, series D 951.

84 See Dulles and Dubofsky, 324–25.

85 Merle Fainsod, Lincoln Gordon, and Joseph C. Palamountain, Jr., *Government and the American Economy*, 3rd ed (New York: W.W. Norton & Co., 1959), 208, 850.

86 Donald M. Nelson, *Arsenal of Democracy: The Story of American War Production* (New York: Harcourt, Brace and Co., 1946), 205.

87 Richard Polenberg, *War and Society: The United States, 1941–1945* (Philadelphia: J.B. Lippincott, 1972), 219.

88 See the discussion of reconversion in Gregory Hooks, *Forging the Military-Industrial Complex: World War II's Battle of the Potomac* (Urbana: University of Illinois Press, 1991).

89 Brian Waddell, *The War Against the New Deal: World War II and American Democracy* (DeKalb: Northern Illinois Press, 2001), 126.

90 R. Elberton Smith, *The Army and Economic Mobilization* (Washington, D.C.: Center for Military History, United States Army, 1991), 683–93.

91 Ibid., 686–94.

92 John Morton Blum, *V was for Victory: Politics and American Culture During World War II* (San Diego: Harcourt Brace Javanovich, 1976), 130.

93 William F. Shughart II, "Bending before the Storm: The U.S. Supreme Court in Economic Crisis, 1935–37," *The Independent Review* 9, no.1 (2004): 55–83.

94 See Theodore J. Lowi, *The Personal President: Power Invested, Promise Unfulfilled* (Ithaca, NY: Cornell University Press, 1985).

95 Quoted in John W. Sloan, *Eisenhower and the Management of Prosperity* (Lawrence: University Press of Kansas, 1991), 62.

96 George H. Mayer, *The Republican Party, 1854–1966*, 2nd ed (New York: Oxford University Press, 1967), 498.

5 The Postwar Consolidation of the New Deal Regime

1 Bureau of the Census, *Historical Statistics of the United States*, series D-85.
2 John Maynard Keynes, *The General Theory of Employment, Interest, and Money* (New York: Harcourt Brace Javanovich Publishers, 1964), 249–50.
3 Herbert Stein, *The Fiscal Revolution in America*, revised edition (Washington, D.C.: The American Enterprise Institute, 1990), 165.
4 Franklin D. Roosevelt, "State of the Union Message to Congress, January 11, 1944." Available at http://www.presidency.ucsb.edu/ws/?pid=16518
5 Quoted in Alvin H. Hansen, *Economic Policy and Full Employment* (New York: McGraw Hill, 1947), 107.
6 Quoted in James E. Murray, "A Practical Approach," *The American Political Science Review* 39, no. 6 (1945): 1122.
7 William P. Quigley, *Ending Poverty as We Know It: Guaranteeing a Right to a Job at a Living Wage* (Philadelphia: Temple University Press, 2003), 110.
8 Murray, 1123.
9 Mark Blyth, *Great Transformations: Economic Ideas and Institutional Change in the Twentieth Century* (Cambridge: Cambridge University Press, 2002), 82.
10 Murray, 1120.
11 J. Bradford De Long, "Keynesianism, Pennsylvania Avenue Style: Some Economic Consequences of the Employment Act of 1946," *The Journal of Economic Perspectives* 10, no. 3 (1996): 42.
12 Seymour E. Harris, "Some Aspects of the Murray Full Employment Bill," *The Review of Economics and Statistics* 27, no. 3 (1945): 104.
13 Sumner H. Slichter, "Comments on the Murray Bill," *The Review of Economics and Statistics* 27, no. 3 (1945): 110.
14 E. E. Schattschneider, "Party Government and Employment Policy," *The American Political Science Review* 39, no. 6 (1945): 1148–49, 1150, 1156.
15 See Robert M. Collins, *The Business Response to Keynes, 1929–1964* (New York: Columbia University Press, 1981), 100–5.
16 Margaret Weir, *Politics and Jobs: The Boundaries of Employment Policy in the United States* (Princeton: Princeton University Press, 1992), 52. See the discussion of the debates in Stein, 197–204, and Collins, 100–1.
17 See G.J. Santoni, "The Employment Act of 1946: Some History Notes," Federal Reserve Bank of St. Louis, November (1986): 5–16.
18 Jacob Viner, "The Employment Act of 1946 in Operation," *The Review of Economics and Statistics* 29, no. 2 (1947): 77.
19 Alvin H. Hansen, "The First Reports Under the Employment Act of 1946," *The Review of Economics and Statistics* 29, no. 2 (1947): 69, 70.
20 Viner, 78.
21 See Douglas Hibbs, "Political Parties and Macroeconomic Policy," *American Political Science Review* 71, no. 4 (1977): 1467–87.
22 Keynes, 372.
23 De Long, 47.
24 Committee for Economic Development, *Taxes and the Budget: A Program for Prosperity in a Free Economy* (New York: Committee for Economic Development, 1947).
25 Stein, 223. See Albert G. Hart, "Timing and Administering Fiscal Policy: How to Give Relevant Counsel," *The American Economic Review* 38, no. 2 (1948): 430–42.
26 Office of Management and Budget, Table 1–2, calculations by author.
27 Richard E. Neustadt, *Presidential Power: The Politics of Leadership From FDR to Carter* (New York: John Wiley & Sons. 1980), 26.
28 James A. Thurber, "The Consequences of Budget Reform for Congressional-

Presidential Relations," *Annals of the American Academy of Political and Social Science* 499 (1988): 104.

29 See John T. Woolley, *Monetary Politics: The Federal Reserve and the Politics of Monetary Policy* (Cambridge: Cambridge University Press, 1986).

30 Paul Peretz, *The Political Economy of Inflation in the United States* (Chicago: University of Chicago Press, 1983), 165.

31 Tyler Cowan, "The Marshall Plan: Myths and Realities," in *US Aid to the Developing World: A Free Market Agenda*, ed. Doug Bandow (Washington, D.C.: The Heritage Foundation, 1985), 63.

32 James M. Boughton, "Why White, Not Keynes? Inventing the Postwar International Monetary System," IMF Working Paper No. 02/52 (Washington, D.C.: International Monetary Fund, 2002), 4.

33 Henry Morgenthau Jr., "Bretton Woods and International Cooperation," *Foreign Affairs* 23, no. 2 (1945): 185.

34 Mabel Newcomer, "Bretton Woods and a Durable Peace," *Annals of the American Academy of Political and Social Science* 240 (1945): 40.

35 John W. Pehle, "The Bretton Woods Institutions," *The Yale Law Journal* 55, no. 5 (1946): 1130, 1131.

36 Eugene Staley, "The Economic Side of Stable Peace," *Annals of the American Academy of Political and Social Science* 240 (1945): 34.

37 Newcomer, 39–40.

38 Valdemar Carlson, "Bretton Woods and Wall Street," *The Antioch Review* 4, no. 3 (1944): 352.

39 B. H. Beckhart, "The Bretton Woods Proposal for an International Monetary Fund," *Political Science Quarterly* 59, no. 4 (1944): 518.

40 Carlson, 375.

41 Alvin H. Hansen, "A Brief Note on Fundamental Disequilibrium," *The Review of Economics and Statistics* 26, no. 4 (1944): 183.

42 William Fellner, "The Commercial Policy Implications of the Fund and Bank," *The American Economic Review* 35, no. 2, (1945): 265, 269–70.

43 See Joseph Stiglitz, *Globalization and Its Discontents* (New York: W.W. Norton, 2002).

44 Harry D. White, "The International Monetary Fund: The First Year," *Annals of the American Academy of Political and Social Science* 252 (1947): 28.

45 Leicester Webb, "The Future of International Trade," *World Politics* 5, no. 4 (1953): 429.

46 John W. Evans, "United States Foreign Trade Policy: A Practical Approach," *Journal of Farm Economics* 31, no. 1 (1949): 505.

47 Margaret S. Gordon, "The Character and Significance of the General Commitments That Nations will Make Under the ITO," *The American Economic Review* 39, no. 3, (1949): 244, 250.

48 Webb, 430.

49 Barry Eichengreen, *Globalizing Capital: A History of the International Monetary System*, 2nd ed (Princeton: Princeton University Press, 2008), 99.

50 See Robert Kuttner, *The End of Laissez-Faire: National Purposes and the Global Economy After the Cold War* (New York: Alfred A. Knopf, 1991), 40–43.

51 George Bronz, "An International Trade Organization: The Second Attempt," *Harvard Law Review* 69, no. 3 (1956): 453.

52 Quoted in Irving B. Kravis, "The Trade Agreements Escape Clause," *The American Economic Review* 44, no. 3 (1954): 321.

53 See Kumiko Koyama, "The Passage of the Smoot-Hawley Tariff Act: Why Did the President Sign the Bill?" *Journal of Policy History* 21, No. 2 (2009): 163–86.

54 Joan Edelman Spero, *The Politics of International Economic Relations* (New York: St. Martin's Press, 1977), 70–71.
55 Douglas A. Irwin, "The GATT in Historical Perspective," *The American Economic Review* 85, no. 2 (1995), 327.
56 World Trade Organization, "Press Brief: Fiftieth Anniversary of the Multilateral Trading System." http://www.wto.org/english/theWTO_e/minist_e/min96_e/chrono.htm
57 J. Michael Donnelly, "US-World Merchandise Trade Data: 1948–2006," CRS Report for Congress, RS22612 (Washington, D.C.: Congressional Research Service, 2007), 3.
58 Department of Commerce, Bureau of Economic Analysis, US International Trade in Goods and Services. http://www.bea.gov/newsreleases/international/trade/trad_time_series.xls
59 Bureau of the Census, series D-935, 949, 977–78.
60 Robert A. Taft, "The Taft-Hartley Act: A Favorable View," *Annals of the American Academy of Political and Social Science* 274 (1951): 198, 199.
61 William Green, "The Taft-Hartley Act: A Critical View," *Annals of the American Academy of Political and Social Science* 274, (1951): 201.
62 John B. Judis, *The Paradox of American Democracy: Elites, Special Interests, and the Betrayal of Public Trust* (New York: Routledge, 2001), 70.
63 Foster Rhea Dulles and Melvyn Dubofsky, *Labor in America: A History*, 4th ed (Arlington Heights, IL: Harlan Davidson, 1984), 345–46.
64 Henry S. Farber, "Union Membership in the United States: The Divergence between the Public and Private Sectors," Working Paper #503, Princeton University Industrial Relations Section, 2005, 11.
65 Aaron Levenstein, "Interfederation Warfare and Its Prospects," *Annals of the American Academy of Political and Social Science* 248 (1946): 49, 53.
66 See James B. Carey, "Organized Labor in Politics," *Annals of the American Academy of Political and Social Science* 319 (1958): 52–62.
67 John Harris Howell, *The Right to Manage: Industrial Relations Policies of American Business in the 1940s* (Madison: University of Wisconsin Press, 1982), 150.
68 Alan Wolfe, *America's Impasse: The Rise and Fall of the Politics of Growth* (New York: Pantheon Books, 1981), 59.
69 Howell, 156.
70 Michael French, *US Economic History Since 1945* (Manchester: Manchester University Press, 1997), 101.
71 James T. Bennett, Bruce E. Kaufman, "Introduction," in *The Future of Private Sector Unionism in the United States*, ed. James T. Bennett, Bruce E. Kaufman (Armonk, N.Y.: M.E. Sharpe, 2002), 6.

6 The Rise and Pause of the Keynesian Welfare State

1 "Democratic Platform, 1960," in *National Party Platforms, 1840–1960*, ed. Kirk H. Porter and Donald Bruce Johnson (Urbana: University of Illinois Press, 1961), 583.
2 Council of Economic Advisers, *Economic Report of the President, 1963* (Washington, D.C.: Government Printing Office, 1963), xxiv–v, 74.
3 Council of Economic Advisers, *Economic Report of the President, 1965* (Washington, D.C.: Government Printing Office,1965), 38. See Herbert Stein, *Presidential Economics: The Making of Economic Policy from Roosevelt to Reagan and Beyond* (Washington, D.C.: American Enterprise Institute, 1988), 112.

4 Council of Economic Advisers, *Economic Report of the President, 1964* (Washington, D.C.: Government Printing Office 1964), 15, 16.

5 Sheldon Danziger and Robert D. Plotnick, "Poverty and Policy: Lessons of the Last Two Decades," *The Social Service Review* 60, no. 1(1986): 48.

6 Council of Economic Advisers, *Economic Report of the President, 1967* (Washington, D.C.: Government Printing Office, 1967), 10.

7 See Marc Allen Eisner, Jeff Worsham, and Evan J. Ringquist, *Contemporary Regulatory Policy*, 2nd ed (Boulder, CO: Lynne Rienner, 2006), chapter 1.

8 Richard M. Nixon, "Annual Message on the State of the Union, January 22, 1970." Available at http://www.presidency.ucsb.edu/ws/index.php?pid=2921

9 See Samuel P. Huntington, "The Marasmus of the ICC: The Commission, the Railroads, and the Public Interest," *Yale Law Journal* 61 (1952): 467–509; Gabriel Kolko, *The Triumph of Conservatism: A Reinterpretation of American History, 1900–1916* (New York: Free Press, 1963), and Marver H. Bernstein, *Regulating Business by Independent Commission* (Princeton: Princeton University Press, 1955).

10 See Richard B. Stewart, "The Reformation of American Administrative Law," *Harvard Law Review* 88, no. 8 (1975): 1667–1813.

11 See Patrick G. Donnelly, "The Origins of the Occupational Safety and Health Act of 1970." *Social Problems* 30, no. 1 (1982): 13–25.

12 See Eisner et al., 91–92.

13 Kevin L. Yuill, *Richard Nixon and the Rise of Affirmative Action: The Pursuit of Racial Equality in an Era of Limits* (Lanham, MD: Rowman & Littlefield, 2006), 135–58, and Joan Hoff, *Nixon Reconsidered* (New York: Basic Books, 1994), 92–93.

14 See William Poole, "Gradualism: A Mid-Course View," *Brookings Papers on Economic Activity* 1970, no. 2 (1970): 271–301.

15 Andrew Rudalevige, *The New Imperial Presidency: Renewing Presidential Power after Watergate* (Ann Arbor: University of Michigan Press, 2005), 91.

16 See Leondard Silk, *Nixonomics*, 2nd ed (New York: Praeger, 1973), 53–69, and Robert R. Keller and Ann Mari May, "The Presidential Political Business Cycle of 1972," *The Journal of Economic History* 44, no. 2 (1984): 269–70.

17 Robert L. Hetzel, *The Monetary Policy of the Federal Reserve: A History* (Cambridge: Cambridge University Press, 2008), 84–86.

18 Arnold Weber, "The Continuing Courtship: Wage-Price Policy through Five Administrations," in *Exhortation and Controls: The Search for a Wage-Price Policy, 1945–1971*, ed. Craufurd D. Goodwin (Washington, D.C.: Brookings Institution, 1975), 252.

19 Silk, 75–79.

20 Fritz W. Scharpf, "Economic and Institutional Constraints of Full-Employment Strategies: Sweden, Austria, and West Germany, 1973–82," in *Order and Conflict in Contemporary Capitalism: Studies in the Political Economy of Western European Nations*, ed. John H. Goldthorpe (Oxford: Oxford University Press, 1984), 271, 274.

21 See Keller and May.

22 Daniel J. B. Mitchell, "Wage-Price Controls and Inflation," *Proceedings of the Academy of Political Science* 31, no. 4 (1975): 120–22.

23 Gerald Ford, "Address to a Joint Session of the Congress, August 12, 1974." Available at http://www.presidency.ucsb.edu/ws/index.php?pid=4694

24 Alan S. Blinder, *Economic Policy and the Great Stagflation* (New York: Academic Press, 1979), 209–16.

25 Robert M. Collins, *More: the Politics of Economic Growth in Postwar America* (New York: Oxford University Press, 2000), 168–69.

26 Margaret Weir, *Politics and Jobs: The Boundaries of Employment Policy in the United States* (Princeton: Princeton University Press, 1992), 136–39; Stephen Woolcock, "The Economic Policies of the Carter Administration," in *The Carter Years: The Presidency and Policy Making*, ed. M. G. Abernathy, D. M. Hill and P. Williams (New York: St. Martin's Press, 1984), 37–38.

27 See Erwin C. Hargrove, *Jimmy Carter as President: Leadership and the Politcs of the Public Good* (Baton Rouge: Louisiana State University Press, 1988), ch. 4.

28 Weir, 134–41.

29 Collins, 170.

30 J. Bradford De Long, "Keynesianism, Pennsylvania Avenue Style: Some Economic Consequences of the Employment Act of 1946," *The Journal of Economic Perspectives* 10, no. 3 (1996): 42.

31 W. Carl Biven, *Jimmy Carter's Economy: Policy in an Age of Limits.* (Chapel Hill: University of North Carolina Press, 2002), 200–2.

32 Stein, 219; Hargrove, 95–96; and Charles E. Jacob, "Macroeconomic Policy Choices of Postwar Presidents," in *The President and Economic Policy*, ed. J. P. Pfiffner. (Philadelphia: Institute for the Study of Human Issues, 1986), 75.

33 Biven, 204; John T. Woolley, *Monetary Politics: The Federal Reserve and the Politics of Monetary Policy* (Cambridge: Cambridge University Press, 1986), 103–4, 111–14.

34 William Greider, *Secrets of the Temple: How the Federal Reserve Runs the Country* (New York: Simon and Schuster, 1987), 184–85, and Andrew H. Bartels, "Volcker's Revolution at the Fed," *Challenge* 28, no. 4 (1985): 35–42.

35 Collins, 160, 162.

36 Frank E. Morris, "Opening Remarks," in *After The Phillips Curve: The Persistence of High Inflation and High Unemployment* (Boston: Federal Reserve Bank of Boston. 1978), 7.

37 Arthur M. Okun, "The Great Stagflation Swamp," *Challenge* 20, no. 6 (1977): 6.

38 Arthur M. Okun, "Political Economy: The Lessons of the Seventies," in *Current Issues in Political Economy*, ed. Arthur M. Okun and Robert Solomon (Toronto: Ontario Economic Council, 1979), 4.

39 See Henry C. Wallich and Sidney Weintraub, "A Tax-Based Incomes Policy," *Journal of Economic Issues* 5, no. 2 (1971): 1–19.

40 See Alfred S., Eichner and J. A. Kregel, "An Essay on Post-Keynesian Theory: A New Paradigm in Economics," *Journal of Economic Literature* 13, no. 4 (1975):1293–1314; and J. A. Kregel, "Post-Keynesian Theory: An Overview," *The Journal of Economic Education* 14, no. 4 (1983): 32–43.

41 Bureau of the Census, *Statistical History of the United States*, series D 127–32; Dean Baker, *The United States Since 1980* (Cambridge: Cambridge University Press, 2007), 30.

42 Otis L. Graham, Jr., *Losing Time: The Industrial Policy Debate* (Cambridge: Harvard University Press, 1992), 10–11.

43 Barry Bluestone and Bennett Harrison, *The Deindustrialization of America: Plant Closings, Community Abandonment, and the Dismantling of Basic Industry* (New York: Basic Books, 1982), 193, 195.

44 Graham, 43–45.

45 Milton Friedman and Rose Friedman, *Free to Choose: A Personal Statement* (New York: Harcourt Brace Javanovich, 1980), 271, 282. See Phillip Cagan, *Persistent Inflation: Historical and Policy Essays* (New York: Columbia University Press, 1979).

46 Robert E. Lucas and Thomas J. Sargent, "After Keynesian Macroeconomics," in *After The Phillips Curve*, 63, 70.

47 See Jude Wanniski, *The Way the World Works: How Economies Fail—and Succeed* (New York: Basic Books, 1978).

48 See David R. Cameron, "The Politics and Economics of the Business Cycle," in *The Political Economy: Readings in the Politics and Economics of American Public Policy*, ed. Thomas Ferguson and Joel Rogers (Armonk, NY: M.E. Sharpe, 1984), and Leon N. Lindberg and Charles S. Maier, eds., *The Politics of Inflation and Economic Stagnation: Theoretical Approaches and International Case Studies* (Washington, D.C.: The Brookings Institution, 1985).

49 See Charles S. Maier, "Preconditions for Corporatism," In *Order and Conflict in Contemporary Capitalism*, and Graham K. Wilson, "Why Is There No Corporatism in the United States," in *Patterns of Corporatist Policy Making*, ed. G. Lehmbruch and P. C. Schmitter (Beverley Hills, CA: Sage, 1982).

50 See Martha Derthick and Paul J. Quirk, *The Politics of Deregulation* (Washington, D.C.: The Brookings Institution, 1985) and Elizabeth E. Bailey, "Deregulation: Causes and Consequences," *Science*, 234 no. 4781 (1986): 1211–16.

51 See Thomas O. McGarity, *Reinventing Rationality: The Role of Regulatory Analysis in the Federal Bureaucracy* (Cambridge: Cambridge University Press, 1991), and Robert V. Percival, "Checks without Balance: Executive Office Oversight of the Environmental Protection Agency," *Law and Contemporary Problems* 54, no. 4 (1991): 127–204.

52 Theodore Caplow, Howard M. Bahr, Bruce A. Chadwick, John Modell, *Recent Social Trends in the United States, 1960–1990* (Montreal: McGill-Queen's Press, 1984), 348.

53 David Vogel, "The Power of Business in America: A Re-Appraisal," *British Journal of Political Science* 13, no. 1 (1983), 36. See David Vogel, *Fluctuating Fortunes: The Political Power of Business in America* (New York: Beard Books, 2003).

54 Kay Lehman Schlozman and John T. Tierney, *Organized Interests and American Politics* (New York: Harper & Row, 1986), 249, 77. See Kay Lehman Schlozman, "What Accent the Heavenly Chorus? Political Equality and the American Pressure System," *The Journal of Politics* 46, 4 (1984): 1006–32.

55 Charles B. Craver, *Can Unions Survive? The Rejuvenation of the American Labor Movement* (New York: NYU Press, 1995), 35.

56 Schlozman and Tierney, 77, 249.

57 Andrew Rich, "War of Ideas: Why Mainstream and Liberal Foundations and the Think Tanks they Support are Losing in the War of Ideas in American Politics," *Stanford Social Innovation Review*, Spring (2005), 21.

7 The Neoliberal Regime and the Return of the Market

1 Council of Economic Advisers, *Economic Report of the President, 2009.* (Washington, D.C.: Government Printing Office, 2009), Tables B-4, B-43, B-2.

2 Ibid., Table B-79, B-32, B-74.

3 Ibid., Table Table B-2.

4 Ibid., Table Table B-46, B-12.

5 Edward N. Wolff, *Does Education Really Help? Skill, Work, and Inequality* (New York: Oxford University Press, 2006), chapter 3. See Jelle Visser, "Union Membership Statistics in 24 Countries," *Monthly Labor Review* 129, no. 1 (2006): 38–49, and Lawrence Mishel and Matthew Walters, "How Unions Help All Workers," EPI Briefing Paper No. 143 (Washington, D.C.: Economic Policy Institute, 2003).

6 U.S. Bureau of the Census, *Current Population Survey*, Annual Social and Economic Supplements, Table 2.

7 Ibid., Table F-4.
8 Ronald Reagan, "Inaugural Address, January 20, 1981." Available at http://www.presidency.ucsb.edu/ws/index.php?pid=43130
9 Herbert Stein, *Presidential Economics: The Making of Economic Policy from Roosevelt to Clinton* (Washington, D.C.: American Enterprise Institute, 1994), 403.
10 J. Craig Jenkins and Craig M. Eckert, "The Right Turn in Economic Policy: Business Elites and the New Conservative Economics," *Sociological Forum* 15, 2 (2000): 316–17.
11 Jerry Tempalski, "Revenue Effects of Major Tax Bills," U.S. Department Of The Treasury, OTA Working Paper 81 (2006), 16–17.
12 Ibid., William A. Niskanen, Jr., *Reaganomics: An Insider's Account of the Policies and the People* (New York: Oxford University Press, 1988), 99–101, and Congressional Budget Office, "Economic Impacts of the Tax Reform Act of 1986: Short-run and Long-run Perspectives." Staff Working Paper, June 1987.
13 See Lance T. Leloup, "After the Blitz: Reagan and the U. S. Congressional Budget Process," *Legislative Studies Quarterly* 7, no. 3 (1982): 321–39, and Jean Peters, "Reconciliation 1982: What Happened?" *PS* 14, no. 4 (1981): 732–36.
14 Office of Management and Budget, *Historical Tables, Fiscal Year 2009*, Table 3–1.
15 Paul E. Peterson and Mark Rom, "Lower Taxes, More Spending, and Budget Deficits," in *The Reagan Legacy: Promise and Performance*, ed. Charles O. Jones (Chatham, NJ: Chatham House, 1988), 28–35, and Phil Williams, "The Reagan Administration and Defence Policy," in *The Reagan Presidency: An Incomplete Revolution?*, ed. Dilys M. Hill, Raymond A. Moore, and Phil Williams (New York: St. Martin's Press, 1990), 201–5.
16 Office of Management and Budget, Table 3–1 and 8–3.
17 Ibid., Table 1–2.
18 For a discussion of the debates surrounding monetary policy, see Jenkins and Eckert, 314–15.
19 Charles Murray, *Losing Ground: American Social Policy, 1950–1980* (New York: Basic Books, 1984), 227–28.
20 Ira Moscovice and William Craig, "The Omnibus Budget Reconciliation Act and the Working Poor," *The Social Service Review* 58, no. 1 (1984): 51.
21 See Robert Moffitt and Douglas A. Wolf, "The Effect of the 1981 Omnibus Budget Reconciliation Act on Welfare Recipients and Work Incentives," *The Social Service Review* 61, no. 2 (1987): 247–60, and Paul A. Smith, "The Effect of the 1981 Welfare Reforms on AFDC Participation and Labor Supply," University of Wisconsin–Madison Institute for Research on Poverty Discussion Paper no. 1117–97 (January 1997).
22 David Stoesz, "Social Policy: Reagan and Beyond," in *The Handbook of Social Policy*, 2nd ed, ed. James Midgley and Michelle Livermore (Beverly Hills, CA: Sage, 2008), 171.
23 See Edward T. Jennings, "Administration of Welfare in the States," in *Handbook of State Government Administration*, ed. John J. Gargan (Washington, D.C.: CRC Press, 1999), 483–518.
24 Mark E. Rushefsky, *Public Policy in the United States: At the Dawn of the Twenty-First Century*, 3rd ed (Armonk, NY: M.E. Sharpe, 2002), 187.
25 See Michael J. Boskin, ed., *The Crisis in Social Security: Problems and Prospects* (San Francisco: Institute for Contemporary Studies, 1978).
26 Steven M. Teles and Martha Derthick, "Social Security from 1980 to the Present: From Third Rail to Presidential Commitment—and Back?" in

Conservatism and American Political Development, ed. Brian J. Glenn and Steven M. Teles (New York: Oxford University Press, 2009), 264–67. See *Report of the National Commission on Social Security Reform* (Washington, D.C.: Government Printing Office, 1983). www.ssa.gov/history/reports/gspan.html

27 See Norman J. Vig, "Presidential Leadership and the Environment," in *Environmental Policy: New Directions for the Twenty-First Century,* ed. Norman J. Vig and Michael E. Kraft (Washington, D.C.: *Congressional Quarterly,* 2003), 107–9.

28 See Robert V. Percival, "Checks without Balance: Executive Office Oversight of the Environmental Protection Agency," *Law and Contemporary Problems* 54, no. 4 (1991):127–204.

29 Council of Economic Advisers, *Economic Report of the President, 1981* (Washington, D.C.: Government Printing Office, 1981), 182, 213.

30 Vladimir N. Pregelj, "Caribbean Basin Interim Trade Program: CBI/NAFTA Parity." CRS Issue Brief for Congress (Washington, D.C.: Congressional Research Service, 2005), 2.

31 See Stephen D. Cohen, "The Route To Japan's Voluntary Export Restraints On Automobiles: An Analysis Of The U.S. Government's Decision-Making Process In 1981," U.S-Japan project Working Paper No. 20 (Washington, D.C.: American University School of International Service, 2000).

32 I.M. Destler, *American Trade Politics,* 2nd ed (New York: NYU Press, 1992), 160–61.

33 William Anthony Lovett, Alfred E. Eckes, and Richard L. Brinkman, *U.S. Trade Policy: History, Theory, and the WTO,* 2nd ed (Armonk, NY: M.E. Sharpe, 2004), 78.

34 *Economic Report of the President, 2009,* Table B-2. Calculations by author.

35 Congressional Research Service, "Statutory Individual Income Tax Rates and Other Elements of the Tax System: 1988 through 2008," (RL34498) May 21, 2008.

36 Office of Management and Budget, Table 1–2, calculations by author.

37 Council of Economic Advisers, *Economic Report of the President, 1996* (Washington, D.C.: Government Printing Office, 1996), 23–24.

38 *Bowsher v. Synar,* 478 U.S. 714 (1986).

39 Darrell M. West, "Gramm-Rudman-Hollings and the Politics of Deficit Reduction," *Annals of the American Academy of Political and Social Science* 499 (1988): 90–100.

40 See Sung Deuk Hahm, Mark S. Kamlet, David C. Mowery, Tsai-Tsu Su, "The Influence of the Gramm-Rudman-Hollings Act on Federal Budgetary Outcomes, 1986–89," *Journal of Policy Analysis and Management* 11, no. 2 (1992): 207–34.

41 Bill Clinton and Al Gore, "Reinventing Environmental Regulation 1995," quoted in Eisner, 96.

42 See Eisner, chapters 6–7.

43 Frances Fox Piven and Richard A. Cloward, "The Historical Sources of the Contemporary Relief Debate," in Fred Block, Richard A. Cloward, Barbara Ehrenreich, and Fraces Fox Piven, *The Mean Season: The Attack on the Welfare State* (New York: Pantheon Books, 1987), 42.

44 William J. Clinton, "Inaugural Address, January 20, 1993." Available at http://www.presidency.ucsb.edu/ws/?pid=47232

45 V. Joseph Hotz, John Karl Scholz, "The Earned Income Tax Credit." NBER Working Paper No. 8078 (Cambridge, MA: National Bureau of Economic Research, 2001), 7–8.

46 Congressional Budget Office, *The Effects of NAFTA on U.S.-Mexican Trade and GDP* (Washington, D.C.: Congressional Budget Office, 2003).
47 Gary Clyde Hufbauer and Jeffrey J. Schott, *NAFTA Revisited: Achievements and Challenges* (Washington, D.C.: Peterson Institute, 2005), 62.
48 See Ian F. Fergusson, "The World Trade Organization: Background and Issues." CRS Report for Congress, 98–928. Washington, D.C.: Congressional Research Service, 2007.
49 Roberto Zagha and Gobind T. Nankani, *Economic Growth in the 1990s: Learning from a Decade of Reform* (Washington, D.C.: World Bank Publications, 2005), 63–64.
50 *Economic Report of the President, 2009,* Table B-2.
51 Ibid., Table B-79.
52 Alan Greenspan, *The Age of Turbulence: Adventures in a New World* (New York: Penguin Press, 2007), 217.
53 For a discussion of the internal debates, see Ron Suskind, *The Price of Loyalty: George W. Bush, the White House, and the Education of Paul O'Neill* (New York: Simon & Schuster, 2004).
54 See Tempalski.
55 William G. Gale and Peter Orszag, "The Great Tax Shift," *The American Prospect,* April 22, 2004. http://www.prospect.org/cs/articles?articleId=7641
56 *Economic Report of the President, 2009,* Table B-79.
57 See, for example, Robert J. Barro, "Are Government Bonds Net Wealth?" *Journal of Political Economy* 82, no. 6 (1974): 1095–117.
58 See William G. Gale and Peter R. Orszag, "Budget Deficits, National Saving, and Interest Rates," *Brookings Papers on Economic Activity* 2004, no. 2 (2004): 101–87.
59 Derek Hunter, "Medicare Drug Cost Estimates: What Congress Knows Now," *Backgrounder* no. 1484 (Washington, D.C.: The Heritage Foundation, 2005), and The Boards of Trustees, Federal Hospital Insurance and Federal Supplementary Medical Insurance Trust Funds, *The 2008 Annual Report of the Boards of Trustees of the Federal Hospital Insurance and Federal Supplementary Medical Insurance Trust Funds* (Washington, D.C.: Centers For Medicare And Medicaid Services, 2008), 24.
60 Quoted in Guy L. Clifton, *Flatlined: Resuscitating American Medicine* (New Brunswick, N.J.: Rutgers University Press, 2009), 209.
61 *Economic Report of the President, 2009,* Table B-43.

8 The Two Welfare States and the Coming Entitlement Crisis

1 Ronald Reagan, "Address Before a Joint Session of Congress on the State of the Union January 25, 1988." Available at http://www.presidency.ucsb.edu/ws/?pid=36035
2 U.S. Bureau of the Census, *Current Population Survey, Annual Social and Economic Supplement,* Historical Poverty Tables, Table 2.
3 Garth L. Mangum, Stephen L. Mangum, Andrew Sum and Sar A. Levitan, *The Persistence of Poverty in the United States* (Baltimore: Johns Hopkins University Press, 2003), 49.
4 See James K. Galbraith and Vidal Garza Cantú, "Inequality in American Manufacturing Wages, 1920–98: A Revised Estimate," University of Texas Inequality Project, Working Paper Number 8, 1999.
5 Sandra Polaski, "U.S. Living Standards in an Era of Globalization," Carnegie Policy Brief 53, Washington, D.C.: Carnegie Endowment for International Peace, 2007, 5.

6 Benjamin I. Page and James Roy Simmons, *What Government Can Do: Dealing with Poverty and Inequality* (Chicago: University of Chicago Press, 2002), 135.

7 Caseload data from Department of Health and Human Services, Administration for Children and Families, http://www.acf.hhs.gov/programs/ofa/data-reports/caseload/caseload_recent.html

8 Cynthia Miller, "Leavers, Stayers, and Cyclers: An Analysis of the Welfare Caseload," 5. Available at http://aspe.hhs.gov/HSP/leavers99/Miller-MDRC-02.pdf

9 Dorothy Rosenbaum, "Families' Food Stamp Benefits Purchase Less Food Each Year,"Washington, D.C.: Center On Budget And Policy Priorities, 2007.

10 See David G. Wood, "Public Housing: Information on the Roles of HUD, Public Housing Agencies, Capital Markets, and Service Organizations," Testimony before the Subcommittee on Federalism and the Census, Committee on Government Reform, House of Representatives (Washington, D.C.: Government Accountability Office, 2006).

11 Margery Austin Turner and G. Thomas Kingsley, *Federal Programs for Addressing Low-Income Housing Needs: A Policy Primer* (Washington, D.C.: The Urban Institute, 2008), 3.

12 Georgetown University Health Policy Institute, Center for Children and Families, "Medicaid and State Budgets: Looking at the Facts," May 2008. http://ccf.georgetown.edu/index/cms-filesystem-action?file=ccf%20publications/about%20medicaid/nasbo%20final%205-1-08.pdf

13 Lynn Etheredge, "Reagan, Congress, and Health Spending," *Health Affairs* 2, no. 1 (1983): 14–24.

14 Kant Patel and Mark E. Rushefsky, *Health Care Politics and Policy in America* (Armonk, NY: M.E. Sharpe, 1999), 58.

15 Leighton Ku and Teresa A. Coughlin, "How the New Welfare Reform Law Affects Medicaid." *New Federalism: Issues and Options for States*, No. A-5. Washington, D.C.: The Urban Institute, 1997.

16 Robert Pear, "Obama Signs Children's Health Insurance Bill," *New York Times*, February 4, 2009, A1.

17 Office of Management and Budget, *Budget for Fiscal Year 2010, Historical Tables* (Washington, D.C.: Office of Management and Budget, 2009), Tables 8–5 and 8–6.

18 E.E. Schattschneider, *The Semisovereign People: A Realist's View of Democracy in America* (New York: Holt, Rinehart and Winston, 1960), 35.

19 Christopher Howard, *The Hidden Welfare State: Tax Expenditures and Social Policy in the United States* (Princeton: Princeton University Press, 1999), 31.

20 Office of Management and Budget, *Analytical Perspectives, Fiscal Year 200.* (Washington, D.C.: Office of Management and Budget, 2009), Table 19–2.

21 U.S. Congress, Joint Committee on Taxation, *Estimates of Federal Tax Expenditures for Fiscal Years 2008–2012* (Washington, D.C.: Government Printing Office, 2008), 70–76, calculations by author.

22 See Cato Institute, *Cato Handbook for Policymakers*, 7th ed (Washington, D.C.: the Cato Institute, 2009), 279, and http://www.citizen.org/congress/welfare/index.cfm

23 Congressional Budget Office, *Corporate Income Tax Rates: International Comparisons* (Washington, D.C.: Congressional Budget Office, 2005), 13.

24 See Aviva Aron-Dine, "Well-Designed, Fiscally Responsible Corporate Tax Reform Could Benefit the Country: Unpaid-For Rate Cuts Would Likely Hurt Most Americans In The Long Run," Washington D.C.: Center on Budget and Policy Priorities, 2008.

25 Geoffrey Kollmann, "Summary of Major Changes in the Social Security Cash Benefits Program: 1935–96," *CRS Report for Congress* (Washington, D.C.: Congressional Research Service, 1996), 23.

26 Data from Social Security Administration, http://www.ssa.gov/history/ lifeexpect.html and Office of Management and Budget, *Budget for Fiscal Year 2010*, Table 8–6.

27 All data from http://www.ssa.gov/OACT/

28 See Mary Williams Walsh, "Social Security to See Payout Exceed Pay-In This Year," *New York Times*, March 25, 2010, A1.

29 Office of Management and Budget, *Budget for Fiscal Year 2010*, Tables 8–6 and 8–7. The Boards of Trustees, Federal Hospital Insurance And Federal Supplementary Medical Insurance Trust Funds, *2009 Annual Report of the Boards of Trustees of the Federal Hospital Insurance and Federal Supplementary Medical Insurance Trust Funds*, 3.

30 The Boards of Trustees, Federal Hospital Insurance and Federal Supplementary Medical Insurance Trust Funds, 4, 38.

31 Mangum, Mangum, Sum and Levitan, 49.

32 Martha Ozawa, "Social Security," in *The Handbook of Social Policy*, ed. James Midgley and Michelle Livermore (Beverly Hills, CA: Sage, 2008), 362–63.

33 U.S. Census Bureau, Table 3, calculations by author.

34 Duncan Lindsey, *The Welfare of Children* (New York: Oxford University Press, 2004), 238.

35 David M. Walker, "Long-Term Budget Outlook: Saving Our Future Requires Tough Choices Today," Testimony before the Committee on the Budget, U.S. Senate (Washington, D.C.: Government Accountability Office, 2007), 10.

36 Ibid., 8.

37 Ibid., 12

38 Congressional Budget Office, *Long-Term Budget Outlook, June 2009* (Washington D.C.: Congressional Budget Office, 2009), 39, 21, 7.

39 Ibid., xii.

40 Office of Management and Budget, *Analytical Perspectives, Budget of the United States, Fiscal Year 2000* (Washington, D.C.: U.S. Government Printing Office, 1999), 337.

41 Office of Management and Budget, *Analytical Perspectives, Budget of the United States, Fiscal Year 2004* (Washington, D.C.: U.S. Government Printing Office, 2003), 48.

42 C. Eugene Steuerle, "Alternatives To Strengthen Social Security," Statement before the Committee on Ways and Means, United States House of Representatives, May 12, 2005, 1–2.

43 http://www.ssa.gov/legislation/testimony_020205.html

44 See Social Security Administration, Provisions Affecting OASDI Contribution and Benefit Base. http://www.ssa.gov/OACT/solvency/provisions/ wagebase. html

45 Peter A. Diamond and Peter R. Orszag, "Saving Social Security: The Diamond-Orszag Plan," *The Economists' Voice* 2, no. 1 (2005): 1–8. See Eric R. Kingson, "Setting the Agenda for Social Security Reform," in *Challenges of an Aging Society: Ethical Dilemmas, Political Issues*, ed. Rachel Pruchno and Michael A. Smyer (Baltimore: Johns Hopkins University Press, 2007), 335–36.

46 Cynthia M. Fagnoni, "Social Security and Minorities: Current Benefits and Implications of Reform." Testimony before the Subcommittee on Social Security, Committee on Ways and Means, House of Representatives (Washington, D.C.: General Accounting Office, 1999), 4–5.

47 See Social Security Administration, Provisions Affecting Taxation of Benefits, http://www.ssa.gov/OACT/solvency/provisions/charts/chart_run217. html

48 Diamond and Orszag, 3.

49 Geoffrey Kollmann, "Social Security: Taxation of Benefits," *CRS Report for Congress* (Washington, D.C.: Congressional Research Service, 2000), 12.

50 Patrick Purcell, Laura Haltzel, and Neela Ranade, "Indexing Social Security Benefits: The Effects of Price and Wage Indexes," *CRS Report for Congress* (Washington, D.C.: Congressional Research Service, 2005), 14, 21, 17.

51 Government Accountability Office, *Social Security: Answers to Key Questions* (Washington, D.C.: Government Accountability Office, 2005), 11–12.

52 Michael Tanner, "The Better Deal: Estimating Rates of Return under a System of Individual Accounts," *Cato Project on Social Security Choice*, No. 31 (Washington, D.C.: The Cato Institute, 2003), 18.

53 See Dawn Nuschler, "Social Security Reform," *CRC Report for Congress.* (Washington, D.C.: Congressional Research Service, 2005), 10–11.

54 See Congressional Budget Office, *Long-Term Analysis of Plan 2 of the President's Commission to Strengthen Social Security* (Washington, D.C.: Congressional Budget Office, 2004).

55 Dean Baker and David Rosnick, *Basic Facts on Social Security and Proposed Benefit Cuts/Privatization* (Washington, D.C.: Center for Economic and Policy Research, 2005), 8.

56 See Robin Toner and Marjorie Connelly, "Poll Shows Dwindling Approval of Bush and Congress," *New York Times*, June 17, 2005, A1, and Jonathan Weisman and Michael Abramowitz, "Katrina's Damage Lingers For Bush: Many See Storm as President's Undoing," *Washington Post*, August 26, 2006, A01.

57 Sandra Christensen and Rick Kasten, "The Medicare Catastrophic Coverage Act of 1988," Washington, D.C.: Congressional Budget Office, 1988, 25.

58 Thomas Rice, Katherine Desmond, and Jon Gabel, "The Medicare Catastrophic Coverage Act: A Post-Mortem," *Health Affairs*, 9, no. 3 (1990), 76.

59 David Hyman, *Medicare Meets Mephistopheles* (Washington, D.C.: Cato Institute, 2006), 43.

60 Office of the Actuary in the Centers for Medicare & Medicaid Services, "National Health Expenditure Projections 2008–18." "http://www.cms. hhs.gov/NationalHealthExpendData/downloads/proj2008.pdf

61 OECD Health Data, 2009.

62 Christian Hagist and Laurence J. Kotlikoff, "Who's Going Broke? Comparing Healthcare Costs in Ten OECD Countries," National Bureau Of Economic Research Working Paper 11833, 2005, 17.

63 Rand Corporation, "The Health Insurance Experiment: A Classic RAND Study Speaks to the Current Health Care Reform Debate," 3. Available at http://www.rand.org/pubs/research_briefs/2006/RAND_RB9174.pdf

64 See Patricia A. Butler, "Revisiting Pay or Play: How States Could Expand Employer-Based Coverage Within ERISA Constraints," National Academy for State Health Policy, 2002.

65 Jonathan Oberlander, "Learning from Failure in Health Care Reform," *New England Journal of Medicine* 357, no. 17 (2007), 1678.

66 Ceci Connolly, "U.S. Firms Losing Health Care Battle, GM Chairman Says," *Washington Post*, February 11, 2005, E01.

67 David M. Herszenhorn and Robert Pear, "Final Votes in Congress Cap Battle on Health Bill," *New York Times*, March 26, 2010, A17.

9 The Global Economy and the Persistence of the State

1 Douglas Kellner, "Theorizing Globalization," *Sociological Theory* 20, no. 3 (2002): 300–301, 286.
2 Daniel W. Drezner, "Globalization and Policy Convergence," *International Studies Review* 3, no. 1 (2001): 53.
3 This discussion draws on Duncan Green and Matthew Griffith, "Globalization and Its Discontents," *International Affairs* 78, no. 1 (2002): 50–52. Helen V. Milner and Keiko Kubota, "Why the Move to Free Trade? Democracy and Trade Policy in the Developing Countries," *International Organization* 59, no. 1 (2005): 110–11.
4 See Ting Gao, "Trade Costs, International Production Shifting, and Growth," *European Economic Review* 51 (2007) 317–35.
5 World Trade Organization, *International Trade Statistics* (Geneva: WTO Publications, 2008), 7.
6 See Jeffrey D. Sachs and Andrew Warner, "Economic Reform and the Process of Global Integration," *Brookings Papers on Economic Activity* 1 (1995): 1–118, and Romain Wacziarg and Karen Horn Welch, "Trade Liberalization and Growth: New Evidence," *The World Bank Economic Review* 22, no. 2 (2008): 187–231.
7 Shaohua Chen and Martin Ravallion, "The Developing World Is Poorer Than We Thought, But No Less Successful in the Fight against Poverty," The World Bank Development Group, Policy Research Working Paper 4703 (Washington, D.C.: The World Bank, 2008), 19, 23.
8 Joseph E. Stiglitz, "Poverty, globalization and growth: perspectives on some of the statistical links," in United Nations Development Programme, *Human Development Report 2003* (New York: Oxford University Press, 2003), 80.
9 Council of Economic Advisers, *Economic Report of the President, 2009*, Table B-2. Calculations by author. World Trade Organization, 10–11.
10 James H. Mittelman, "Globalization: Captors and Captive," *Third World Quarterly* 21, no. 6 (2000): 919.
11 World Trade Organization, 38, 73, 101.
12 Ibid., 80, 86–87, 95.
13 Ibid., 121.
14 Robert B. Reich, *The Work of Nations: Preparing Ourselves for 21st-Century Capitalism* (New York: Alfred A. Knopf, 1991), 178, 302–3.
15 John Goodman and Louis Pauly, "The Obsolescence of Capital Controls?" *World Politics* 46, no. 1 (1993), 50–82.
16 George Ross, "Labor versus Globalization," *Annals of the American Academy of Political and Social Science* 570 (2000): 82.
17 OECD, Growing Unequal? Income Distribution and Poverty in OECD Countries. Country Note: United States. Available at http://www.oecd.org/dataoecd/47/2/41528678.pdf
18 See Wilson B. Brown and Jan S. Hogendorn, *International Economics: In the Age of Globalization* (Toronto: University of Toronto Press, 2000), 367–68, and Nigel Grimwade, *International Trade: New Patterns of Trade, Production and Investment* (New York: Routledge, 2000), 268–70.
19 Adam Harmes, "Institutional Investors and the Reproduction of Neoliberalism," *Review of International Political Economy* 5, no. 1 (1998): 107.
20 See Taimur Baig and Ilan Goldfajn, "Financial Market Contagion in the Asian Crisis." *IMF Staff Papers* 46, no. 2 (1999): 170, and Guillermo Calvo, "Capital Inflows and Macroeconomic Management: Tequila Lessons," *International Journal of Finance and Economics* 1, 3 (1996): 207–23.

21 C. Randall Henning and I. M. Destler, "From Neglect to Activism: American Politics and the 1985 Plaza Accord," *Journal of Public Policy* 8, no. 3/ 4(1988): 321.

22 Ibid., 326. See James Shoch, "Party Politics and International Economic Activism: The Reagan-Bush Years," *Political Science Quarterly* 113, no. 1 (1998): 113–31.

23 Paul Volcker and Toyoo Gyohten, *Changing Fortunes: The World's Money and the Threat to American Leadership* (New York: Times Books, 1992), 268, 269.

24 Leonard Silk, "The United States and the World Economy," *Foreign Affairs* 65, no. 3, (1986): 459.

25 Volcker and Gyohten, *op cit.*, 285.

26 U.S Treasury, Major Foreign Holders of Treasury Securities, July 16, 2009. Available at http://www.treas.gov/tic/mfh.txt

27 Niall Ferguson, "Sinking Globalization," *Foreign Affairs* 84, no. 2 (2005): 70.

28 See Joseph E. Stiglitz, "Capital Market Liberalization and Exchange Rate Regimes: Risk without Reward," *Annals of the American Academy of Political and Social Science* 579, (2002): 219–48.

29 Prakash Aseem, "The East Asian Crisis and the Globalization Discourse," *Review of International Political Economy* 8, no. 1 (2001): 124. This paragraph draws on Aseem's account of the crisis.

30 Paul Bowles, "Asia's Post-Crisis Regionalism: Bringing the State Back in, Keeping the (United) States Out," *Review of International Political Economy* 9, no. 2 (2002): 235–36.

31 Nicola Bullard, Walden Bello, Kamal Mallhotra, "Taming the Tigers: The IMF and the Asian Crisis," *Third World Quarterly* 19, no. 3 (1998): 506, 507.

32 See Michael R. King, "Who Triggered the Asian Financial Crisis?" *Review of International Political Economy* 8, no. 3 (2001): 438–66.

33 See Bowles, *op cit.*

34 Green and Griffith, *op cit.*, 52.

35 Martin Wolf, "Will the Nation-State Survive Globalization?" *Foreign Affairs* 80, no. 1 (2001): 190.

36 Drezner, "Globalization and Policy Convergence," 75.

37 See Amy J. Hillman and Gerald D. Keim, "Shareholder Value, Stakeholder Management, and Social Issues: What's the Bottom Line?" *Strategic Management Journal* 22, no. 2 (2001):125–39; Benjamin Cashore and Ilan Vertinsky, "Policy Networks And Firm Behaviours: Governance Systems And Firm Responses To External Demands For Sustainable Forest Management," *Policy Sciences* 33, no. 1 (2000): 1–30; and Edward Balleisen and Marc Eisner, "The Promise and Pitfall of Co-Regulation: How Governments Can Draw on Private Governance for Public Purposes," in *New Perspectives on Regulation*, ed. David Moss and John Cisternino (Cambridge: The Tobin Project, 2009), 127–50.

38 Madhu Khanna and William Rose Q. Anton, "Corporate Environmental Management: Regulatory and Market-Based Incentives," *Land Economics* 78, no. 4 (November 2002): 555.

39 See Neil Gunningham and Joseph Rees, "Industry Self-Regulation: An Institutional Perspective," *Law & Policy* 19, no. 4 (October 1997): 363–414. On the limitations, see Michael J. Lennox and Jennifer Nash, "Industry Self-Regulation and Adverse Selection: A Comparison Across Four Trade Association Programs," *Business Strategy and the Environment* 12 (2003): 343–56.

40 See the examination of nuclear industry self-regulation in Joseph Rees, *Hostages of Each Other: The Transformation of Nuclear Safety since Three Mile Island* (Chicago: University of Chicago Press, 1994).

41 See Marc Allen Eisner, *Governing the Environment: The Transformation of Environmental Regulation* (Boulder, CO: Lynn Rienner, 2007), chapter 9, and ISO Central Secretariat, *The ISO Survey of Certifications 2007* (Geneva: International Organization for Standardization, 2008).

42 David Vogel, *Trading Up: Consumer and Environmental Regulation in a Global Economy* (Cambridge: Harvard University Press, 1995), 249.

43 Aseem Prakash and Mathew Potoski, *The Voluntary Environmentalists: Green Clubs, ISO 14001, and Voluntary Environmental Regulations* (Cambridge: Cambridge University Press, 2006), 185.

44 Petra Christmann and Glen Taylor, "Globalization and the Environment: Determinants of Firm Self-Regulation in China," *Journal of International Business Studies* 32, no. 3 (2001): 452.

45 Daniel W. Drezner, "Bottom Feeders," *Foreign Policy* No. 121 (2000): 70.

46 See Robert Z. Lawrence, *Regionalism, Multilateralism, and Deeper Integration* (Washington, D.C.: Brookings Institution Press, 1996).

47 United Nations Development Programme, *Human Development Report*, 113.

48 Ibid., 133.

49 See John Whalley and Xian Xin, "Regionalization, Changes In Home Bias, And The Growth Of World Trade," NBER Working Paper 13023. Cambridge, MA: National Bureau of Economic Research, 2007.

50 World Trade Organization, 3–4.

10 The Financial Crisis and the Great Recession

1 See Roger D. Congleton, "On the Political Economy of the Financial Crisis and Bailout of 2008," *Public Choice* 140 (2009): 311–12.

2 See David Moss, "An Ounce of Prevention: The Power of Public Risk Management in Stabilizing the Financial System," *Harvard Business School Working Paper* 09–087, 2009.

3 See George J. Stigler, "The Theory of Economic Regulation," *The Bell Journal of Economics and Management Science* 2, no.1 (1971): 3–21; Richard A. Posner, "Theories of Economic Regulation," *Bell Journal of Economics and Management Science* 5, no. 3 (1974): 337–52; and Sam Peltzman, "Toward a More General Theory of Regulation," *Journal of Law and Economics* 19, no. 2 (1976): 211–40.

4 See Neil Fligstein, "Markets as Politics: A Political-Cultural Approach to Market Institutions," *American Sociological Review* 61, no. 4 (1996): 656–73.

5 Thomas H. Hammond and Jack H. Knott, "The Deregulatory Snowball: Explaining Deregulation in the Financial Industry," *The Journal of Politics* 50, no. 1 (1988): 15.

6 George G. Kaufman, Larry R. Mote, Harvey Rosenblum, "Consequences of Deregulation for Commercial Banking," *The Journal of Finance* 39, no. 3 (1984): 790.

7 See Paul R. Allen and William J. Wilhelm, "The Impact of the 1980 Depository Institutions Deregulation and Monetary Control Act on Market Value and Risk: Evidence from the Capital Markets," *Journal of Money, Credit and Banking* 20, no. 3, (1988): 364–80.

8 Kenneth J. Meier, *Regulation: Politics, Bureaucracy, and Economics* (New York: St. Martin's Press, 1985), 70. For an overview of Garn-St. Germain, see Marcia Millon Cornett and Hassan Tehranian, "An Examination of the Impact of the Garn-St. Germain Depository Institutions Act of 1982 on Commercial Banks and Savings and Loans," *The Journal of Finance* 45, no. 1 (1990): 98–100.

9 Congressional Budget Office, *The Economic Effects of the Savings & Loan Crisis* (Washington, D.C.: The Congressional Budget Office, 1992), 10. Mark Carl Rom, *Public Spirit in the Thrift Tragedy* (Pittsburgh: University of Pittsburgh Press, 1996).

10 Richard J. Cebula and Chao-Shun Hung, "Barth's Analysis of the Savings and Loan Debacle: An Empirical Test," *Southern Economic Journal* 59, no. 2 (1992): 307, 305. Rom, 3.

11 Robert D. Hershey, Jr., "Plan Is Offered To Reorganize Finance Sector," *New York Times*, May 22, 1997, D1.

12 James R. Barth, R. Dan Brumbaugh Jr., and James A. Wilcox, "The Repeal of Glass-Steagall and the Advent of Broad Banking," *The Journal of Economic Perspectives* 14, no. 2 (2000): 196.

13 Barny Frank, "Why America Needs a Little Less Laissez-Faire," *Financial Times*, January 13, 2008.

14 See Franklin Allen and Douglas Gale, "Bubbles and Crises," *The Economic Journal* 110, no 460 (2000): 236–55.

15 This discussion draws on Stan J. Liebowitz, "Anatomy of a Train Wreck: Causes of the Mortgage Meltdown," Independent Policy Report (Oakland, CA: The Independent Institute, 2008).

16 Alicia H. Munnell, Geoffrey M. B. Tootell, Lynn E. Browne, and James McEneaney, "Mortgage Lending in Boston: Interpreting HMDA Data." *The American Economic Review* 86, no. 1 (1996): 25–53.

17 Federal Reserve Bank of Boston, *Closing the Gap: A Guide to Equal Opportunity Lending* (Boston: Federal Reserve Bank of Boston, 1993), 15.

18 See Liebowitz, *op cit.*

19 Vikas Bajaj and David Leonhardt, "Tax Break May Have Helped Cause Housing Bubble," *The New York Times*, December 18, 2008, A1.

20 John B. Taylor, *Getting Off Track: How Government Actions and Interventions Caused, Prolonged, and Worsened the Financial Crisis* (Stanford, CA: Hoover Institution Press, 2009), 11. See Mark Landler, "Chinese Savings Helped Inflate American Bubble," *New York Times*, December 26, 2008, A1.

21 See Congressional Budget Office, "Federal Subsidies and the Housing GSEs," (Washington, D.C.: Congressional Budget Office, 2001).

22 12 U.S.C. § 4501(7).

23 See the discussion of the GSEs in Tim Iglesias and Rochelle E. Lento, *The Legal Guide to Affordable Housing Development* (Chicago: American Bar Association, 2006), 208–10.

24 Nigel Jenkinson, "Ratings in Structured Finance: What Went Wrong and What Can Be Done to Address Shortcomings?" *CGFS Papers 32*, Basel: Committee on the Global Financial System, 2008.

25 Gretchen Morgenson, "Debt Watchdogs: Tamed or Caught Napping?" *The New York Times*, December 6, 2008, A1.

26 Eric Lipton and Raymond Hernandez, "A Champion of Wall Street Reaps Benefits," *The New York Times*, December 13, 2008, A1.

27 Gerald P. O'Driscoll, Jr., "Asset Bubbles and Their Consequences," *Cato Briefing Paper*, 102 (May 20, 2008).

28 Congressional Budget Office, "Federal Subsidies and the Housing GSEs."

29 General Accounting Office, "Financial Derivatives: Actions Needed to Protect the Financial System, GAO/T-GDD-94-15" (Washington, D.C.: General Accounting Office, 1994), 2.

30 Peter S. Goodman, "Taking Hard New Look at a Greenspan Legacy," *The New York Times*, October 8, 2008, A1.

31 Stephen Labaton, "Agency's '04 Rule Let Banks Pile Up New Debt," *The New York Times*, October 2, 2008, A1.

32 Mark Jickling, "Government-Sponsored Enterprises (GSEs): Regulatory Reform Legislation," CRS Report for Congress, RL32795, Washington, D.C.: Congressional Research Service, 2005, 2.

33 See Mark Jickling, "Accounting and Management Problems at Freddie Mac," CRS Report for Congress, RS21567, Washington, D.C.: Congressional Research Service, 2007.

34 International Monetary Fund, *Global Financial Stability Report: Market Developments and Issues* (Washington, D.C.: International Monetary Fund, 2003), 16–17, 22.

35 Office of Management and Budget, *Analytical Perspectives, Budget of the United States Government, Fiscal Year 2005* (Washington, D.C.: Government Printing Office, 2004), 82.

36 See Michael R. Crittenden, "2005 Legislative Summary: Fannie Mae and Freddie Mac Oversight," *CQ Weekly Online* (January 2, 2006): 28 and Michael R. Crittenden, "New GSE Regulator Included in Rewrite," *CQ Weekly Online* (May 28, 2007): 1607.

37 Chairman Ben S. Bernanke, "The Economic Outlook," Testimony before the Committee on the Budget, U.S. House of Representatives, January 17, 2008. http://www.federalreserve.gov/newsevents/testimony/bernanke20080117a.htm

38 Vikas Bajaj, "Markets Limp Into 2009 After a Bruising Year," *New York Times*, December 31, 2008, A1. Bureau of Labor Statistics, Current Population Survey, Table A-1.

39 Congressional Budget Office, *The Troubled Asset Relief Program: Report on Transactions through December 31, 2008* (Washington, D.C.: Congressional Budget Office, 2009), 2–3.

40 http://cato.org/special/stimulus09/cato_stimulus.pdf

41 Paul Krugman, "Fighting Off Depression," *New York Times*, January 4, 2009, A21.

42 Paul Krugman, "The Destructive Center," *New York Times*, February 8, 2009, A23.

43 Joseph E. Stiglitz, "How to Fail to Recover,." http://www.project-syndicate.org/commentary/stiglitz110

44 Congressional Budget Office, *The Troubled Asset Relief Program: Report on Transactions through June 17, 2009* (Washington, D.C.: Congressional Budget Office, 2009), 5.

45 Veronique de Rugy and Melinda Warren, *Regulatory Agency Spending Reaches New Height: An Analysis of the U.S. Budget for Fiscal Years 2008 and 2009* (Fairfax, VA: Mercatus Center at George Mason University, 2008), Table 1, calculations by author.

46 Figures are from Federal Election Commission statistics at opensecrets.com.

47 David Cho and Zachary A. Goldfarb, "U.S. Pushes Ahead With Derivatives Regulation," *Washington Post*, May 14, 2009, 2.

48 U.S. Department of the Treasury, "Fact Sheet: Administration's Regulatory Reform Agenda Moves Forward Credit Rating Agency Reform Legislation Sent to Capitol Hill," July 21, 2009. http://www.ustreas.gov/press/releases/tg223.htm

49 Elizabeth Warren, "Product Safety Regulation as a Model for Financial Service Regulation," *Journal of Consumer Affairs* 42, no. 3 (2008): 452–60.

50 David Moss, "An Ounce of Prevention: The Power of Public Risk Management in Stabilizing the Financial System," Harvard Business School Working Paper 09–087, 2009, 10.

11 Continuity and Change in the American Political Economy

1   Adam Smith, *An Inquiry into the Nature and the Causes of the Wealth of Nations* (Indianapolis, IN: Liberty Fund, 1981), 1:25.
2   John Lie, "Sociology of Markets," *Annual Review of Sociology* 23 (1997): 342.
3   Fred Block, "Political Choice and the Multiple 'Logics' of Capital," *Theory and Society* 15, No. 1/2 (1986): 180.
4   See Peter A. Hall and David Soskice, eds., *Varieties of Capitalism: The Institutional Foundations of Comparative Advantage* (New York: Oxford University Press, 2001).

Index

Note: Page numbers followed by 'f' refer to figures.